WRITER
**G. Willow Wilson**

ARTIST
**Christian Ward**

LETTERER
**Sal Cipriano**

# VOLUME 3

# IN OTHER WORLDS

EDITOR
**Karen Berger**

ASSISTANT EDITOR
**Rachel Boyadjis**

BOOK DESIGNER
**Richard Bruning**

DIGITAL ART TECHNICIAN
**Adam Pruett**

PRESIDENT & PUBLISHER
**Mike Richardson**

With love and thanks to Karen Berger and Richard Bruning,
who have been there since the beginning

• • •

G. Willow Wilson

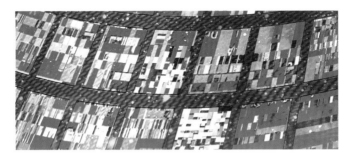

**For Catherine**

• • •

Christian Ward

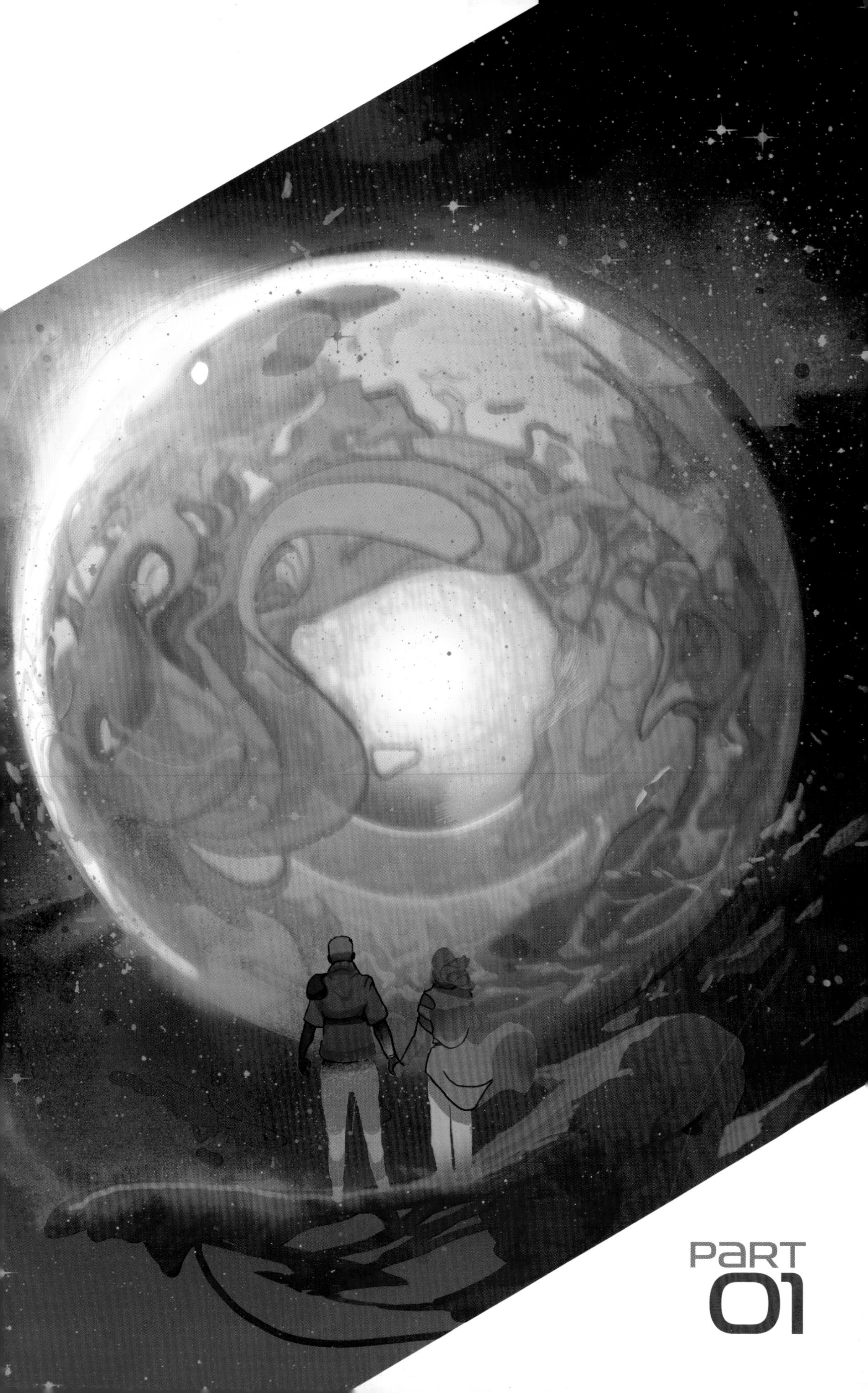

# PART 01

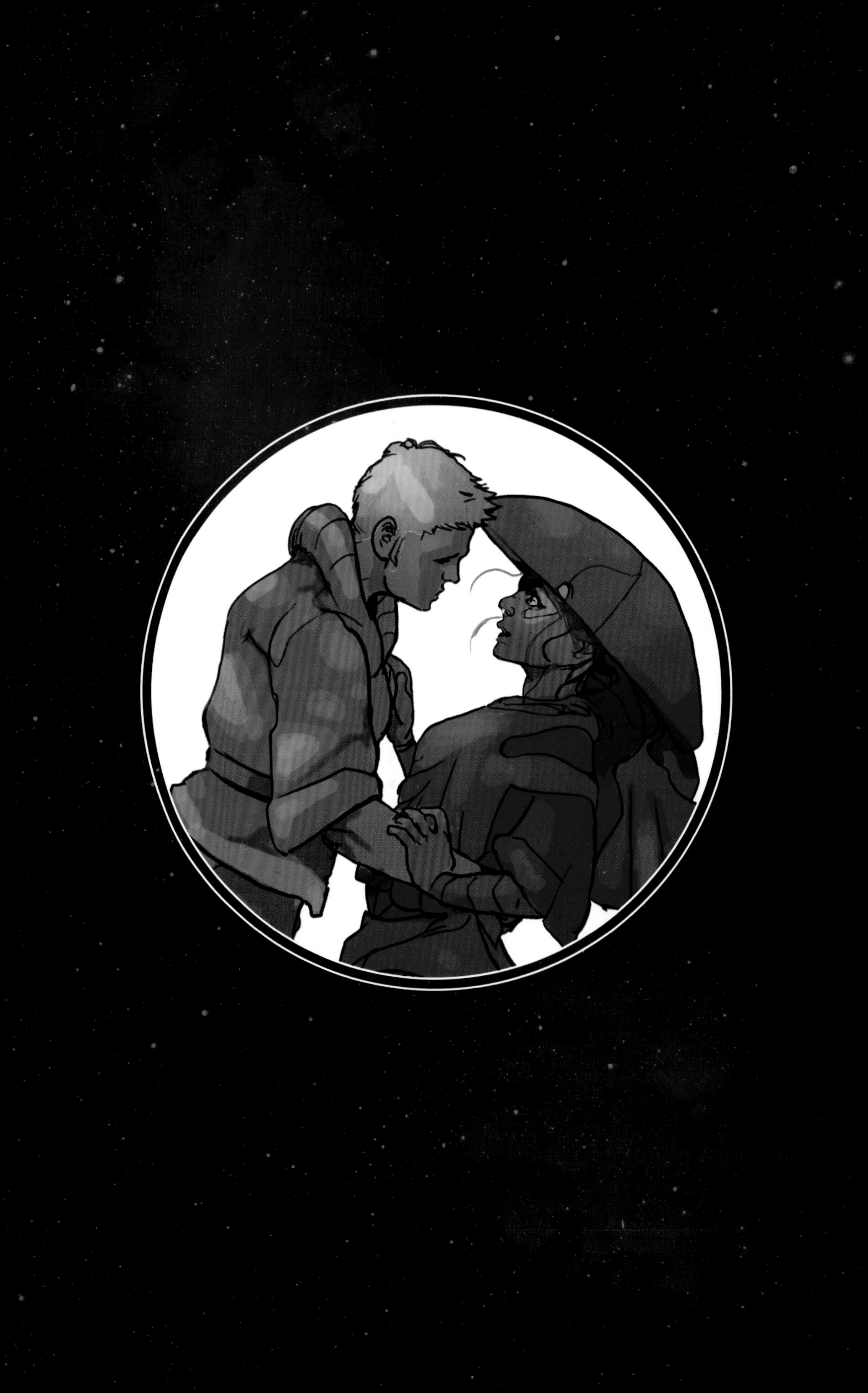

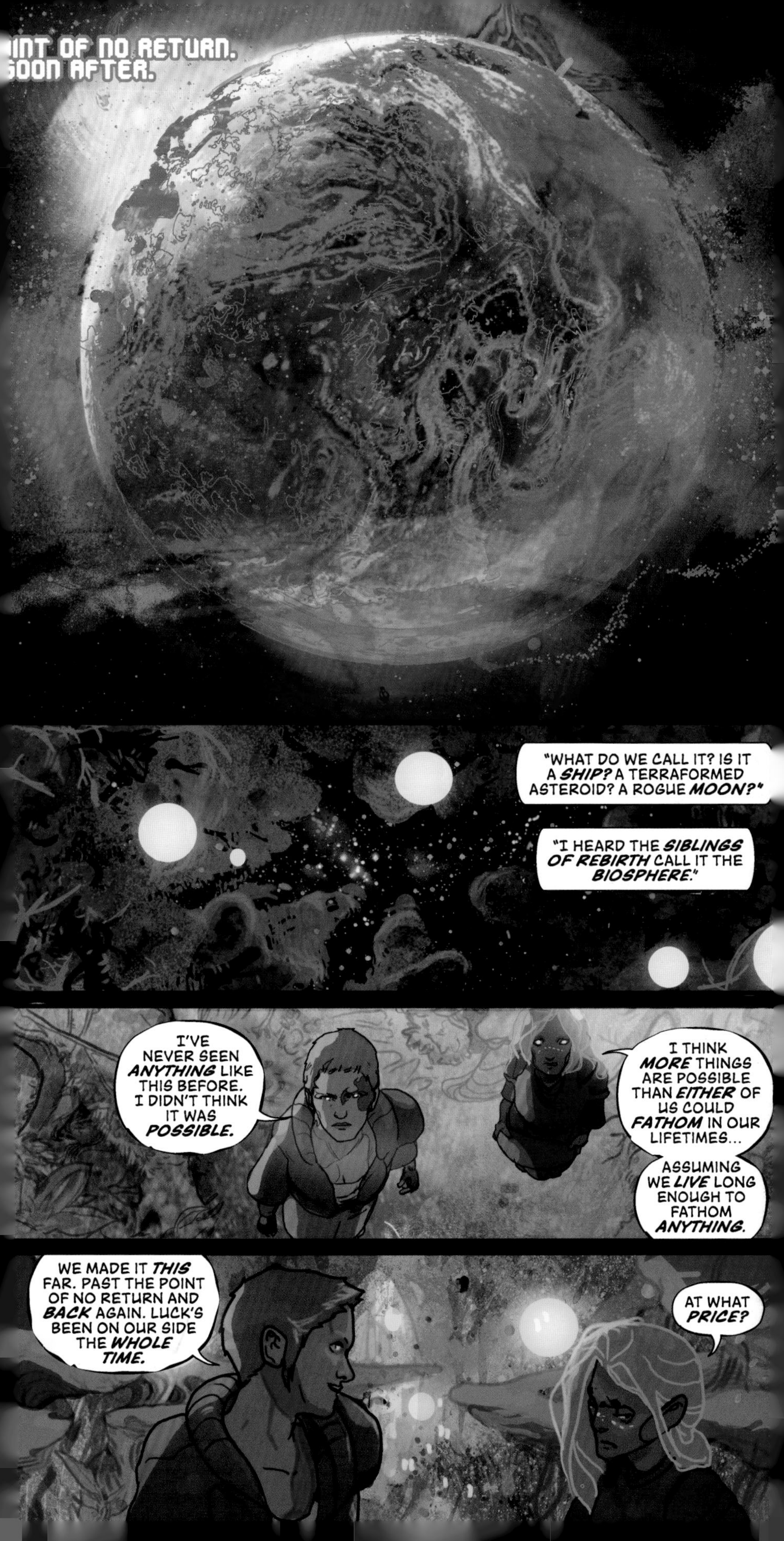
INT OF NO RETURN.
SOON AFTER.
"WHAT DO WE CALL IT? IS IT A SHIP? A TERRAFORMED ASTEROID? A ROGUE MOON?"
"I HEARD THE SIBLINGS OF REBIRTH CALL IT THE BIOSPHERE."
I'VE NEVER SEEN ANYTHING LIKE THIS BEFORE. I DIDN'T THINK IT WAS POSSIBLE.
I THINK MORE THINGS ARE POSSIBLE THAN EITHER OF US COULD FATHOM IN OUR LIFETIMES...
ASSUMING WE LIVE LONG ENOUGH TO FATHOM ANYTHING.
WE MADE IT THIS FAR. PAST THE POINT OF NO RETURN AND BACK AGAIN. LUCK'S BEEN ON OUR SIDE THE WHOLE TIME.
AT WHAT PRICE?

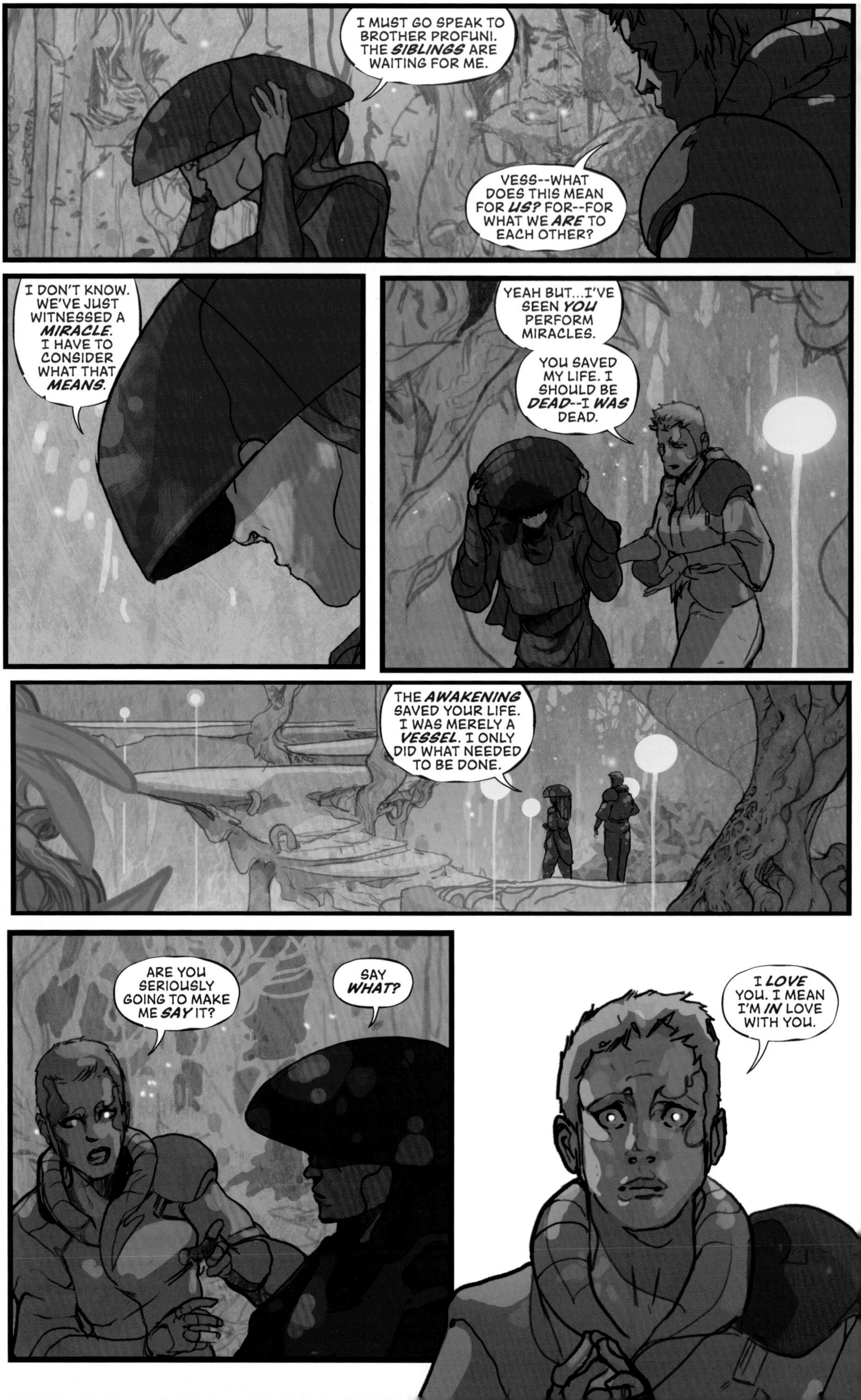
I MUST GO SPEAK TO BROTHER PROFUNI. THE *SIBLINGS* ARE WAITING FOR ME.
VESS--WHAT DOES THIS MEAN FOR *US?* FOR--FOR WHAT WE *ARE* TO EACH OTHER?
I DON'T KNOW. WE'VE JUST WITNESSED A *MIRACLE*. I HAVE TO CONSIDER WHAT THAT *MEANS*.
YEAH BUT...I'VE SEEN *YOU* PERFORM MIRACLES.
YOU SAVED MY LIFE. I SHOULD BE *DEAD*--I *WAS* DEAD.
THE *AWAKENING* SAVED YOUR LIFE. I WAS MERELY A *VESSEL*. I ONLY DID WHAT NEEDED TO BE DONE.
ARE YOU SERIOUSLY GOING TO MAKE ME *SAY* IT?
SAY *WHAT?*
I *LOVE* YOU. I MEAN I'M *IN* LOVE WITH YOU.

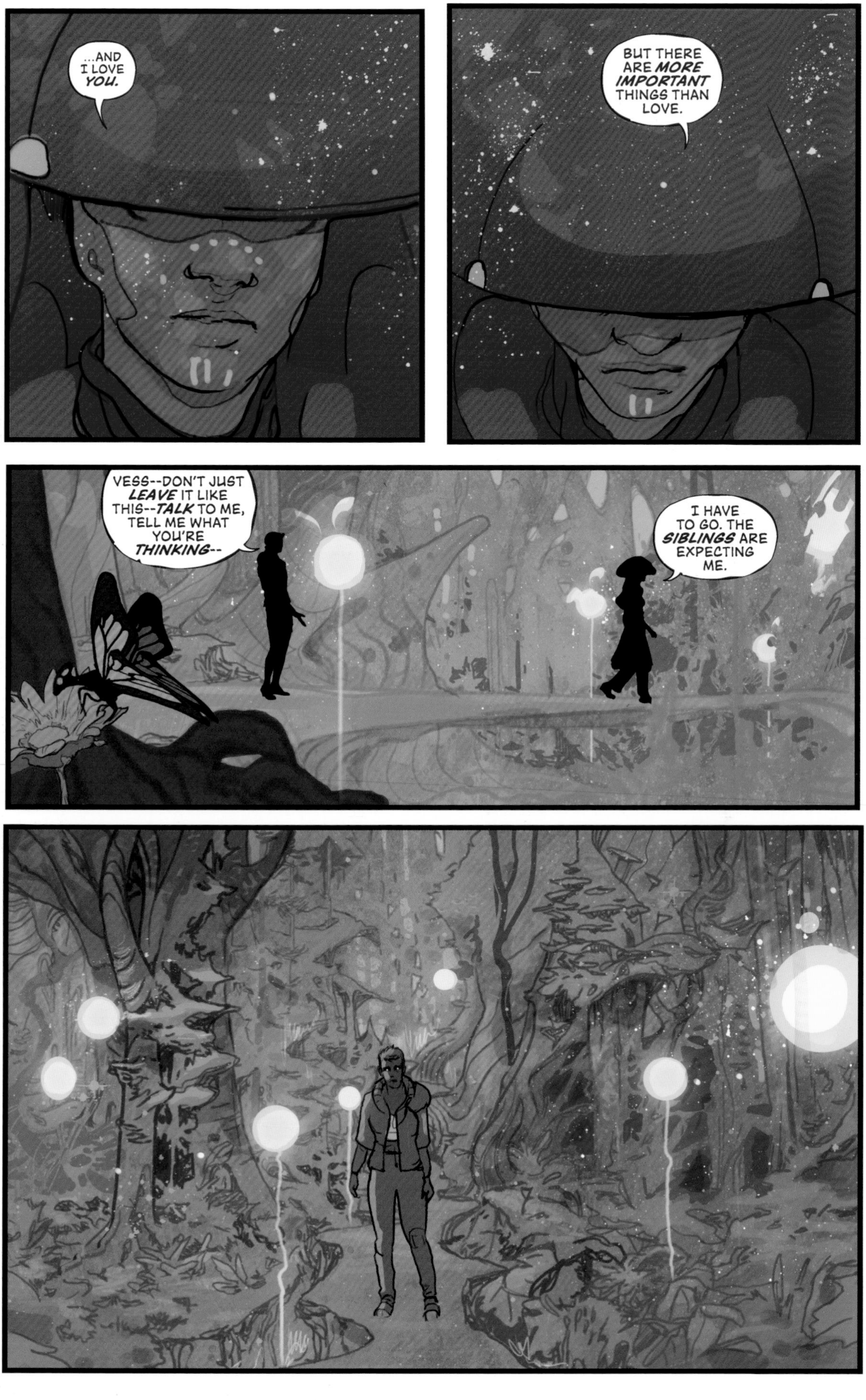
...AND I LOVE *YOU.*
BUT THERE ARE *MORE IMPORTANT* THINGS THAN LOVE.
VESS--DON'T JUST *LEAVE* IT LIKE THIS--*TALK* TO ME, TELL ME WHAT YOU'RE *THINKING*--
I HAVE TO GO. THE *SIBLINGS* ARE EXPECTING ME.

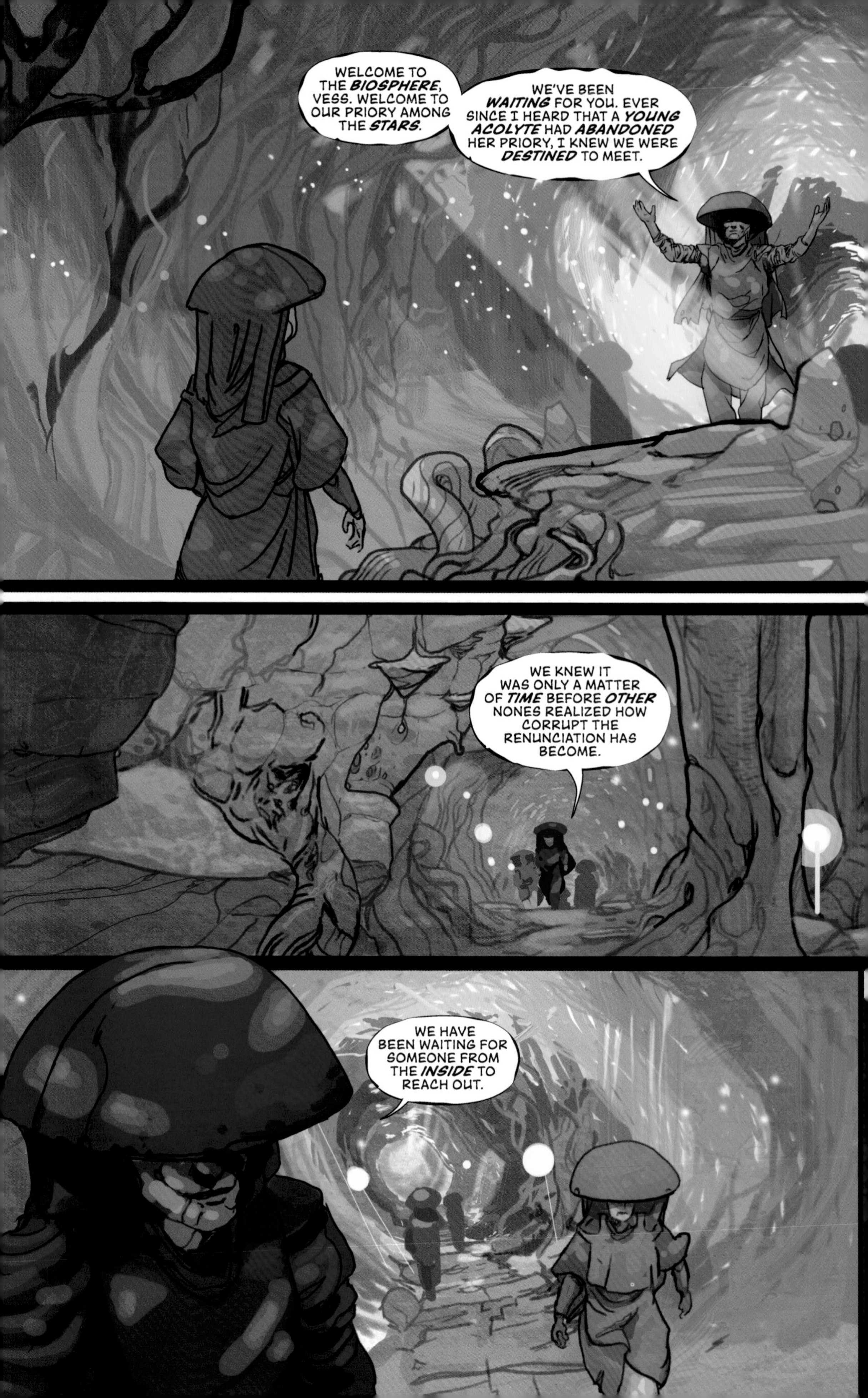
WELCOME TO THE BIOSPHERE, VESS. WELCOME TO OUR PRIORY AMONG THE STARS.
WE'VE BEEN WAITING FOR YOU. EVER SINCE I HEARD THAT A YOUNG ACOLYTE HAD ABANDONED HER PRIORY, I KNEW WE WERE DESTINED TO MEET.
WE KNEW IT WAS ONLY A MATTER OF TIME BEFORE OTHER NONES REALIZED HOW CORRUPT THE RENUNCIATION HAS BECOME.
WE HAVE BEEN WAITING FOR SOMEONE FROM THE INSIDE TO REACH OUT.

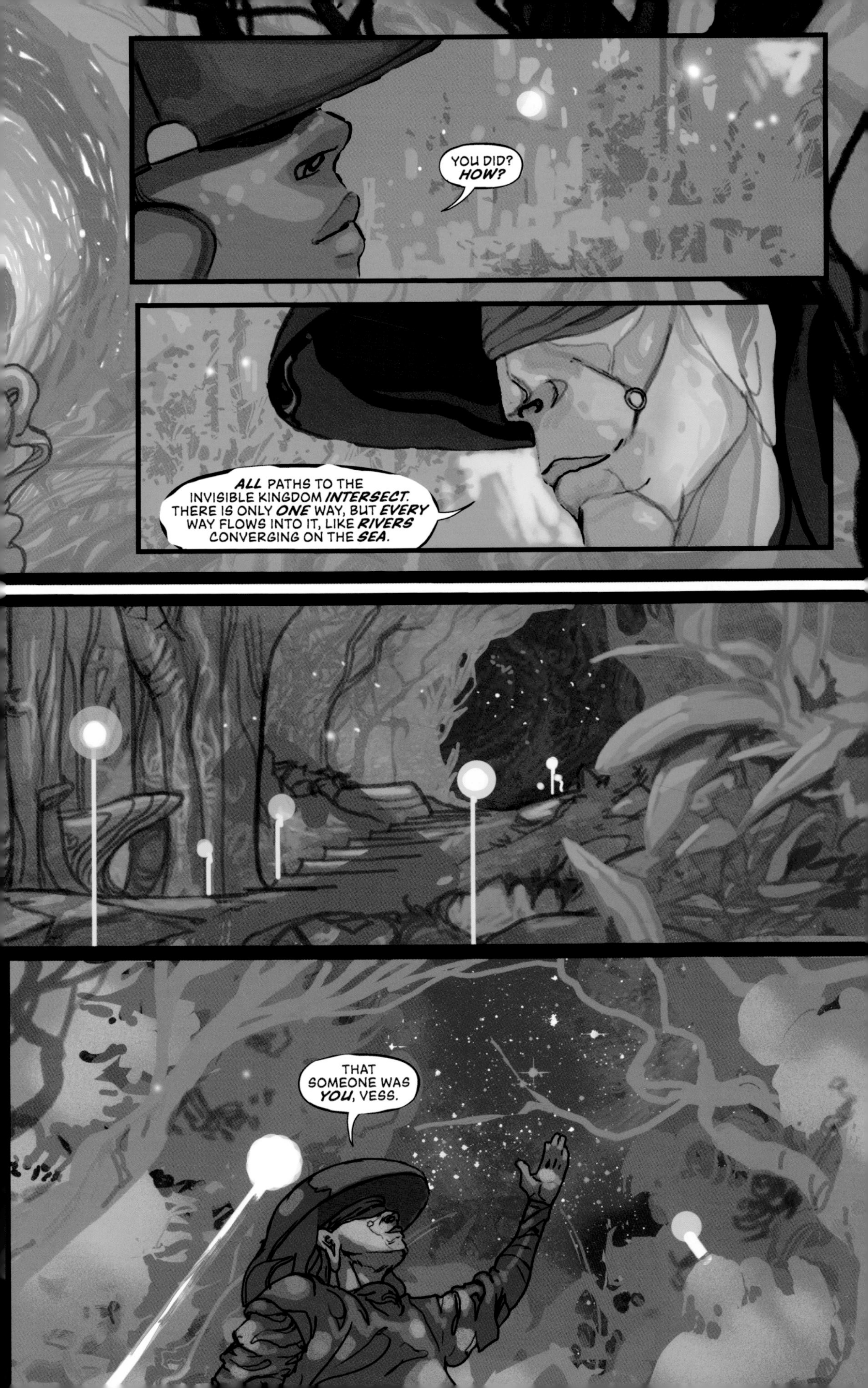
YOU DID? HOW?
ALL PATHS TO THE INVISIBLE KINGDOM INTERSECT. THERE IS ONLY ONE WAY, BUT EVERY WAY FLOWS INTO IT, LIKE RIVERS CONVERGING ON THE SEA.
THAT SOMEONE WAS YOU, VESS.

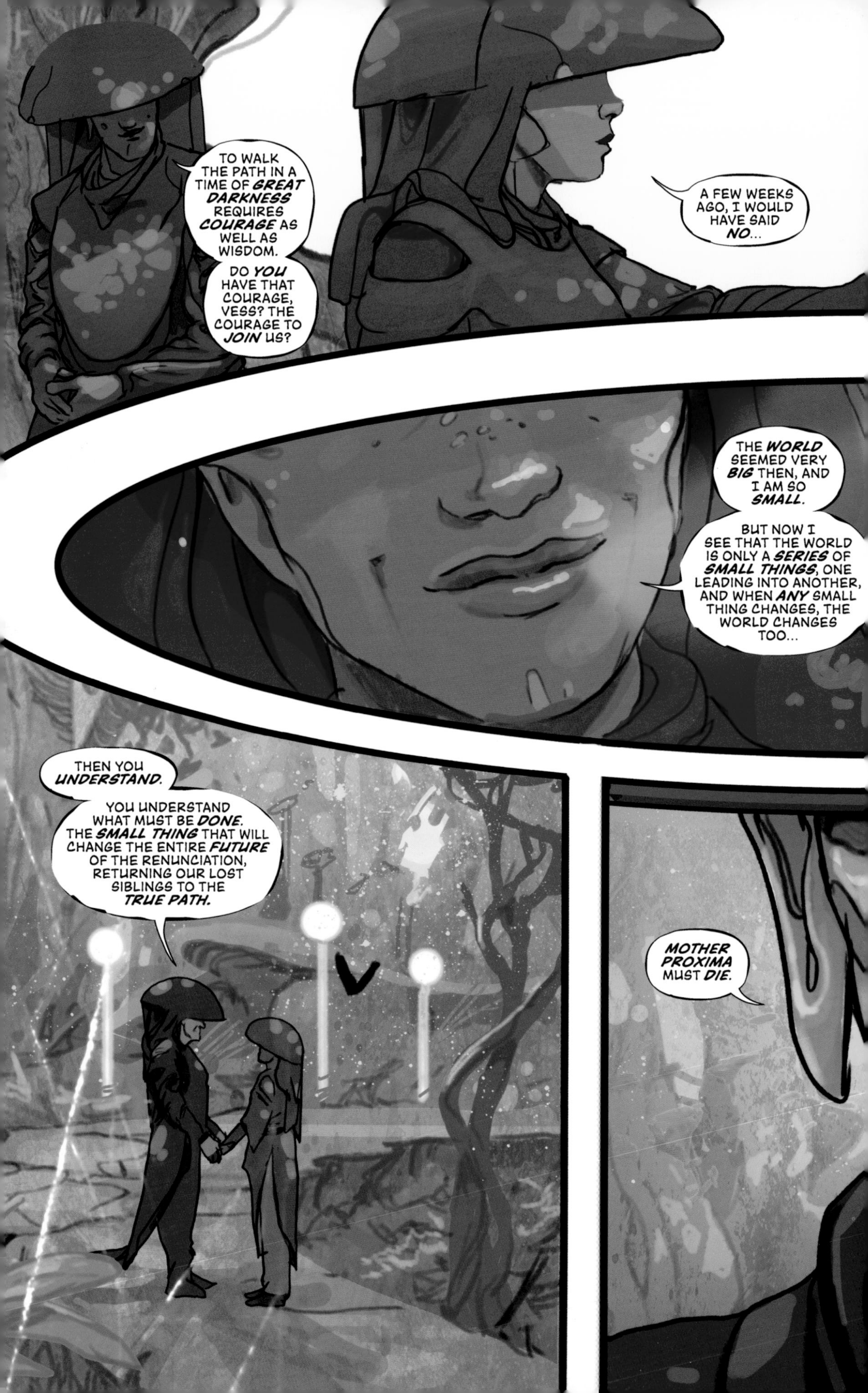
TO WALK THE PATH IN A TIME OF GREAT DARKNESS REQUIRES COURAGE AS WELL AS WISDOM.
DO YOU HAVE THAT COURAGE, VESS? THE COURAGE TO JOIN US?
A FEW WEEKS AGO, I WOULD HAVE SAID NO...
THE WORLD SEEMED VERY BIG THEN, AND I AM SO SMALL.
BUT NOW I SEE THAT THE WORLD IS ONLY A SERIES OF SMALL THINGS, ONE LEADING INTO ANOTHER, AND WHEN ANY SMALL THING CHANGES, THE WORLD CHANGES TOO...
THEN YOU UNDERSTAND.
YOU UNDERSTAND WHAT MUST BE DONE. THE SMALL THING THAT WILL CHANGE THE ENTIRE FUTURE OF THE RENUNCIATION, RETURNING OUR LOST SIBLINGS TO THE TRUE PATH.
MOTHER PROXIMA MUST DIE.

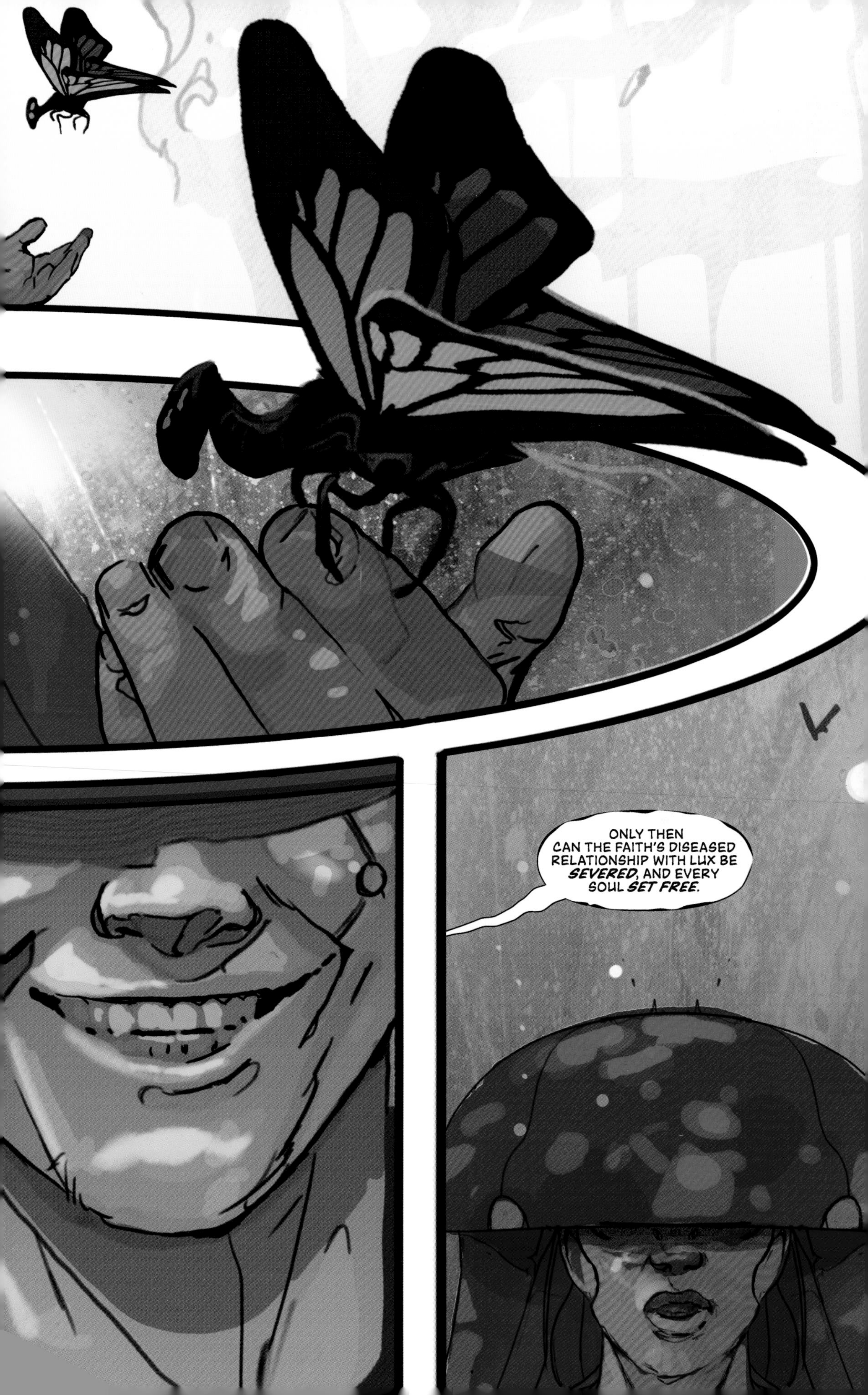
ONLY THEN CAN THE FAITH'S DISEASED RELATIONSHIP WITH LUX BE *SEVERED*, AND EVERY SOUL *SET FREE*.

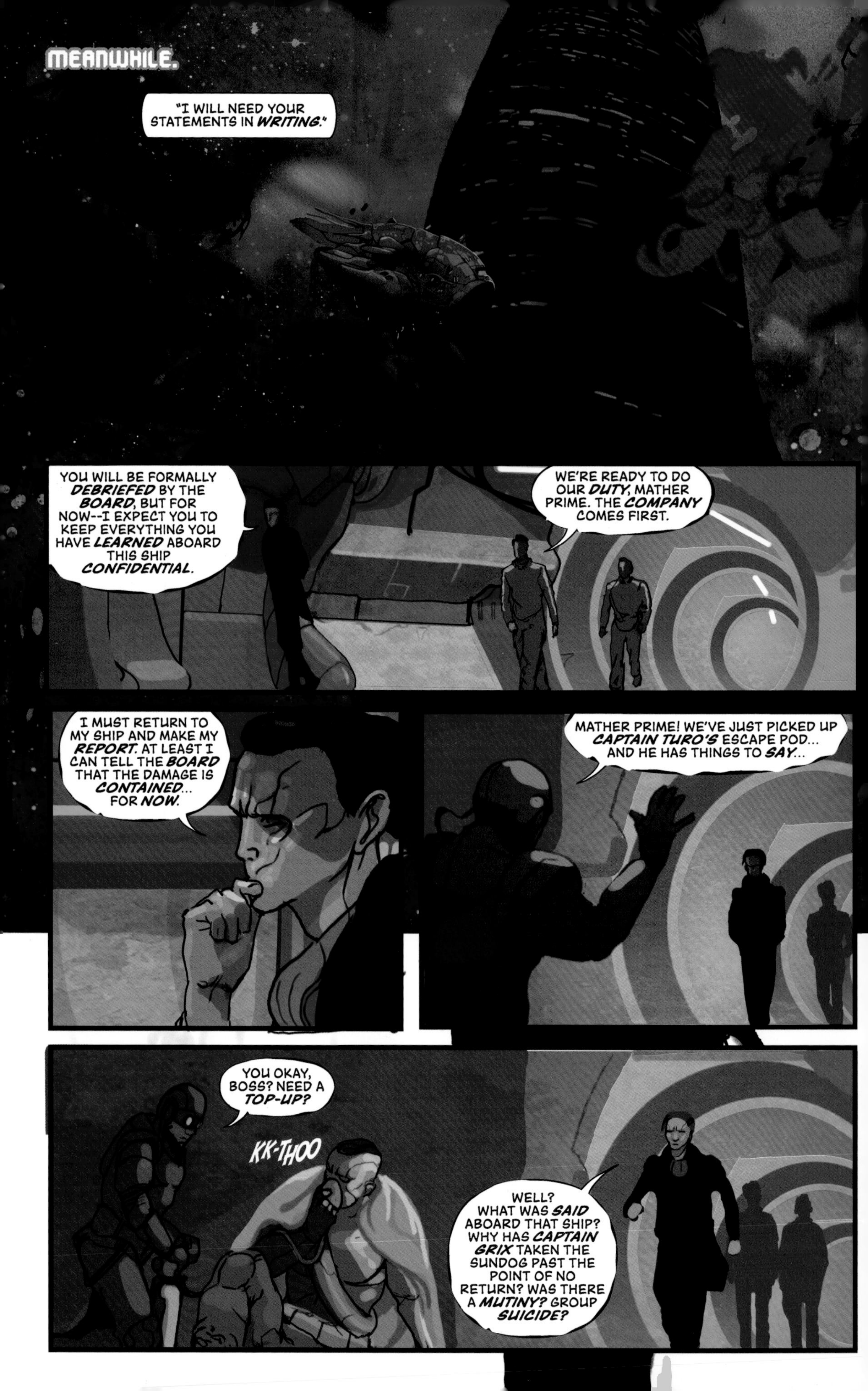
MEANWHILE.
"I WILL NEED YOUR STATEMENTS IN WRITING."
YOU WILL BE FORMALLY DEBRIEFED BY THE BOARD, BUT FOR NOW--I EXPECT YOU TO KEEP EVERYTHING YOU HAVE LEARNED ABOARD THIS SHIP CONFIDENTIAL.
WE'RE READY TO DO OUR DUTY, MATHER PRIME. THE COMPANY COMES FIRST.
I MUST RETURN TO MY SHIP AND MAKE MY REPORT. AT LEAST I CAN TELL THE BOARD THAT THE DAMAGE IS CONTAINED... FOR NOW.
MATHER PRIME! WE'VE JUST PICKED UP CAPTAIN TURO'S ESCAPE POD... AND HE HAS THINGS TO SAY...
YOU OKAY, BOSS? NEED A TOP-UP?
KK-THOO
WELL? WHAT WAS SAID ABOARD THAT SHIP? WHY HAS CAPTAIN GRIX TAKEN THE SUNDOG PAST THE POINT OF NO RETURN? WAS THERE A MUTINY? GROUP SUICIDE?

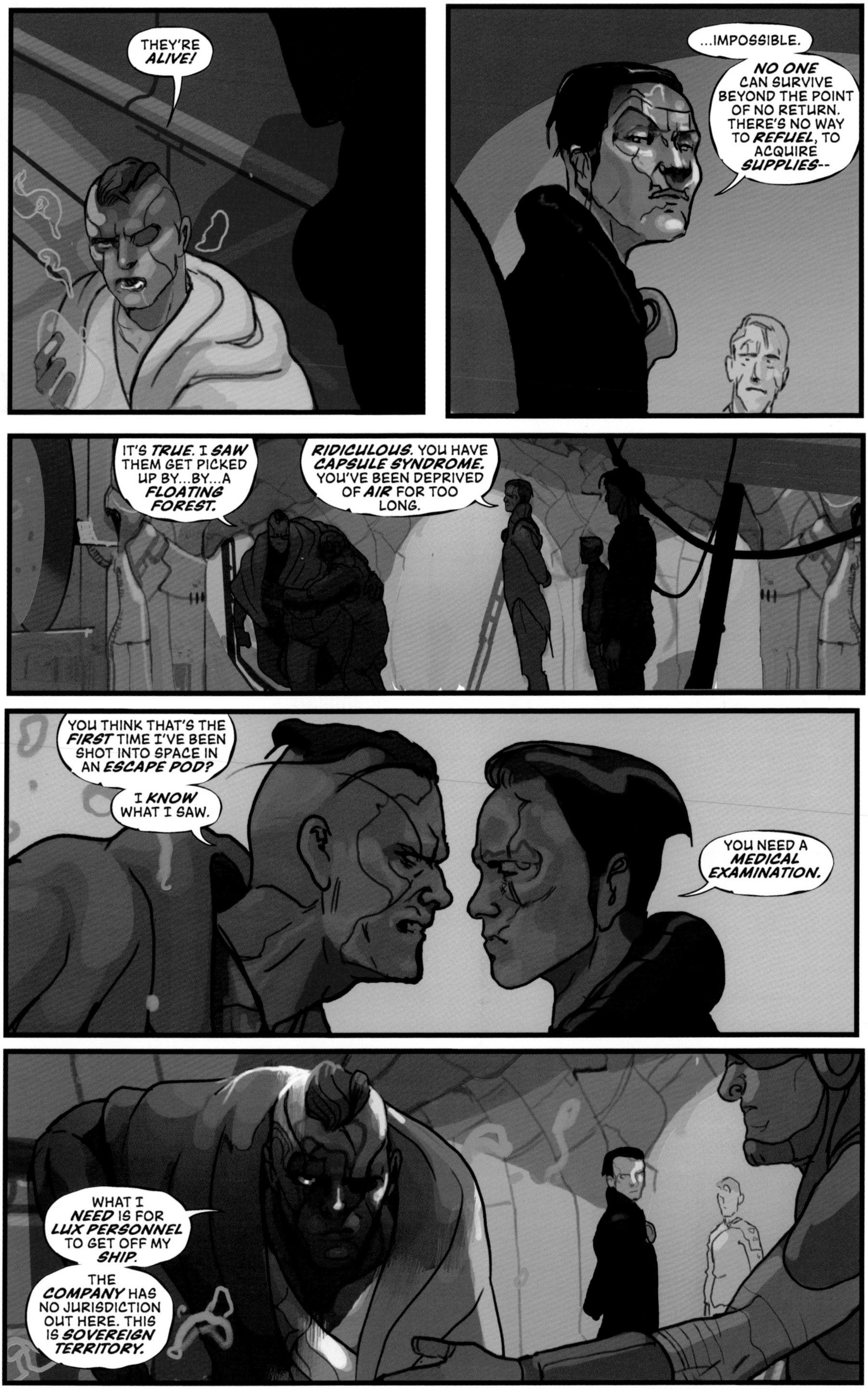
THEY'RE ALIVE!
...IMPOSSIBLE.
NO ONE CAN SURVIVE BEYOND THE POINT OF NO RETURN. THERE'S NO WAY TO REFUEL, TO ACQUIRE SUPPLIES--
IT'S TRUE. I SAW THEM GET PICKED UP BY...BY...A FLOATING FOREST.
RIDICULOUS. YOU HAVE CAPSULE SYNDROME. YOU'VE BEEN DEPRIVED OF AIR FOR TOO LONG.
YOU THINK THAT'S THE FIRST TIME I'VE BEEN SHOT INTO SPACE IN AN ESCAPE POD?
I KNOW WHAT I SAW.
YOU NEED A MEDICAL EXAMINATION.
WHAT I NEED IS FOR LUX PERSONNEL TO GET OFF MY SHIP.
THE COMPANY HAS NO JURISDICTION OUT HERE. THIS IS SOVEREIGN TERRITORY.

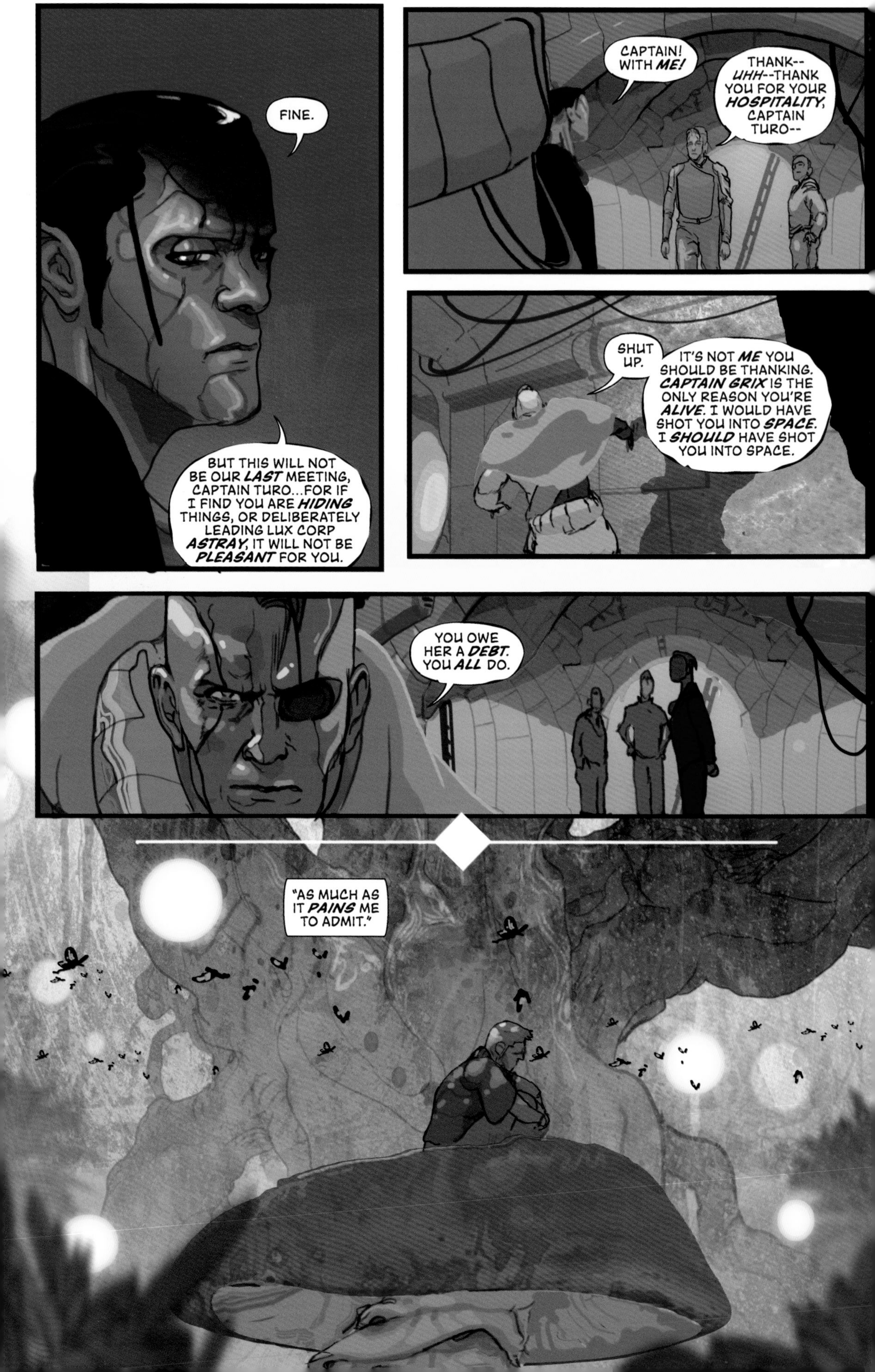
FINE.
BUT THIS WILL NOT BE OUR LAST MEETING, CAPTAIN TURO...FOR IF I FIND YOU ARE HIDING THINGS, OR DELIBERATELY LEADING LUX CORP ASTRAY, IT WILL NOT BE PLEASANT FOR YOU.
CAPTAIN! WITH ME!
THANK-- UHH--THANK YOU FOR YOUR HOSPITALITY, CAPTAIN TURO--
SHUT UP.
IT'S NOT ME YOU SHOULD BE THANKING. CAPTAIN GRIX IS THE ONLY REASON YOU'RE ALIVE. I WOULD HAVE SHOT YOU INTO SPACE. I SHOULD HAVE SHOT YOU INTO SPACE.
YOU OWE HER A DEBT. YOU ALL DO.
"AS MUCH AS IT PAINS ME TO ADMIT."

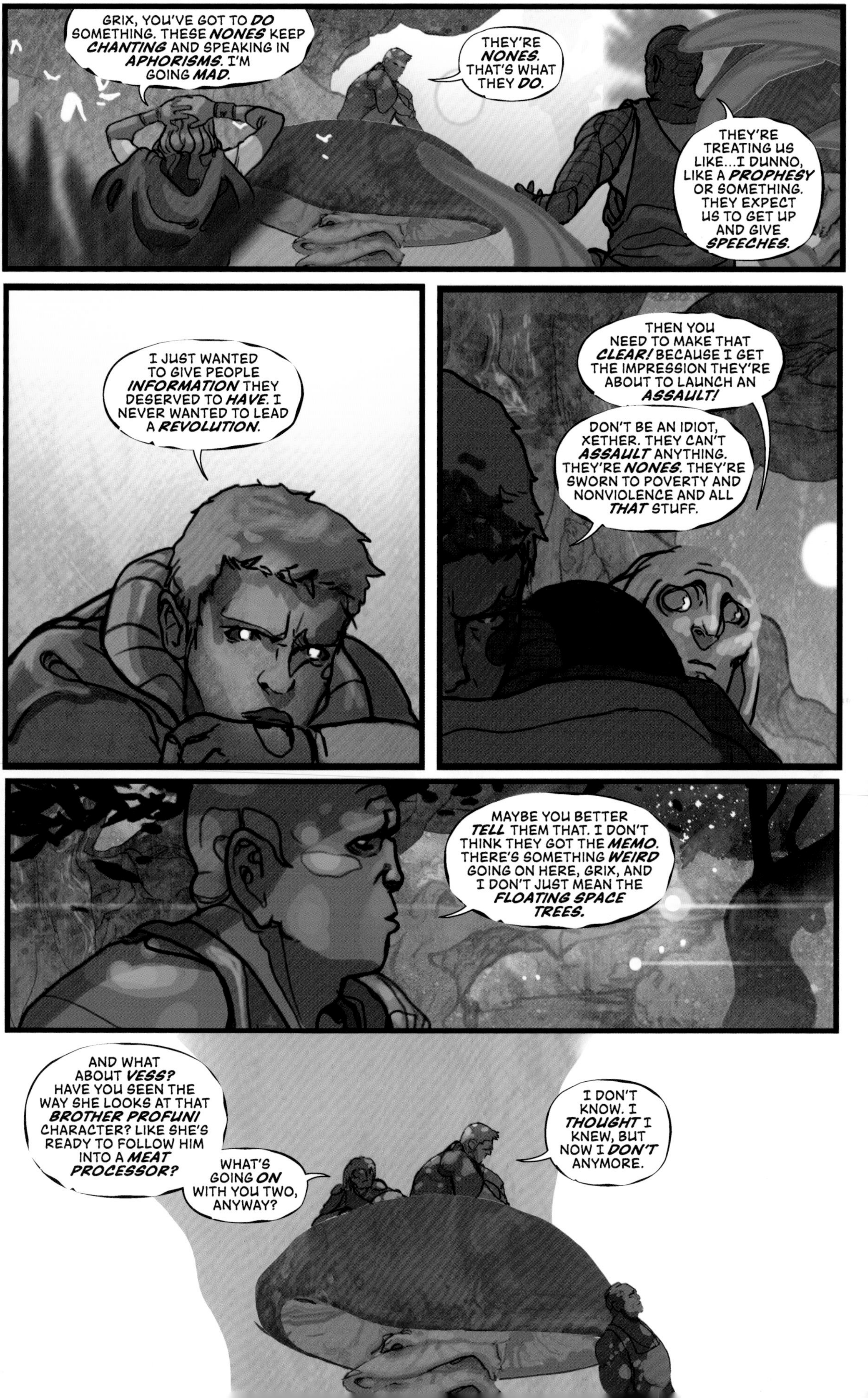
GRIX, YOU'VE GOT TO DO SOMETHING. THESE NONES KEEP CHANTING AND SPEAKING IN APHORISMS. I'M GOING MAD.
THEY'RE NONES. THAT'S WHAT THEY DO.
THEY'RE TREATING US LIKE...I DUNNO, LIKE A PROPHESY OR SOMETHING. THEY EXPECT US TO GET UP AND GIVE SPEECHES.
I JUST WANTED TO GIVE PEOPLE INFORMATION THEY DESERVED TO HAVE. I NEVER WANTED TO LEAD A REVOLUTION.
THEN YOU NEED TO MAKE THAT CLEAR! BECAUSE I GET THE IMPRESSION THEY'RE ABOUT TO LAUNCH AN ASSAULT!
DON'T BE AN IDIOT, XETHER. THEY CAN'T ASSAULT ANYTHING. THEY'RE NONES. THEY'RE SWORN TO POVERTY AND NONVIOLENCE AND ALL THAT STUFF.
MAYBE YOU BETTER TELL THEM THAT. I DON'T THINK THEY GOT THE MEMO. THERE'S SOMETHING WEIRD GOING ON HERE, GRIX, AND I DON'T JUST MEAN THE FLOATING SPACE TREES.
AND WHAT ABOUT VESS? HAVE YOU SEEN THE WAY SHE LOOKS AT THAT BROTHER PROFUNI CHARACTER? LIKE SHE'S READY TO FOLLOW HIM INTO A MEAT PROCESSOR?
WHAT'S GOING ON WITH YOU TWO, ANYWAY?
I DON'T KNOW. I THOUGHT I KNEW, BUT NOW I DON'T ANYMORE.

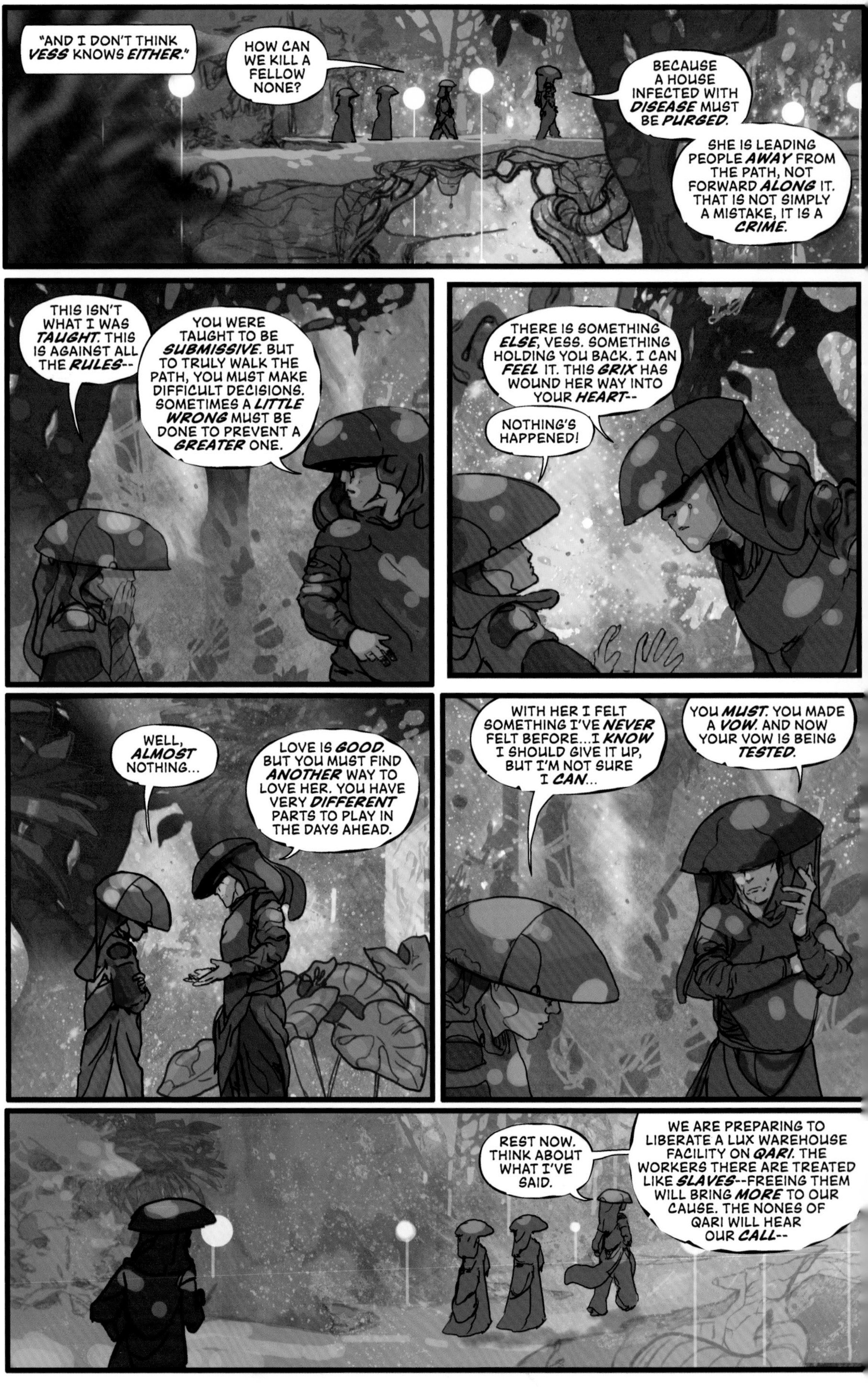
"AND I DON'T THINK VESS KNOWS EITHER."
HOW CAN WE KILL A FELLOW NONE?
BECAUSE A HOUSE INFECTED WITH DISEASE MUST BE PURGED.
SHE IS LEADING PEOPLE AWAY FROM THE PATH, NOT FORWARD ALONG IT. THAT IS NOT SIMPLY A MISTAKE, IT IS A CRIME.
THIS ISN'T WHAT I WAS TAUGHT. THIS IS AGAINST ALL THE RULES--
YOU WERE TAUGHT TO BE SUBMISSIVE. BUT TO TRULY WALK THE PATH, YOU MUST MAKE DIFFICULT DECISIONS. SOMETIMES A LITTLE WRONG MUST BE DONE TO PREVENT A GREATER ONE.
THERE IS SOMETHING ELSE, VESS. SOMETHING HOLDING YOU BACK. I CAN FEEL IT. THIS GRIX HAS WOUND HER WAY INTO YOUR HEART--
NOTHING'S HAPPENED!
WELL, ALMOST NOTHING...
LOVE IS GOOD. BUT YOU MUST FIND ANOTHER WAY TO LOVE HER. YOU HAVE VERY DIFFERENT PARTS TO PLAY IN THE DAYS AHEAD.
WITH HER I FELT SOMETHING I'VE NEVER FELT BEFORE...I KNOW I SHOULD GIVE IT UP, BUT I'M NOT SURE I CAN...
YOU MUST. YOU MADE A VOW. AND NOW YOUR VOW IS BEING TESTED.
REST NOW. THINK ABOUT WHAT I'VE SAID.
WE ARE PREPARING TO LIBERATE A LUX WAREHOUSE FACILITY ON QARI. THE WORKERS THERE ARE TREATED LIKE SLAVES--FREEING THEM WILL BRING MORE TO OUR CAUSE. THE NONES OF QARI WILL HEAR OUR CALL--

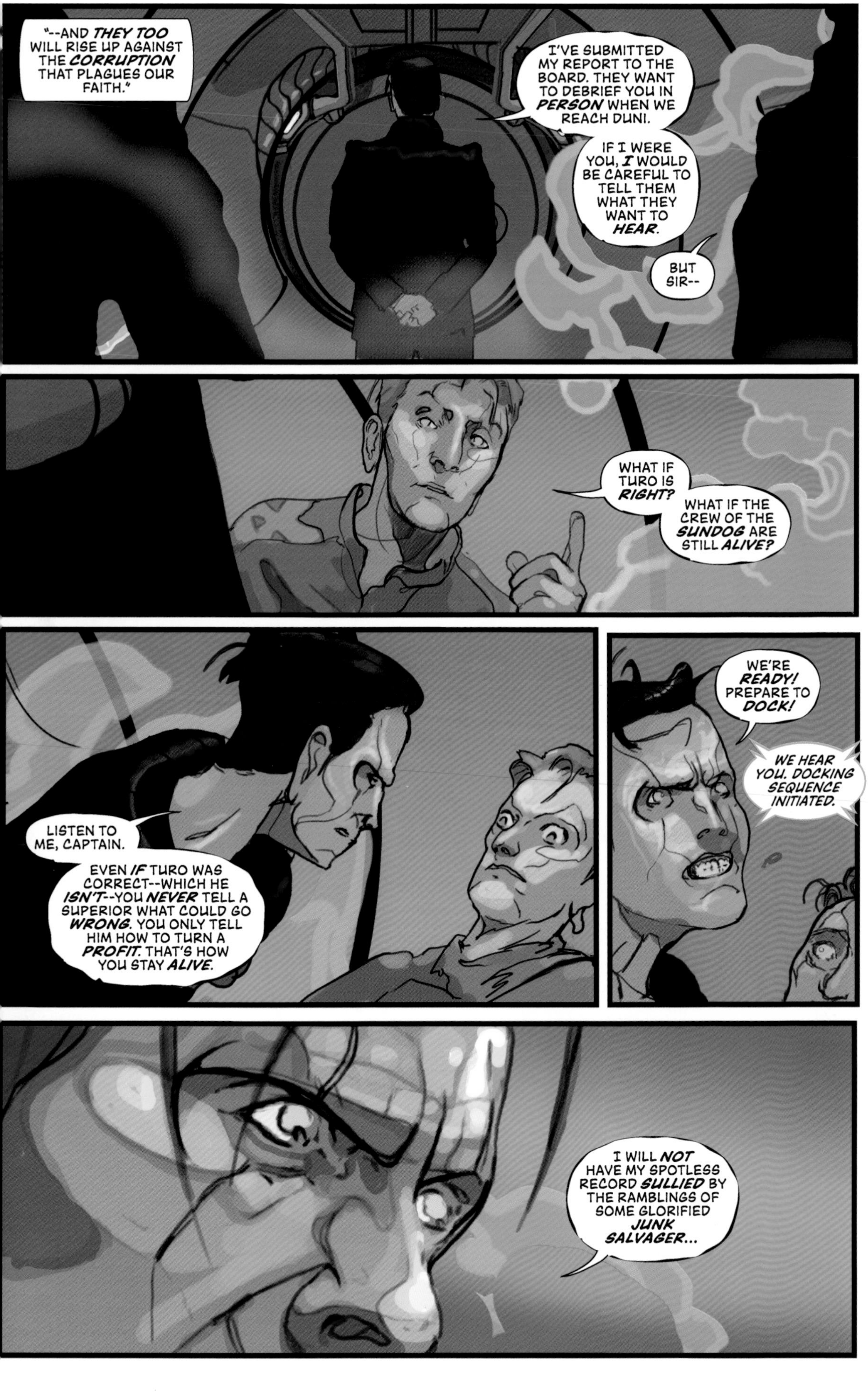
"--AND THEY TOO WILL RISE UP AGAINST THE CORRUPTION THAT PLAGUES OUR FAITH."
I'VE SUBMITTED MY REPORT TO THE BOARD. THEY WANT TO DEBRIEF YOU IN PERSON WHEN WE REACH DUNI.
IF I WERE YOU, I WOULD BE CAREFUL TO TELL THEM WHAT THEY WANT TO HEAR.
BUT SIR--
WHAT IF TURO IS RIGHT?
WHAT IF THE CREW OF THE SUNDOG ARE STILL ALIVE?
LISTEN TO ME, CAPTAIN.
EVEN IF TURO WAS CORRECT--WHICH HE ISN'T--YOU NEVER TELL A SUPERIOR WHAT COULD GO WRONG. YOU ONLY TELL HIM HOW TO TURN A PROFIT. THAT'S HOW YOU STAY ALIVE.
WE'RE READY! PREPARE TO DOCK!
WE HEAR YOU. DOCKING SEQUENCE INITIATED.
I WILL NOT HAVE MY SPOTLESS RECORD SULLIED BY THE RAMBLINGS OF SOME GLORIFIED JUNK SALVAGER...

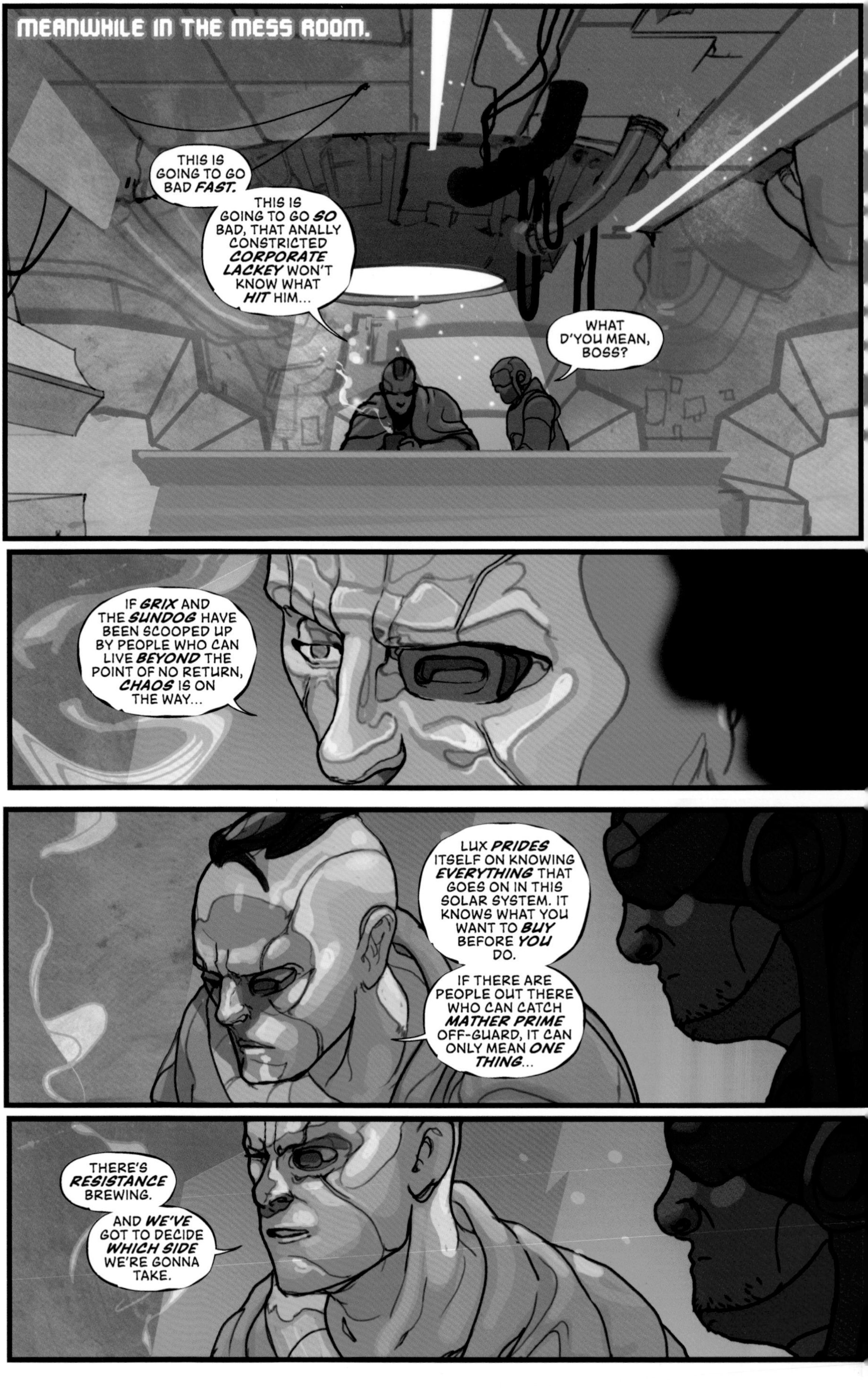
MEANWHILE IN THE MESS ROOM.
THIS IS GOING TO GO BAD FAST.
THIS IS GOING TO GO SO BAD, THAT ANALLY CONSTRICTED CORPORATE LACKEY WON'T KNOW WHAT HIT HIM...
WHAT D'YOU MEAN, BOSS?
IF GRIX AND THE SUNDOG HAVE BEEN SCOOPED UP BY PEOPLE WHO CAN LIVE BEYOND THE POINT OF NO RETURN, CHAOS IS ON THE WAY...
LUX PRIDES ITSELF ON KNOWING EVERYTHING THAT GOES ON IN THIS SOLAR SYSTEM. IT KNOWS WHAT YOU WANT TO BUY BEFORE YOU DO.
IF THERE ARE PEOPLE OUT THERE WHO CAN CATCH MATHER PRIME OFF-GUARD, IT CAN ONLY MEAN ONE THING...
THERE'S RESISTANCE BREWING.
AND WE'VE GOT TO DECIDE WHICH SIDE WE'RE GONNA TAKE.

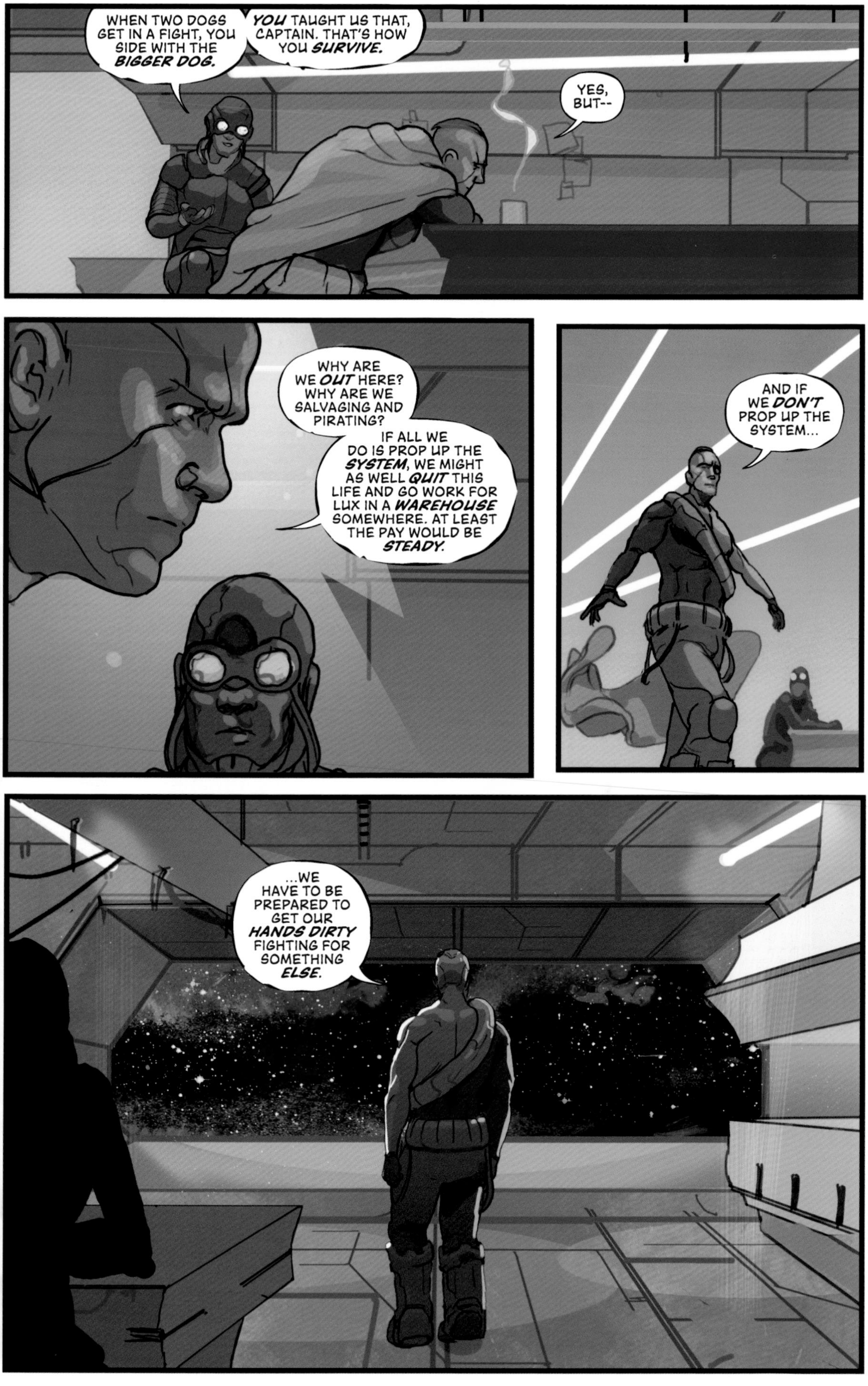
WHEN TWO DOGS GET IN A FIGHT, YOU SIDE WITH THE BIGGER DOG.
YOU TAUGHT US THAT, CAPTAIN. THAT'S HOW YOU SURVIVE.
YES, BUT--
WHY ARE WE OUT HERE? WHY ARE WE SALVAGING AND PIRATING?
IF ALL WE DO IS PROP UP THE SYSTEM, WE MIGHT AS WELL QUIT THIS LIFE AND GO WORK FOR LUX IN A WAREHOUSE SOMEWHERE. AT LEAST THE PAY WOULD BE STEADY.
AND IF WE DON'T PROP UP THE SYSTEM...
...WE HAVE TO BE PREPARED TO GET OUR HANDS DIRTY FIGHTING FOR SOMETHING ELSE.

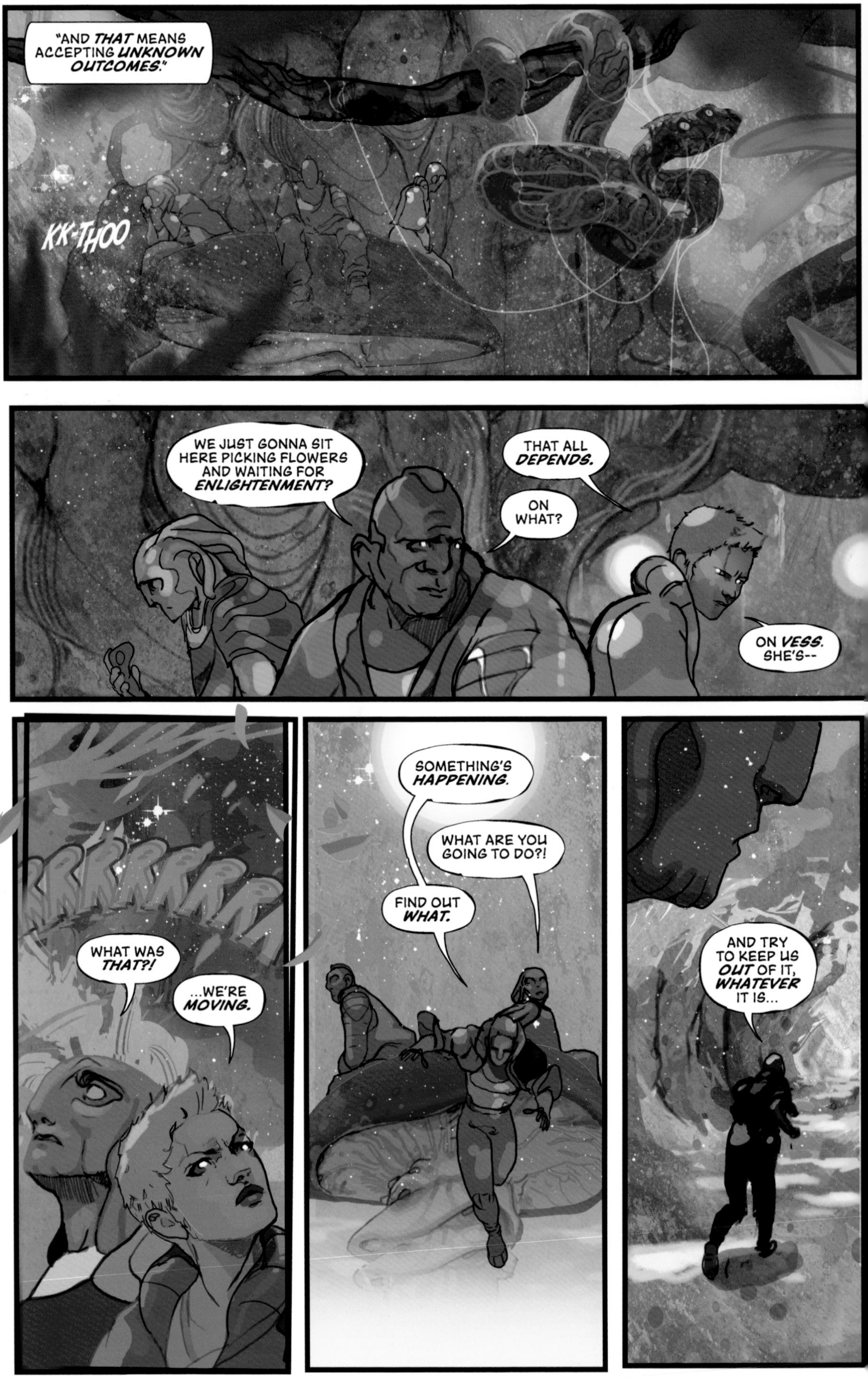
"AND THAT MEANS ACCEPTING UNKNOWN OUTCOMES."
KK-THOO
WE JUST GONNA SIT HERE PICKING FLOWERS AND WAITING FOR ENLIGHTENMENT?
THAT ALL DEPENDS.
ON WHAT?
ON VESS. SHE'S--
RRRRRRR
WHAT WAS THAT?!
...WE'RE MOVING.
SOMETHING'S HAPPENING.
WHAT ARE YOU GOING TO DO?!
FIND OUT WHAT.
AND TRY TO KEEP US OUT OF IT, WHATEVER IT IS...

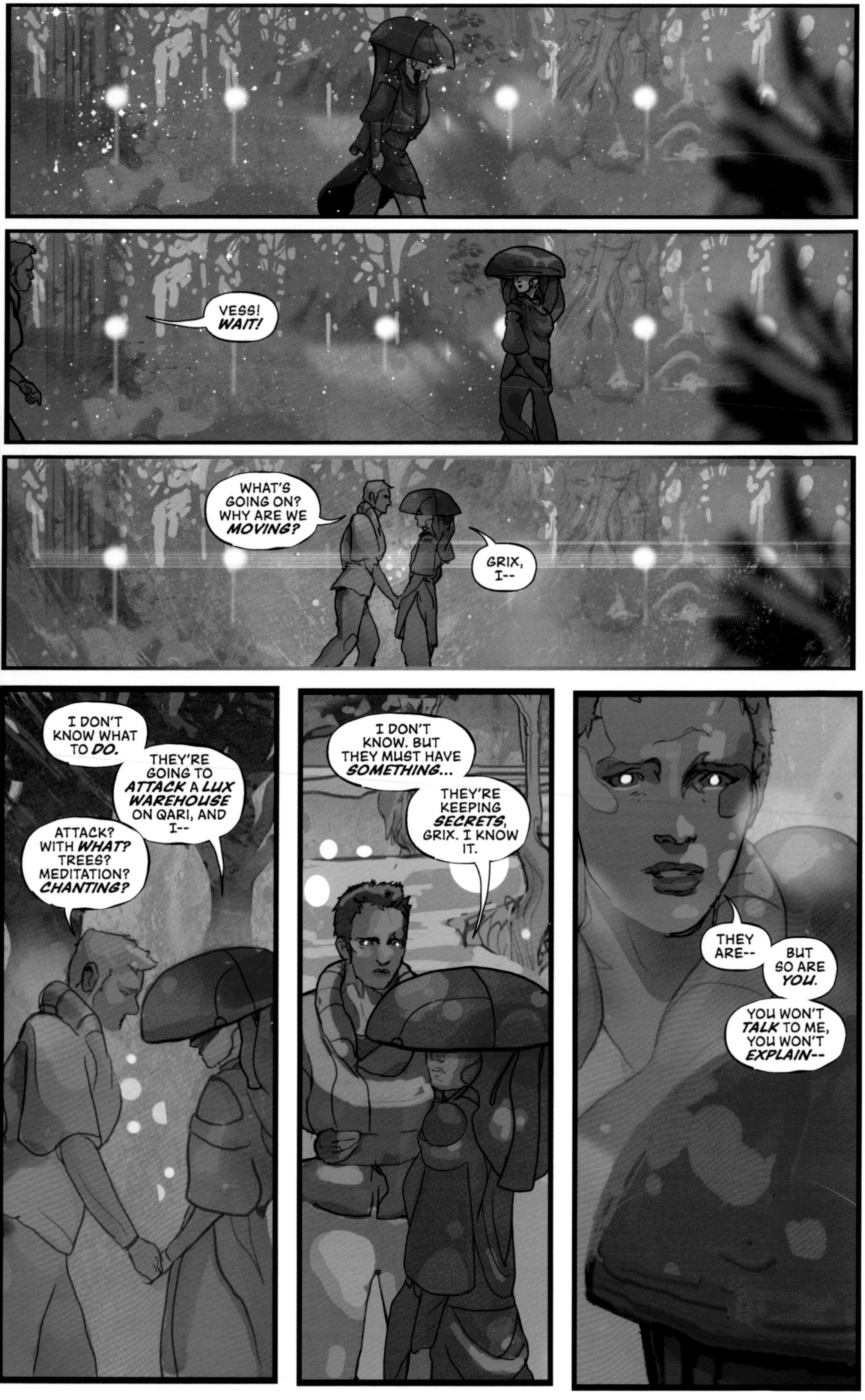
VESS! WAIT!
WHAT'S GOING ON? WHY ARE WE MOVING?
GRIX, I--
I DON'T KNOW WHAT TO DO.
THEY'RE GOING TO ATTACK A LUX WAREHOUSE ON QARI, AND I--
ATTACK? WITH WHAT? TREES? MEDITATION? CHANTING?
I DON'T KNOW. BUT THEY MUST HAVE SOMETHING...
THEY'RE KEEPING SECRETS, GRIX. I KNOW IT.
THEY ARE--
BUT SO ARE YOU.
YOU WON'T TALK TO ME, YOU WON'T EXPLAIN--

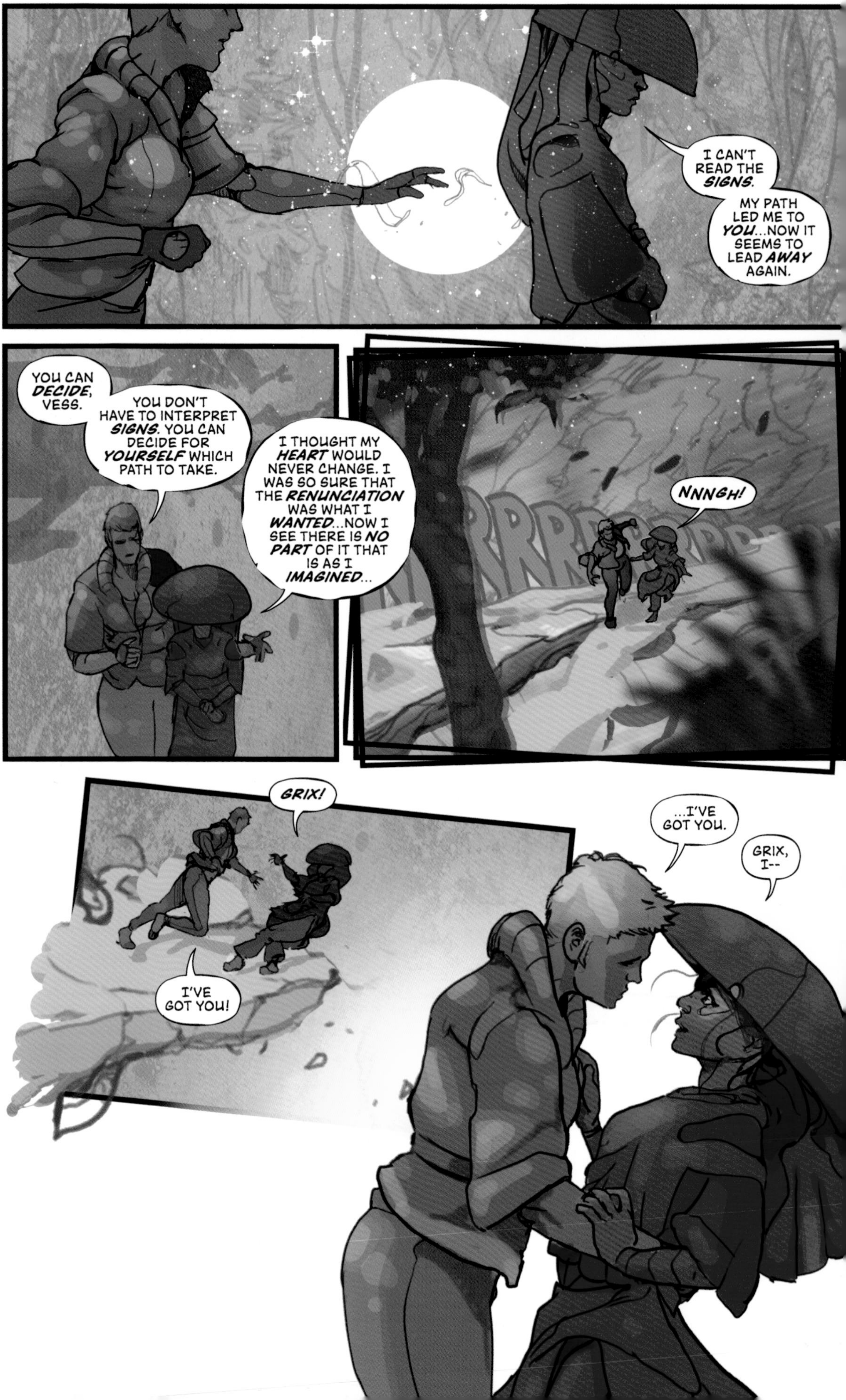
I CAN'T READ THE SIGNS.
MY PATH LED ME TO YOU...NOW IT SEEMS TO LEAD AWAY AGAIN.
YOU CAN DECIDE, VESS.
YOU DON'T HAVE TO INTERPRET SIGNS. YOU CAN DECIDE FOR YOURSELF WHICH PATH TO TAKE.
I THOUGHT MY HEART WOULD NEVER CHANGE. I WAS SO SURE THAT THE RENUNCIATION WAS WHAT I WANTED...NOW I SEE THERE IS NO PART OF IT THAT IS AS I IMAGINED...
NNNGH!
GRIX!
I'VE GOT YOU!
...I'VE GOT YOU.
GRIX, I--

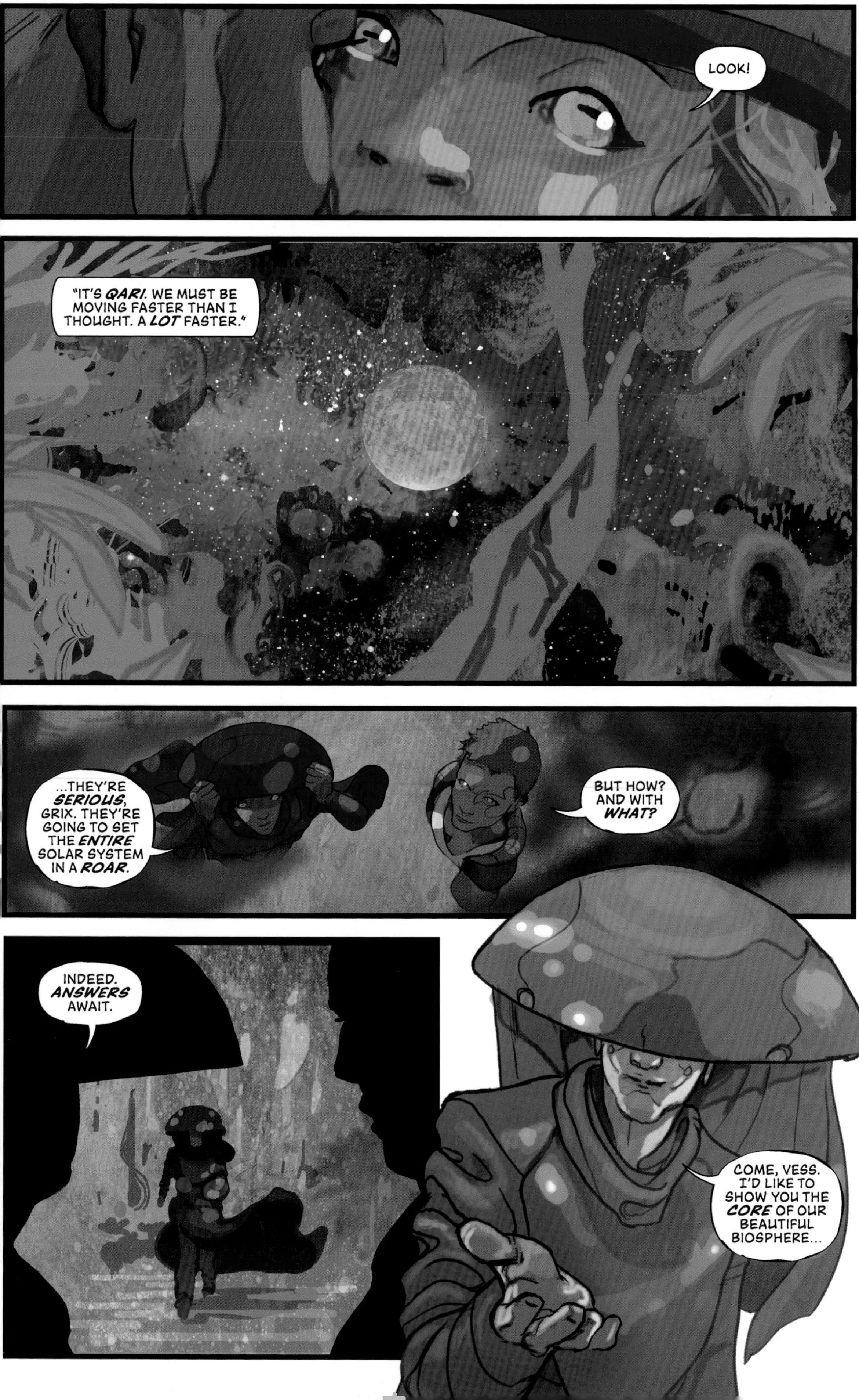
LOOK!
"IT'S QARI. WE MUST BE MOVING FASTER THAN I THOUGHT. A LOT FASTER."
...THEY'RE SERIOUS, GRIX. THEY'RE GOING TO SET THE ENTIRE SOLAR SYSTEM IN A ROAR.
BUT HOW? AND WITH WHAT?
INDEED. ANSWERS AWAIT.
COME, VESS. I'D LIKE TO SHOW YOU THE CORE OF OUR BEAUTIFUL BIOSPHERE...

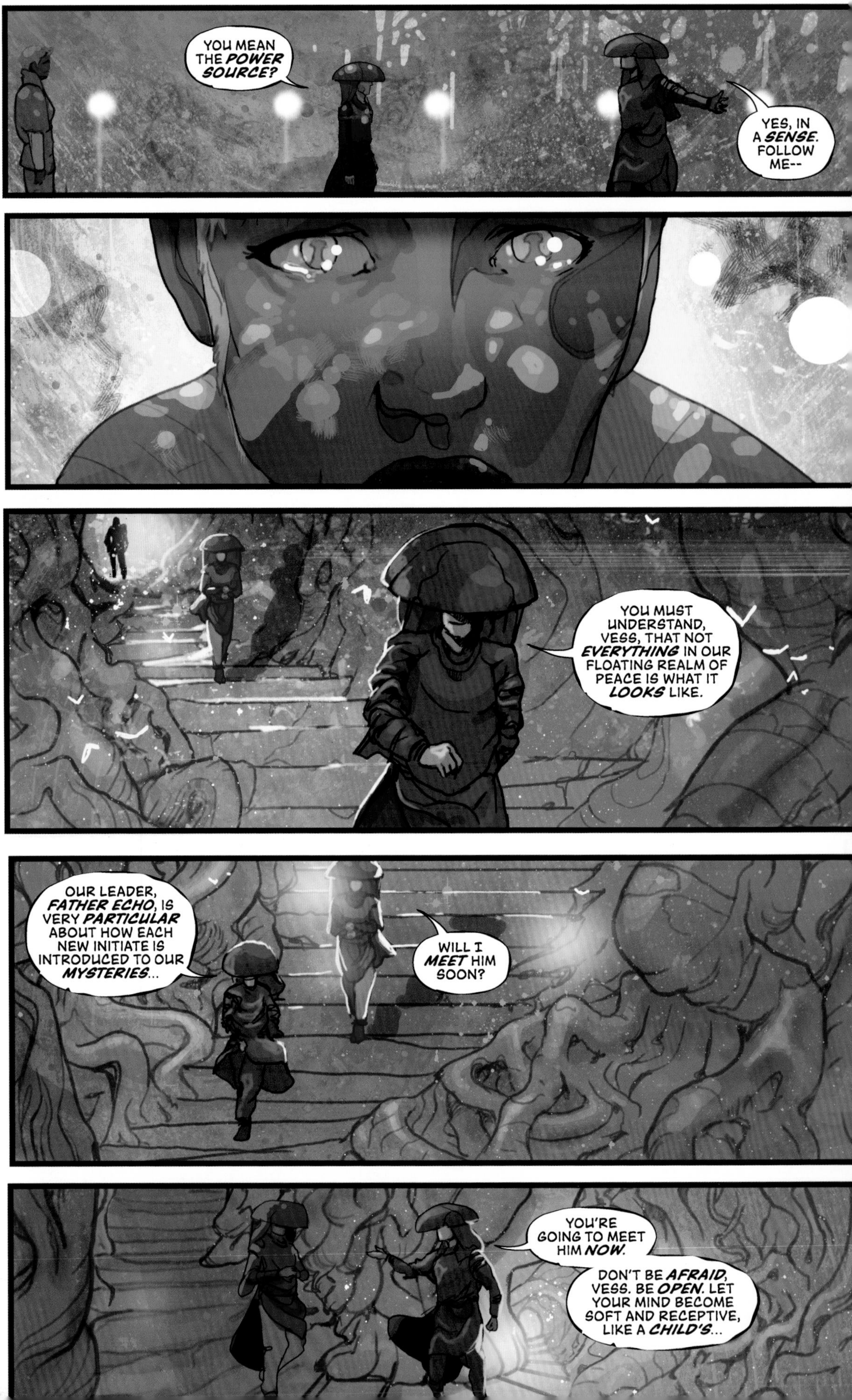

YOU MEAN THE POWER SOURCE?
YES, IN A SENSE. FOLLOW ME--
YOU MUST UNDERSTAND, VESS, THAT NOT EVERYTHING IN OUR FLOATING REALM OF PEACE IS WHAT IT LOOKS LIKE.
OUR LEADER, FATHER ECHO, IS VERY PARTICULAR ABOUT HOW EACH NEW INITIATE IS INTRODUCED TO OUR MYSTERIES...
WILL I MEET HIM SOON?
YOU'RE GOING TO MEET HIM NOW.
DON'T BE AFRAID, VESS. BE OPEN. LET YOUR MIND BECOME SOFT AND RECEPTIVE, LIKE A CHILD'S...

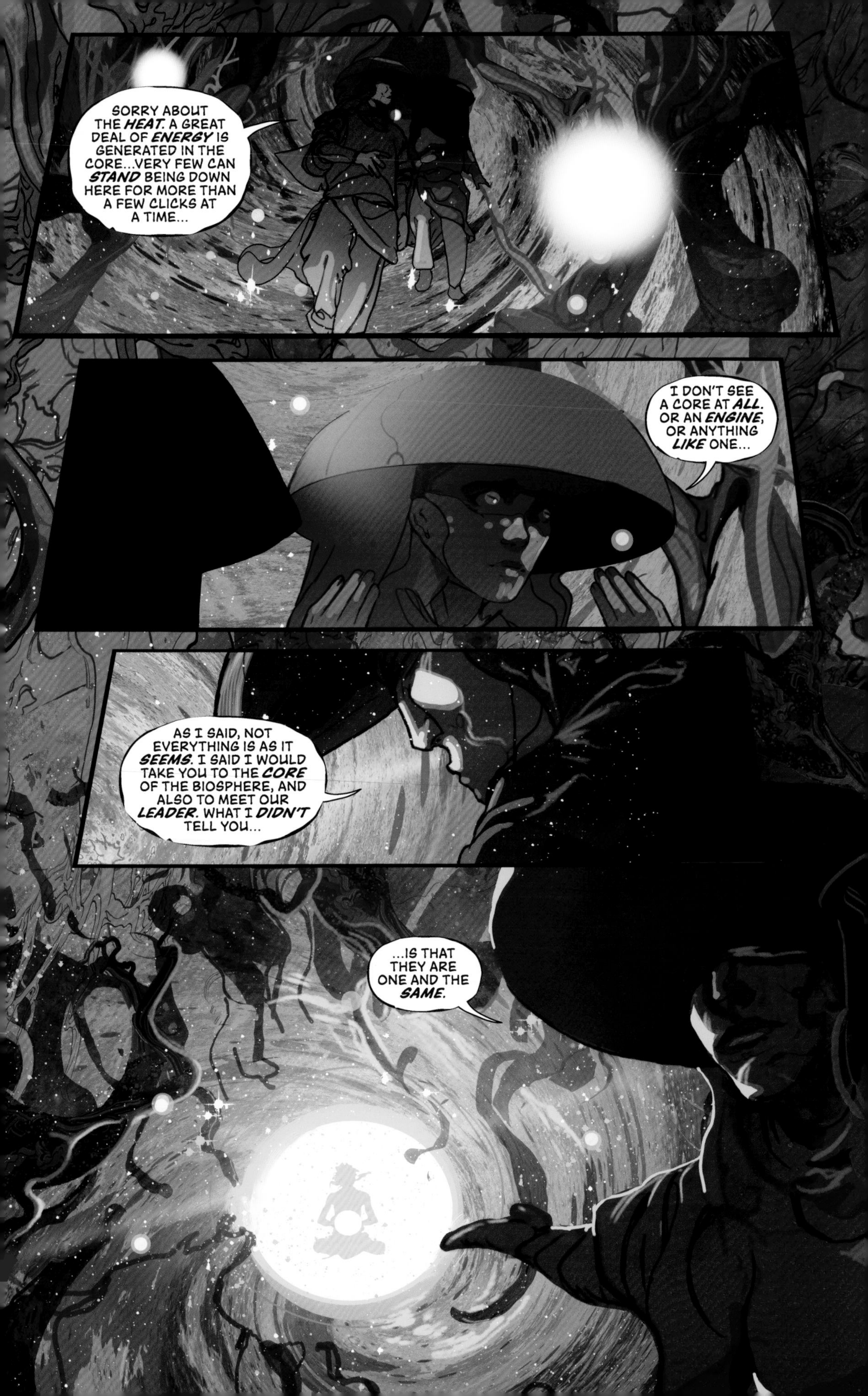
SORRY ABOUT THE HEAT. A GREAT DEAL OF ENERGY IS GENERATED IN THE CORE...VERY FEW CAN STAND BEING DOWN HERE FOR MORE THAN A FEW CLICKS AT A TIME...
I DON'T SEE A CORE AT ALL. OR AN ENGINE, OR ANYTHING LIKE ONE...
AS I SAID, NOT EVERYTHING IS AS IT SEEMS. I SAID I WOULD TAKE YOU TO THE CORE OF THE BIOSPHERE, AND ALSO TO MEET OUR LEADER. WHAT I DIDN'T TELL YOU...
...IS THAT THEY ARE ONE AND THE SAME.

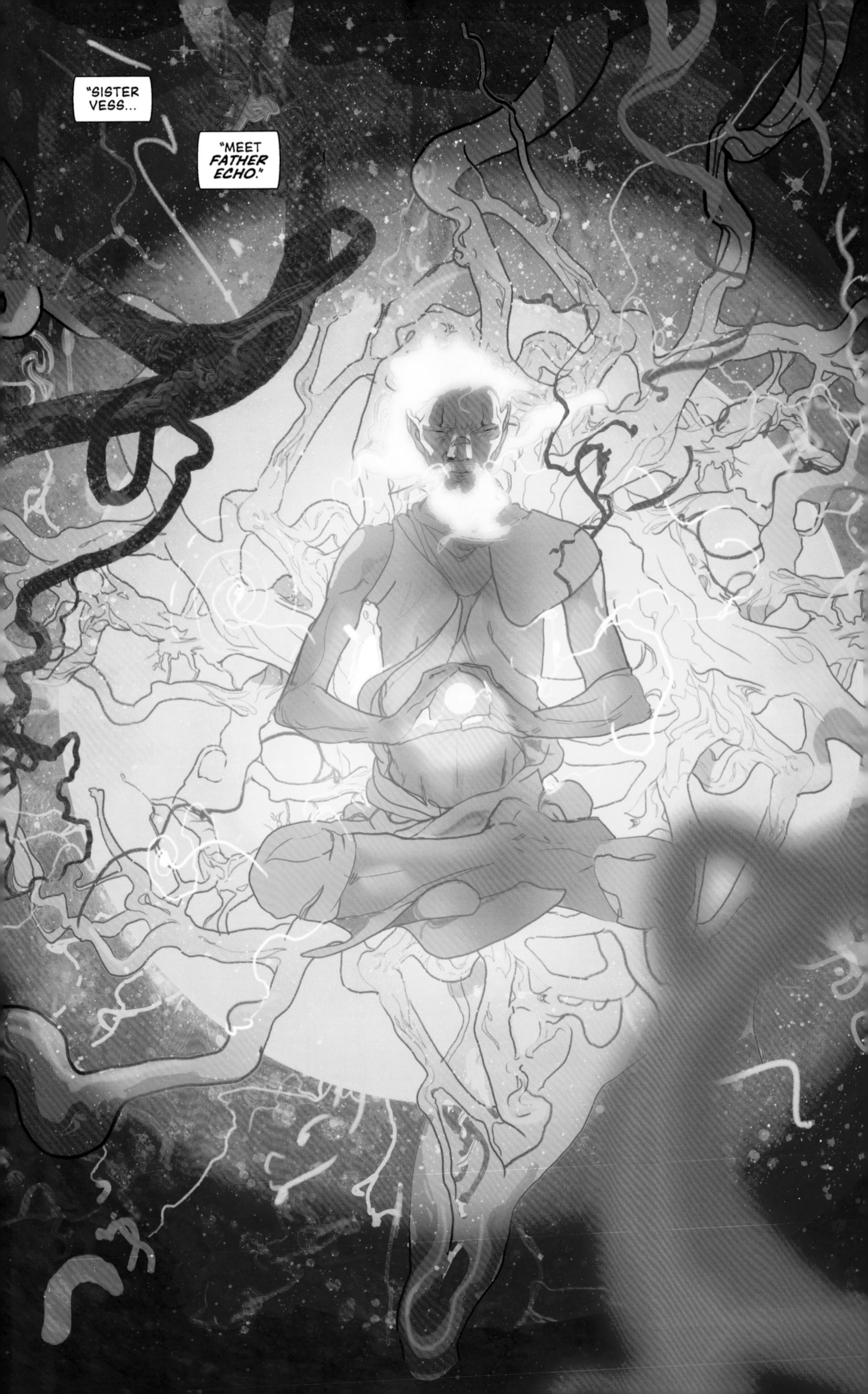
"SISTER VESS...
"MEET *FATHER ECHO*."

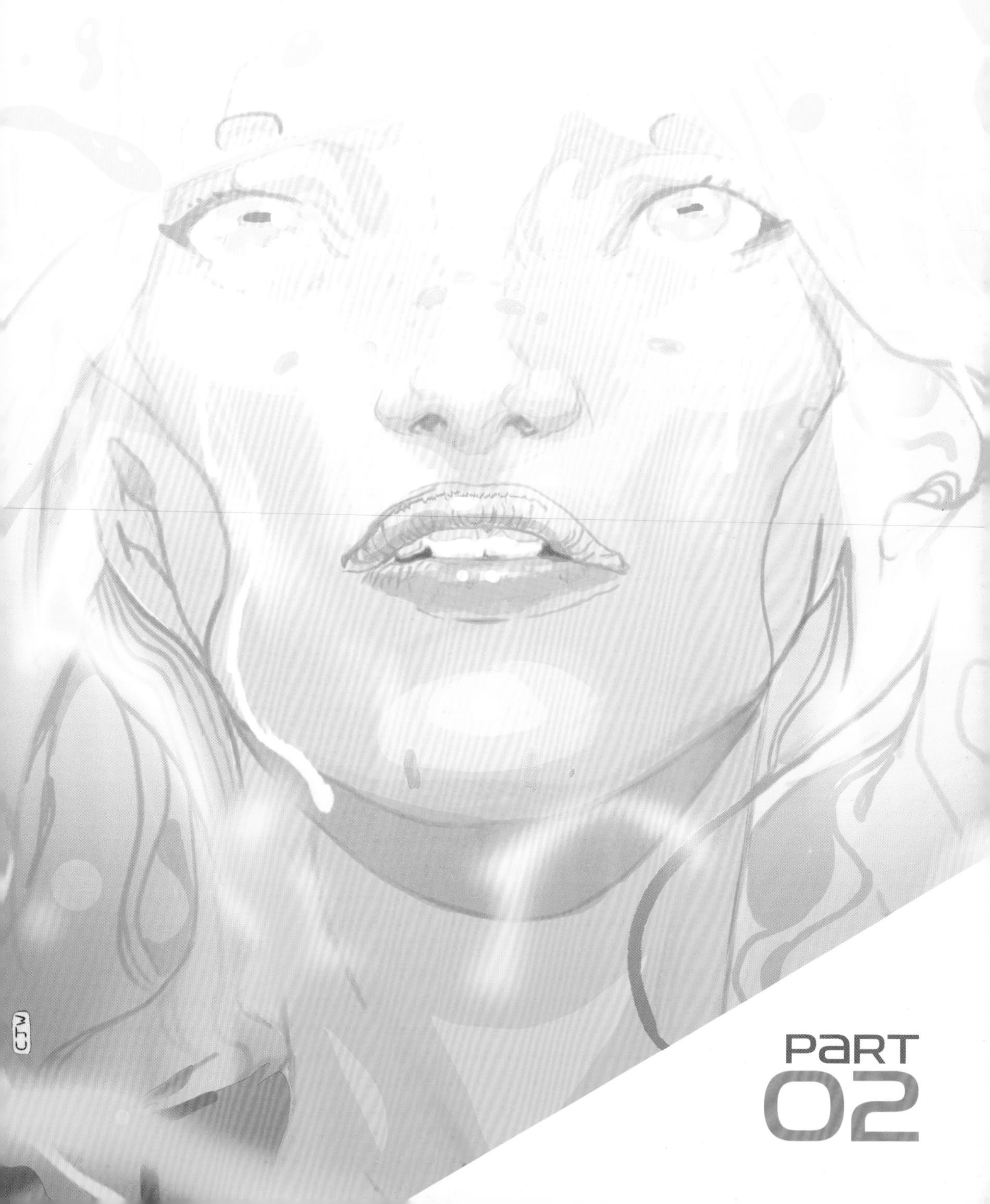

# PART 02

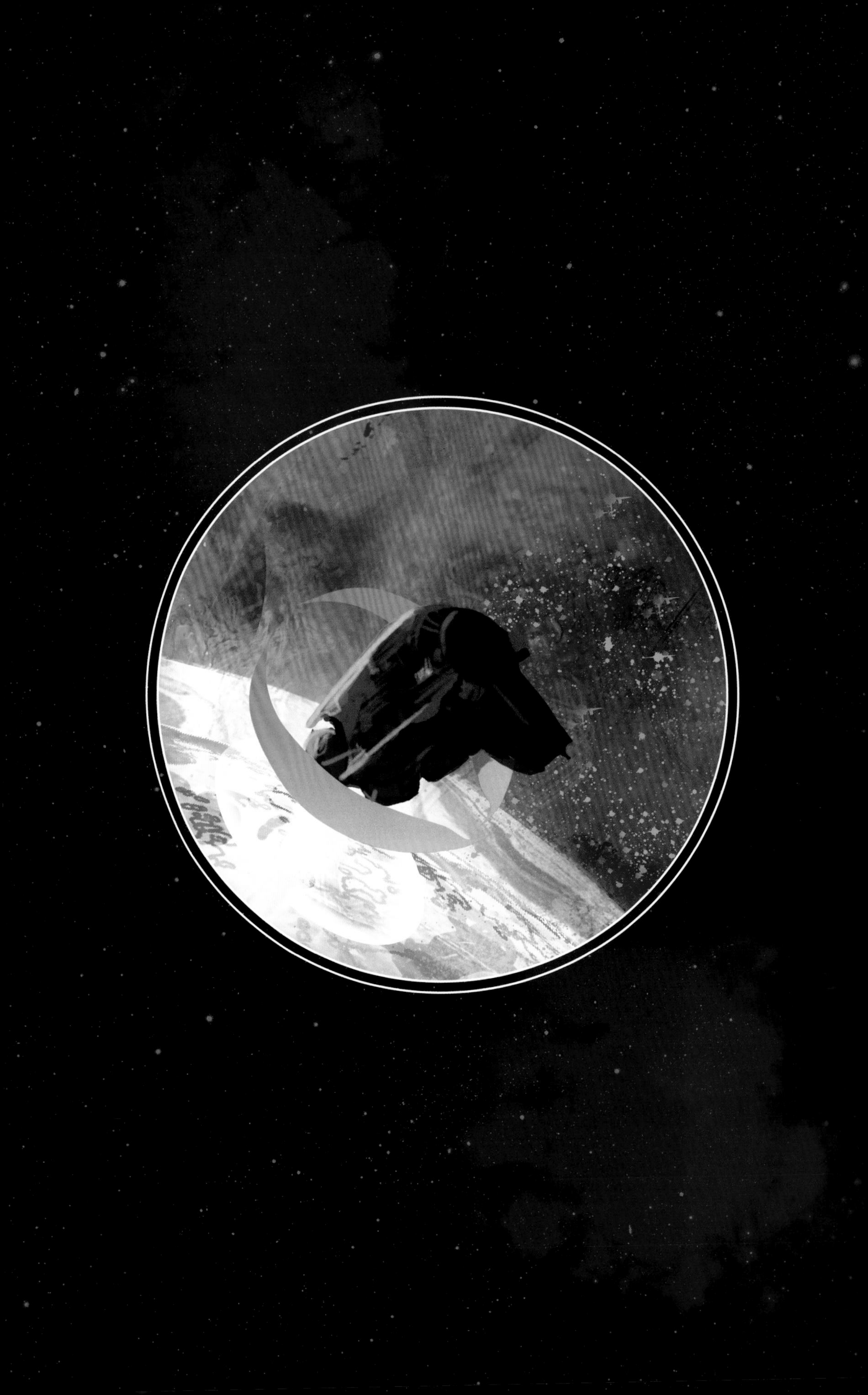

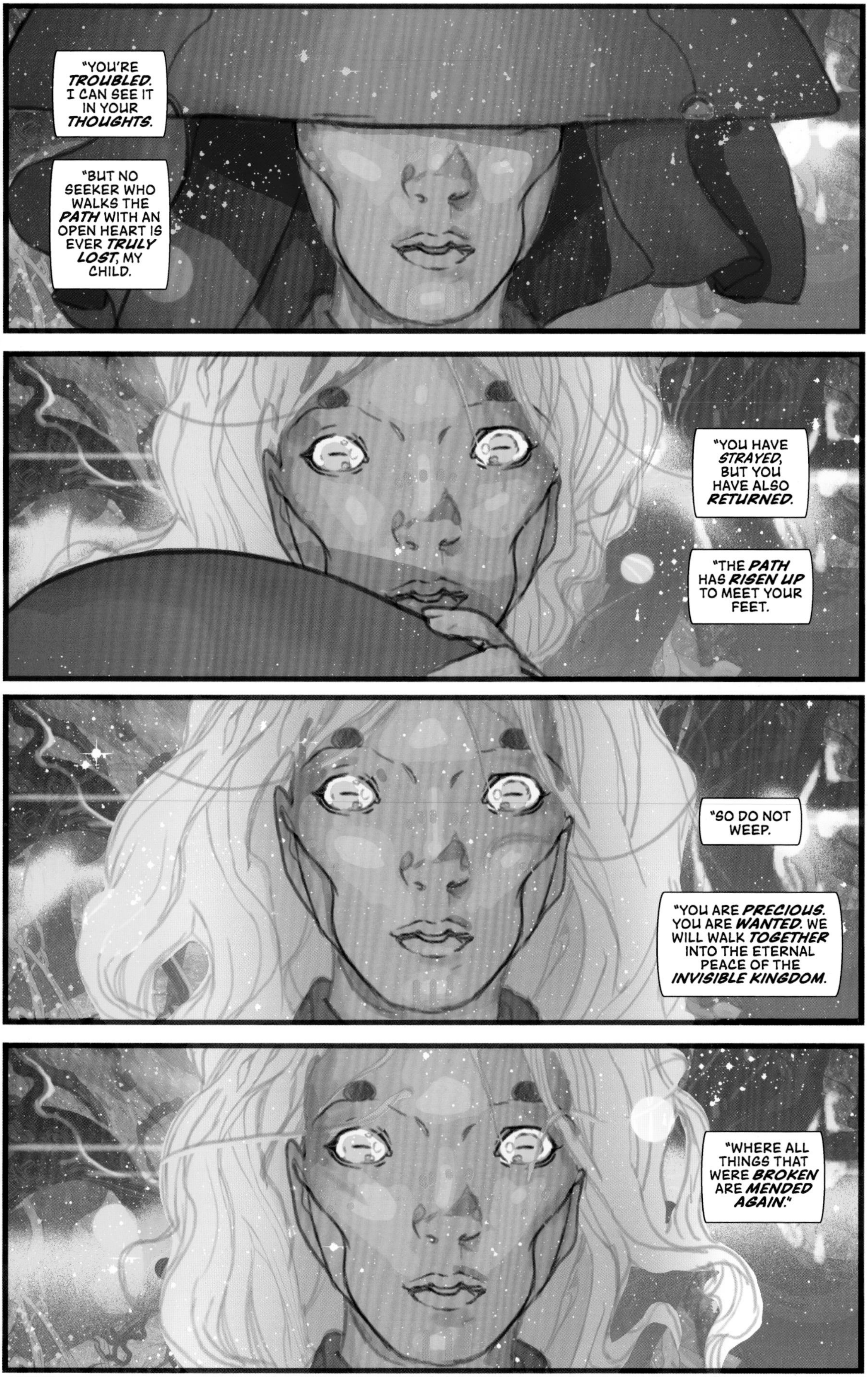
"YOU'RE TROUBLED. I CAN SEE IT IN YOUR THOUGHTS.
"BUT NO SEEKER WHO WALKS THE PATH WITH AN OPEN HEART IS EVER TRULY LOST, MY CHILD.
"YOU HAVE STRAYED, BUT YOU HAVE ALSO RETURNED.
"THE PATH HAS RISEN UP TO MEET YOUR FEET.
"SO DO NOT WEEP.
"YOU ARE PRECIOUS. YOU ARE WANTED. WE WILL WALK TOGETHER INTO THE ETERNAL PEACE OF THE INVISIBLE KINGDOM.
"WHERE ALL THINGS THAT WERE BROKEN ARE MENDED AGAIN."

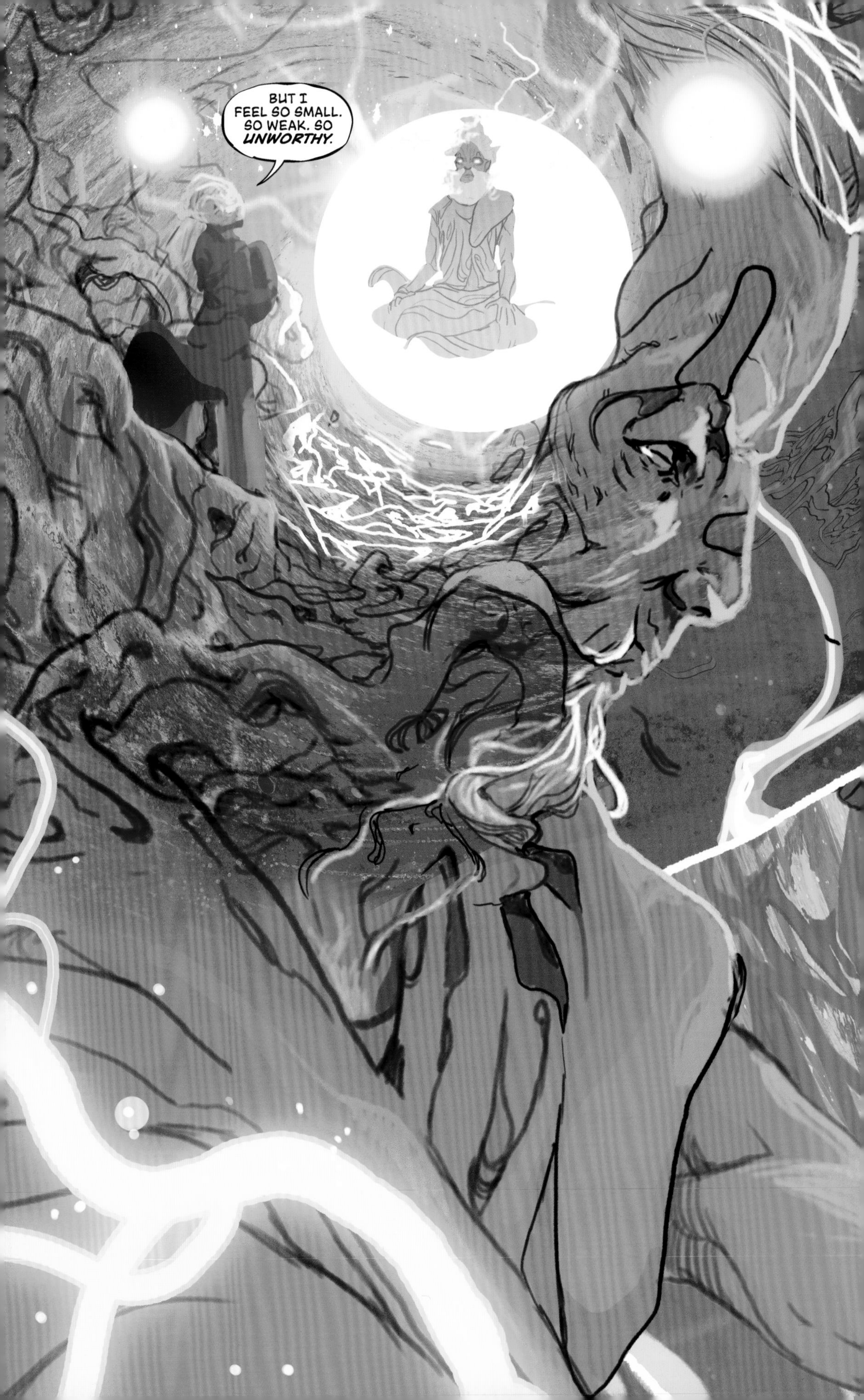
BUT I FEEL SO SMALL. SO WEAK. SO *UNWORTHY*.

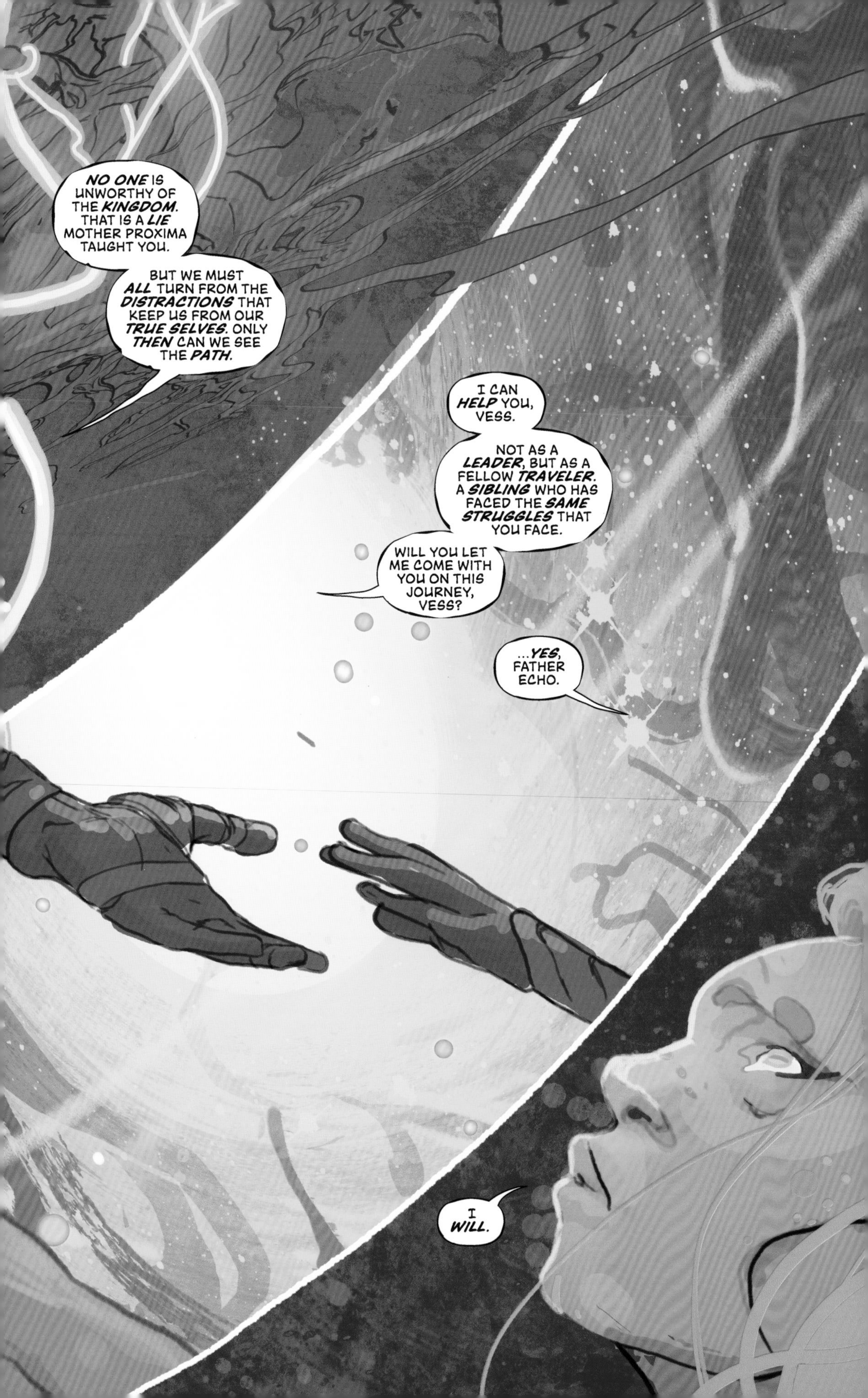
NO ONE IS UNWORTHY OF THE KINGDOM. THAT IS A LIE MOTHER PROXIMA TAUGHT YOU.
BUT WE MUST ALL TURN FROM THE DISTRACTIONS THAT KEEP US FROM OUR TRUE SELVES. ONLY THEN CAN WE SEE THE PATH.
I CAN HELP YOU, VESS.
NOT AS A LEADER, BUT AS A FELLOW TRAVELER. A SIBLING WHO HAS FACED THE SAME STRUGGLES THAT YOU FACE.
WILL YOU LET ME COME WITH YOU ON THIS JOURNEY, VESS?
...YES, FATHER ECHO.
I WILL.

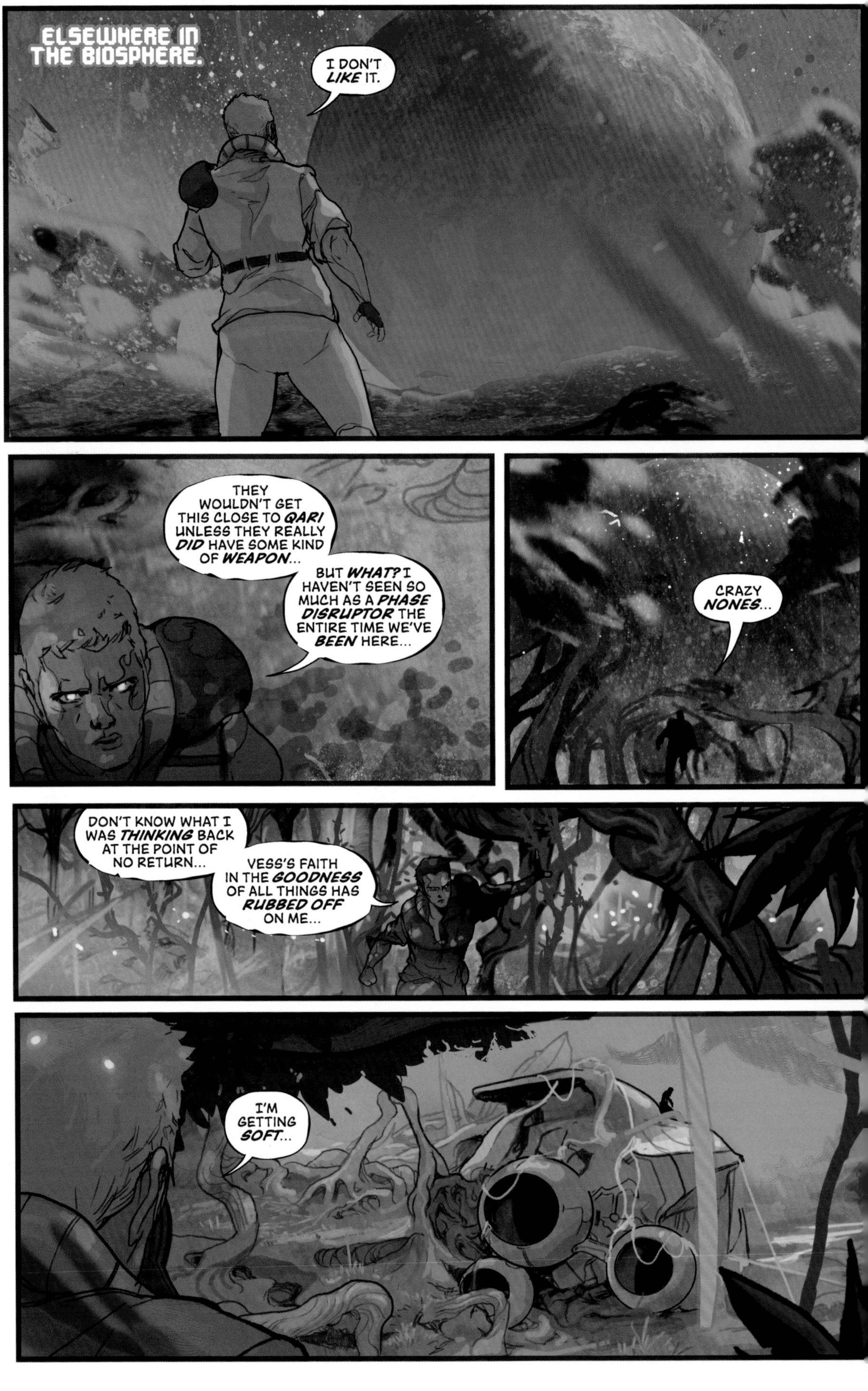
ELSEWHERE IN THE BIOSPHERE.
I DON'T *LIKE* IT.
THEY WOULDN'T GET THIS CLOSE TO *QARI* UNLESS THEY REALLY *DID* HAVE SOME KIND OF *WEAPON*...
BUT *WHAT?* I HAVEN'T SEEN SO MUCH AS A *PHASE DISRUPTOR* THE ENTIRE TIME WE'VE *BEEN* HERE...
CRAZY *NONES*...
DON'T KNOW WHAT I WAS *THINKING* BACK AT THE POINT OF NO RETURN...
VESS'S FAITH IN THE *GOODNESS* OF ALL THINGS HAS *RUBBED OFF* ON ME...
I'M GETTING *SOFT*...

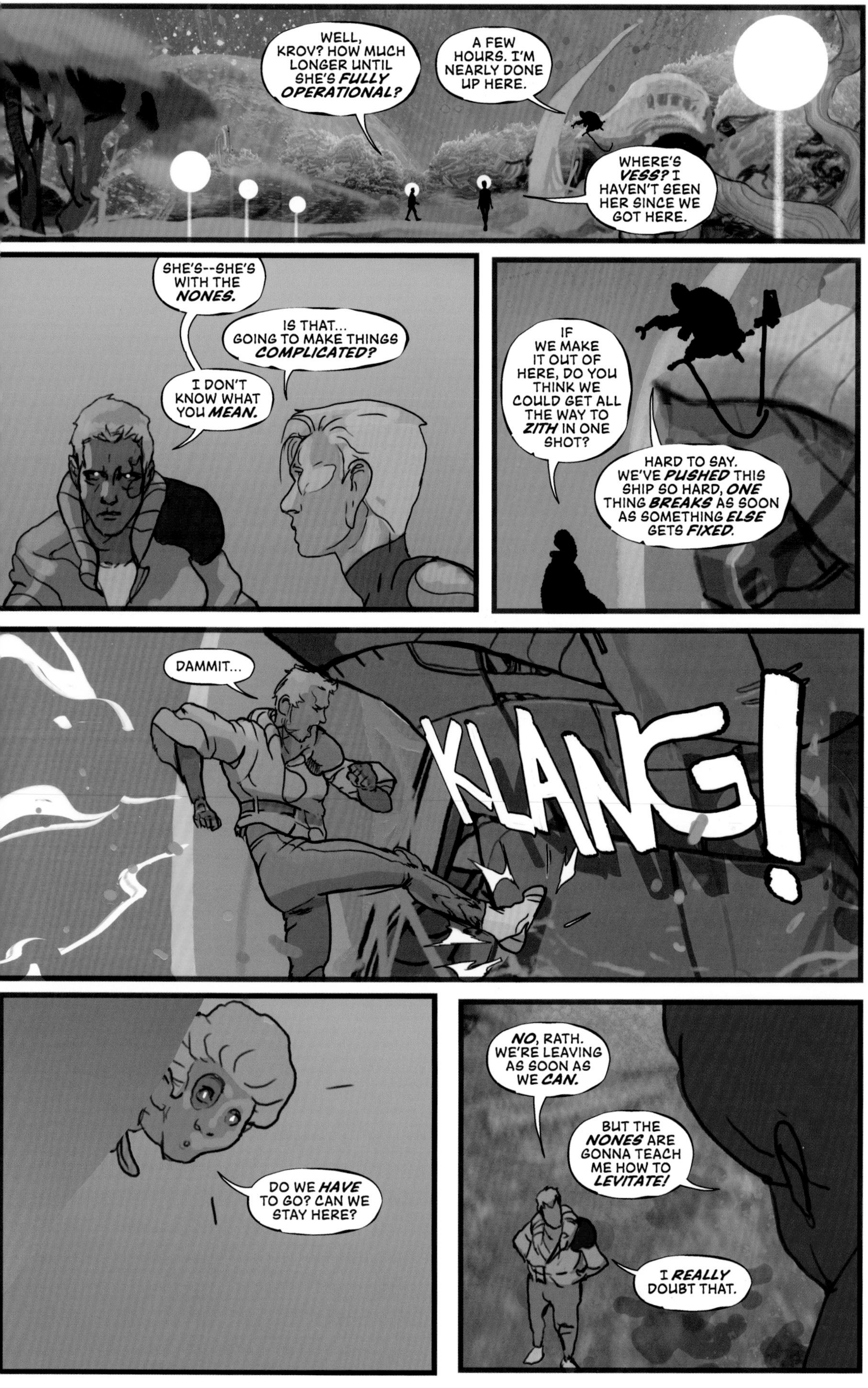
WELL, KROV? HOW MUCH LONGER UNTIL SHE'S *FULLY OPERATIONAL?*
A FEW HOURS. I'M NEARLY DONE UP HERE.
WHERE'S *VESS?* I HAVEN'T SEEN HER SINCE WE GOT HERE.
SHE'S--SHE'S WITH THE *NONES.*
IS THAT... GOING TO MAKE THINGS *COMPLICATED?*
I DON'T KNOW WHAT YOU *MEAN.*
IF WE MAKE IT OUT OF HERE, DO YOU THINK WE COULD GET ALL THE WAY TO *ZITH* IN ONE SHOT?
HARD TO SAY. WE'VE *PUSHED* THIS SHIP SO HARD, *ONE* THING *BREAKS* AS SOON AS SOMETHING *ELSE* GETS *FIXED.*
DAMMIT...
KLANG!
DO WE *HAVE* TO GO? CAN WE STAY HERE?
*NO*, RATH. WE'RE LEAVING AS SOON AS WE *CAN.*
BUT THE *NONES* ARE GONNA TEACH ME HOW TO *LEVITATE!*
I *REALLY* DOUBT THAT.

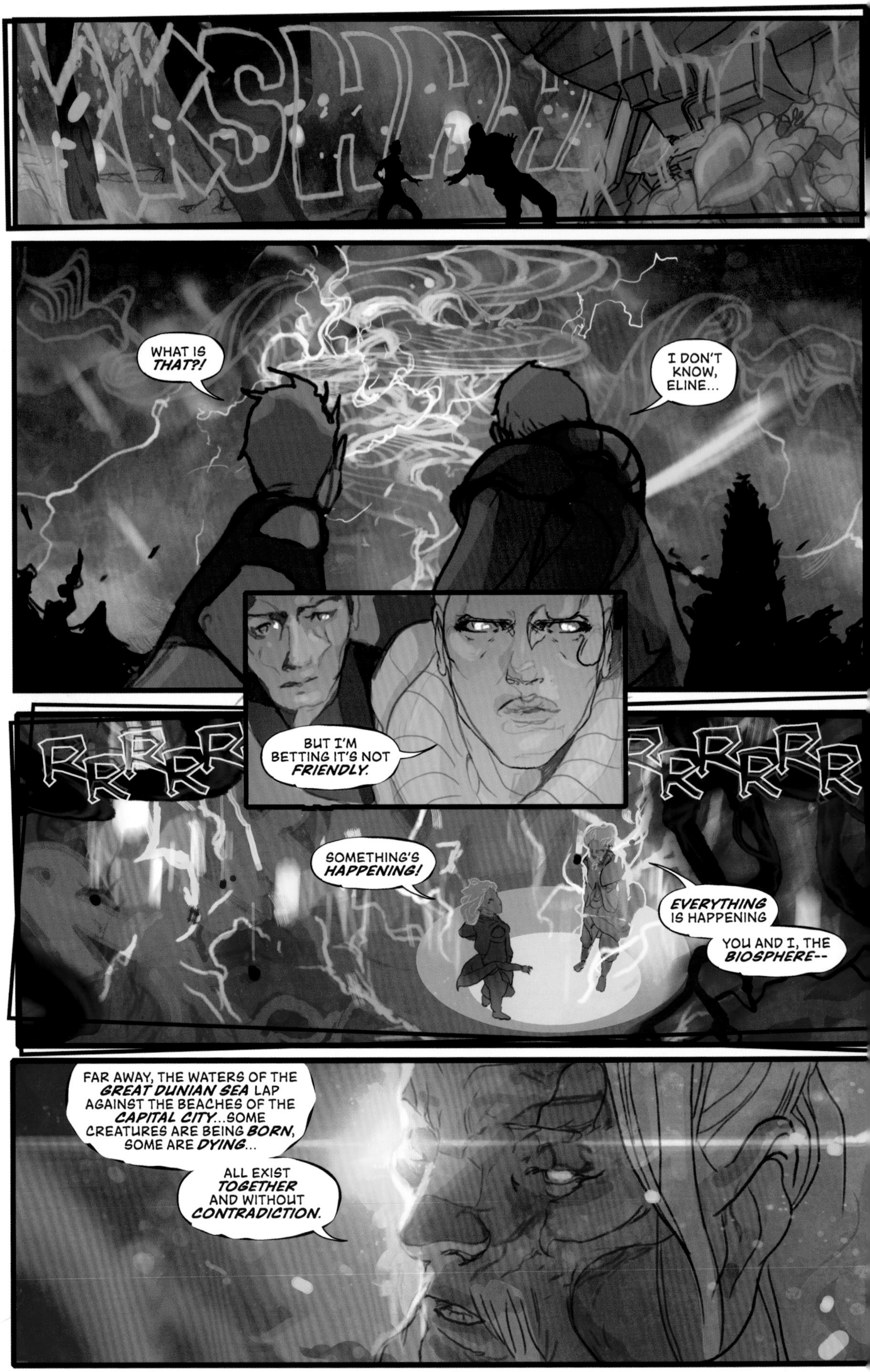
KSHHHH
WHAT IS THAT?!
I DON'T KNOW, ELINE...
BUT I'M BETTING IT'S NOT FRIENDLY.
RRRRRRRRRRRRRR
SOMETHING'S HAPPENING!
EVERYTHING IS HAPPENING
YOU AND I, THE BIOSPHERE--
FAR AWAY, THE WATERS OF THE GREAT DUNIAN SEA LAP AGAINST THE BEACHES OF THE CAPITAL CITY...SOME CREATURES ARE BEING BORN, SOME ARE DYING...
ALL EXIST TOGETHER AND WITHOUT CONTRADICTION.

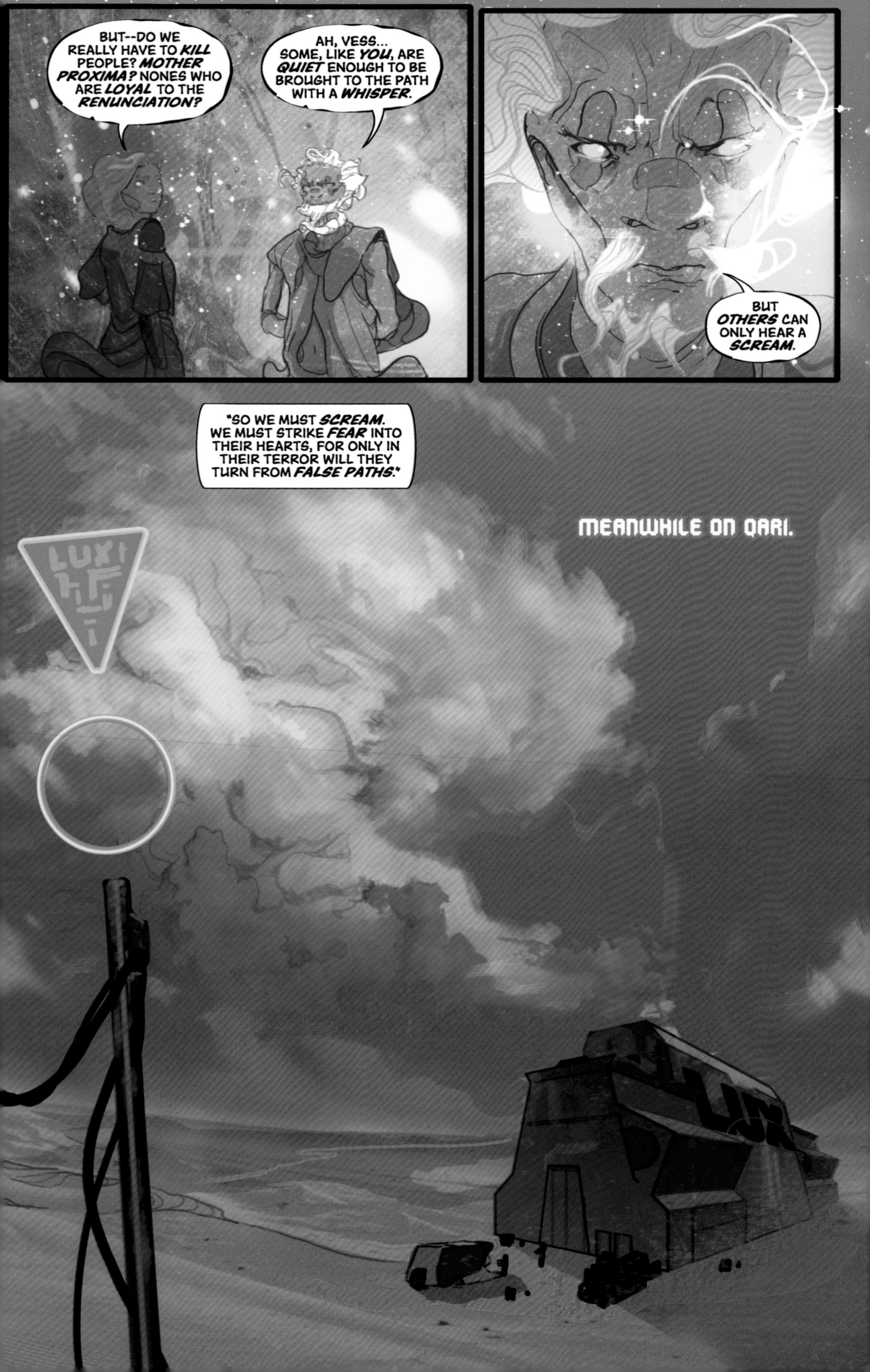
BUT--DO WE REALLY HAVE TO KILL PEOPLE? MOTHER PROXIMA? NONES WHO ARE LOYAL TO THE RENUNCIATION?
AH, VESS... SOME, LIKE YOU, ARE QUIET ENOUGH TO BE BROUGHT TO THE PATH WITH A WHISPER.
BUT OTHERS CAN ONLY HEAR A SCREAM.
"SO WE MUST SCREAM. WE MUST STRIKE FEAR INTO THEIR HEARTS, FOR ONLY IN THEIR TERROR WILL THEY TURN FROM FALSE PATHS."
MEANWHILE ON QARI.
LUX

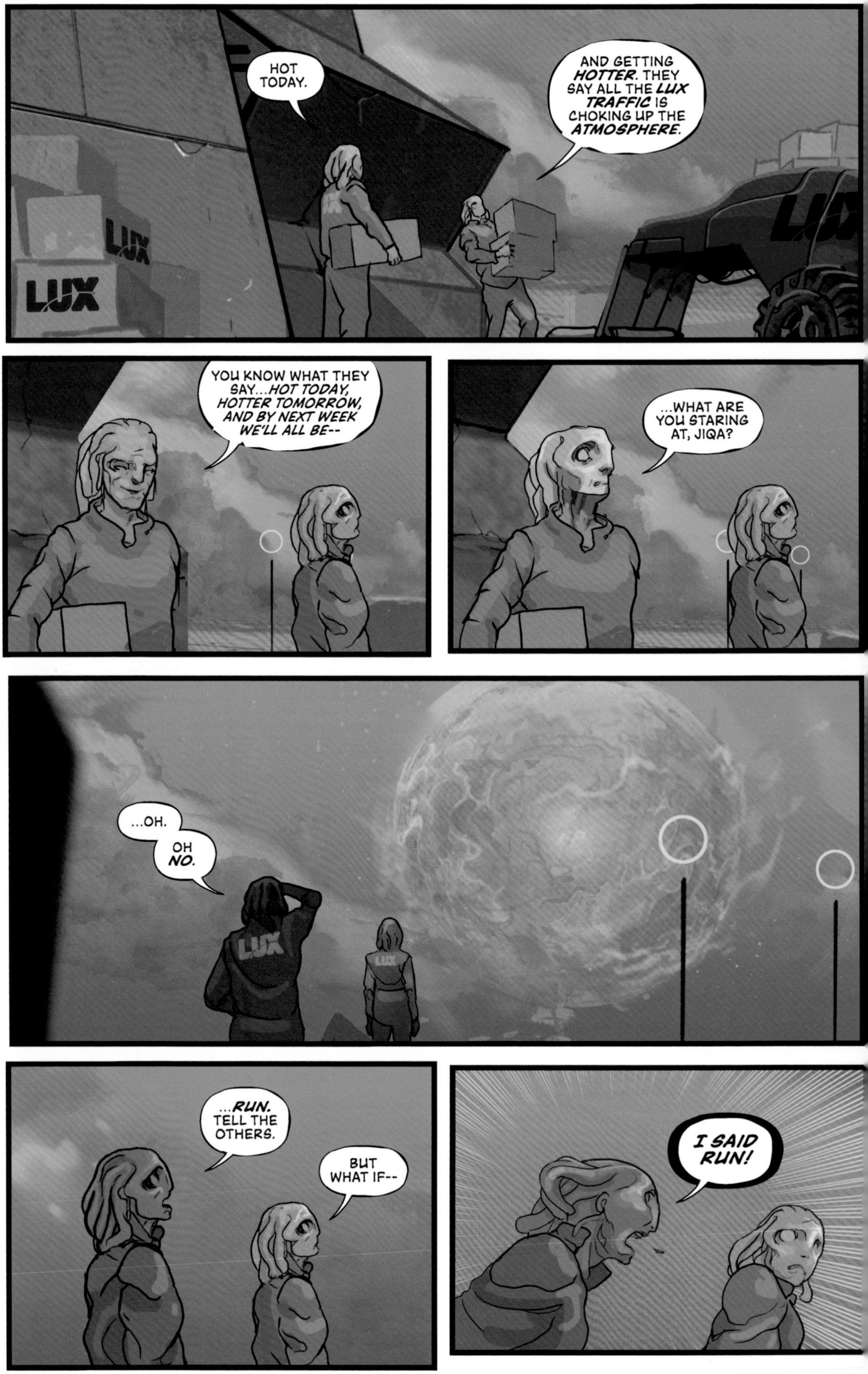
HOT TODAY.
AND GETTING *HOTTER*. THEY SAY ALL THE *LUX TRAFFIC* IS CHOKING UP THE *ATMOSPHERE*.
LUX
LUX
LUX
YOU KNOW WHAT THEY SAY...*HOT TODAY, HOTTER TOMORROW, AND BY NEXT WEEK WE'LL ALL BE--*
...WHAT ARE YOU STARING AT, JIQA?
...OH.
OH *NO.*
LUX
LUX
...*RUN.* TELL THE OTHERS.
BUT WHAT IF--
*I SAID RUN!*

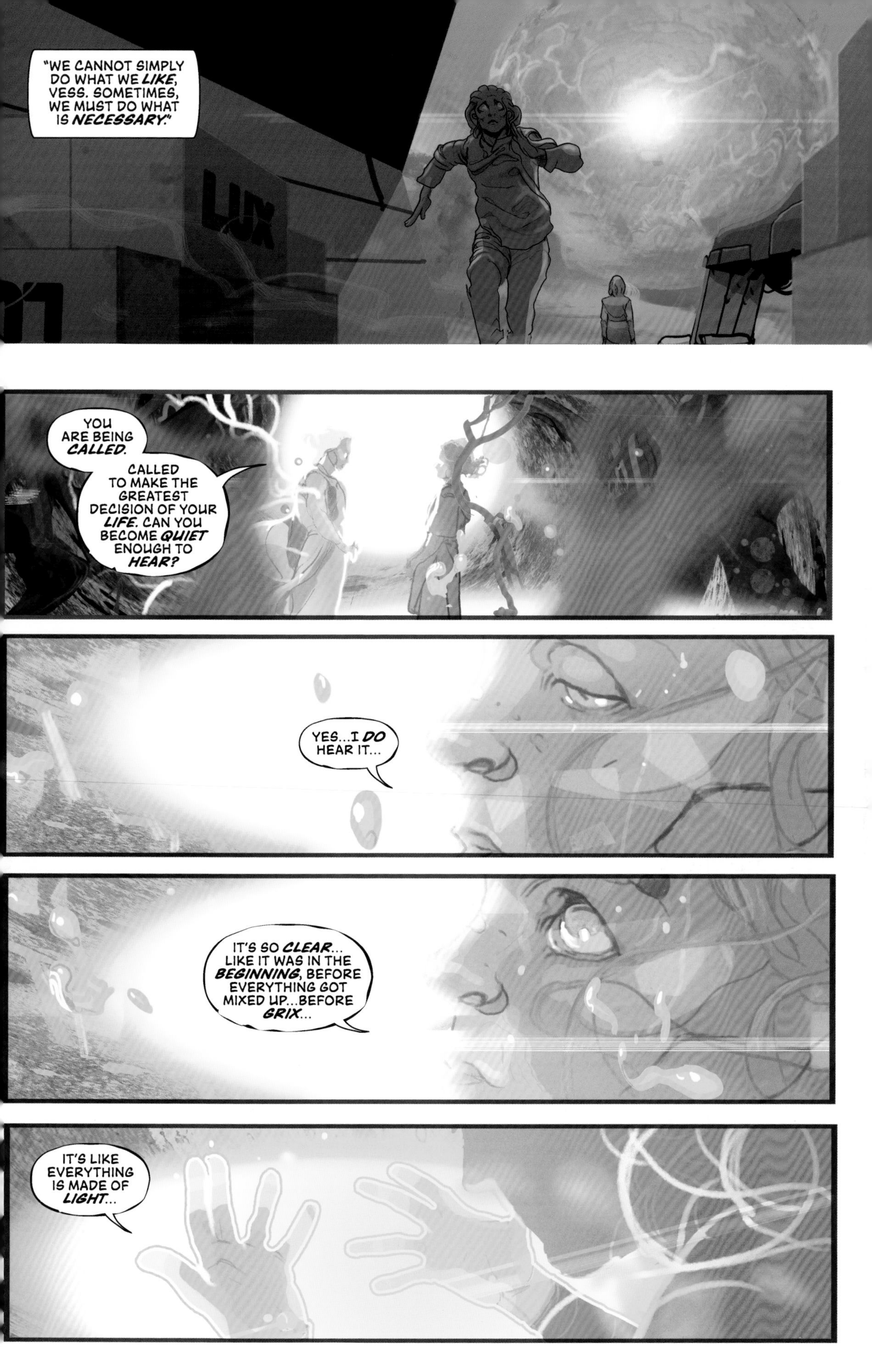
"WE CANNOT SIMPLY DO WHAT WE LIKE, VESS. SOMETIMES, WE MUST DO WHAT IS NECESSARY."
LUX
YOU ARE BEING CALLED.
CALLED TO MAKE THE GREATEST DECISION OF YOUR LIFE. CAN YOU BECOME QUIET ENOUGH TO HEAR?
YES...I DO HEAR IT...
IT'S SO CLEAR... LIKE IT WAS IN THE BEGINNING, BEFORE EVERYTHING GOT MIXED UP...BEFORE GRIX...
IT'S LIKE EVERYTHING IS MADE OF LIGHT...

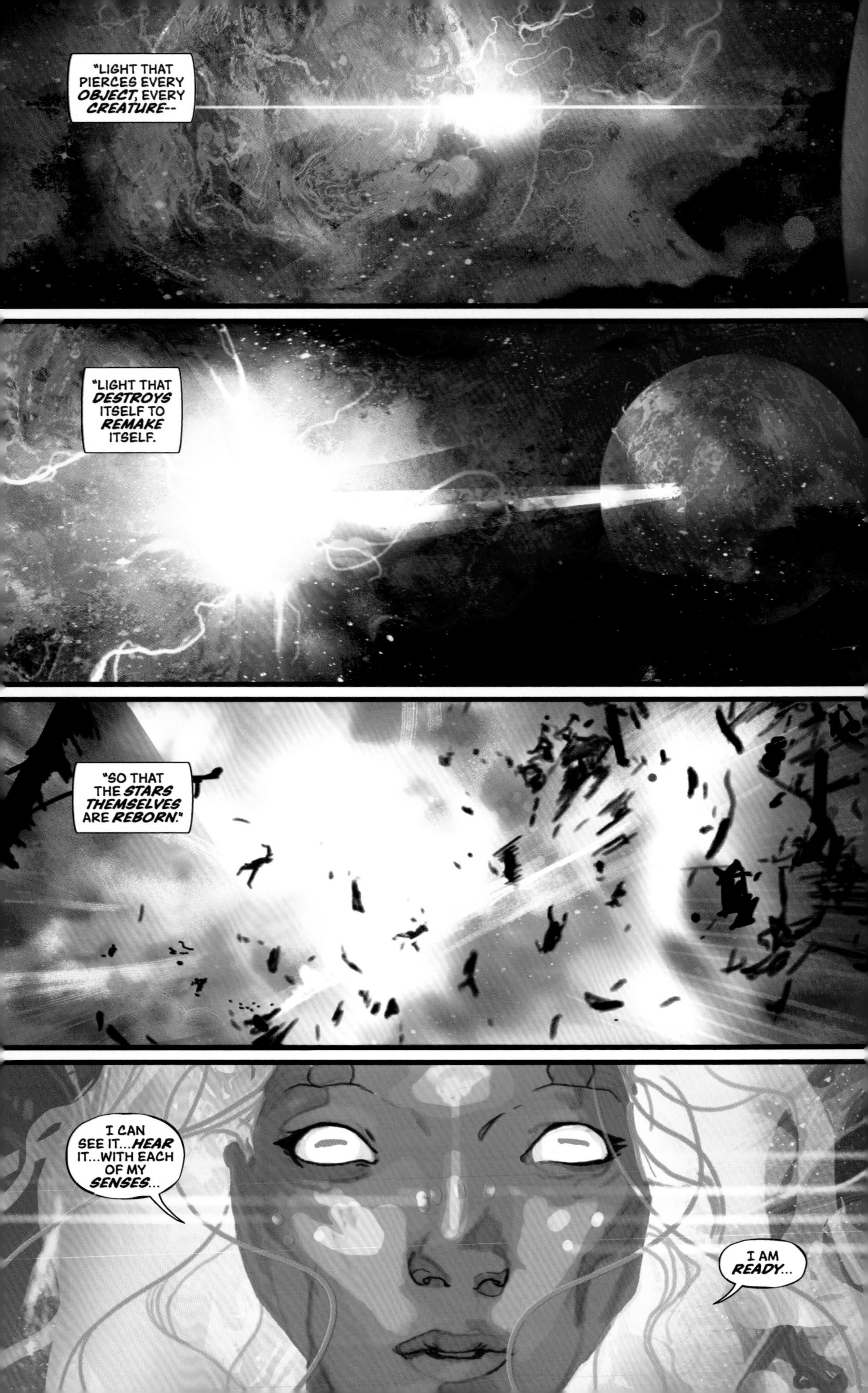
"LIGHT THAT PIERCES EVERY OBJECT, EVERY CREATURE--
"LIGHT THAT DESTROYS ITSELF TO REMAKE ITSELF.
"SO THAT THE STARS THEMSELVES ARE REBORN."
I CAN SEE IT...HEAR IT...WITH EACH OF MY SENSES...
I AM READY...

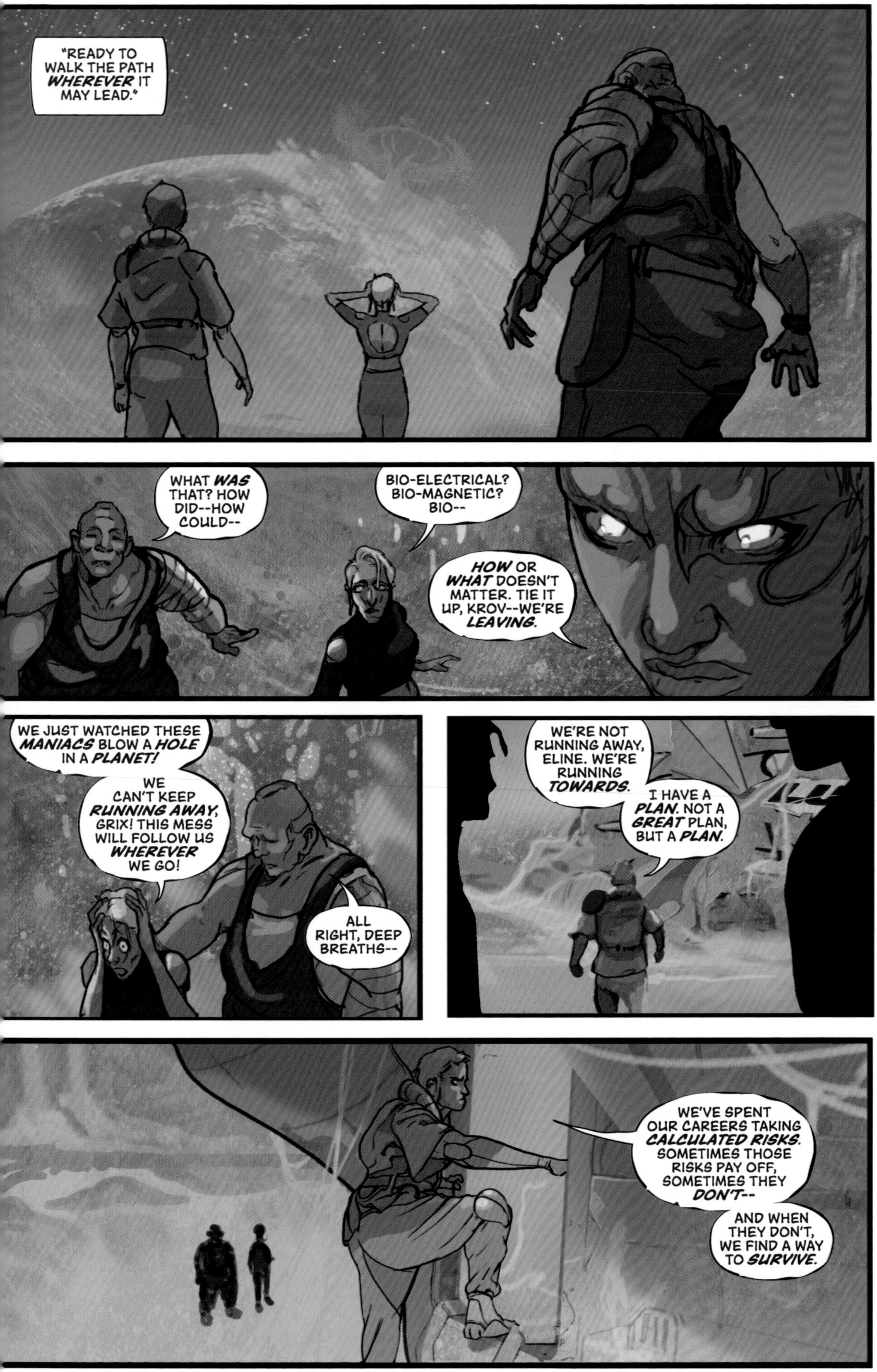
"READY TO WALK THE PATH *WHEREVER* IT MAY LEAD."
WHAT *WAS* THAT? HOW DID--HOW COULD--
BIO-ELECTRICAL? BIO-MAGNETIC? BIO--
*HOW* OR *WHAT* DOESN'T MATTER. TIE IT UP, KROV--WE'RE *LEAVING*.
WE JUST WATCHED THESE *MANIACS* BLOW A *HOLE* IN A *PLANET*!
WE CAN'T KEEP *RUNNING AWAY*, GRIX! THIS MESS WILL FOLLOW US *WHEREVER* WE GO!
ALL RIGHT, DEEP BREATHS--
WE'RE NOT RUNNING AWAY, ELINE. WE'RE RUNNING *TOWARDS*.
I HAVE A *PLAN*. NOT A *GREAT* PLAN, BUT A *PLAN*.
WE'VE SPENT OUR CAREERS TAKING *CALCULATED RISKS*. SOMETIMES THOSE RISKS PAY OFF, SOMETIMES THEY *DON'T*--
AND WHEN THEY DON'T, WE FIND A WAY TO *SURVIVE*.

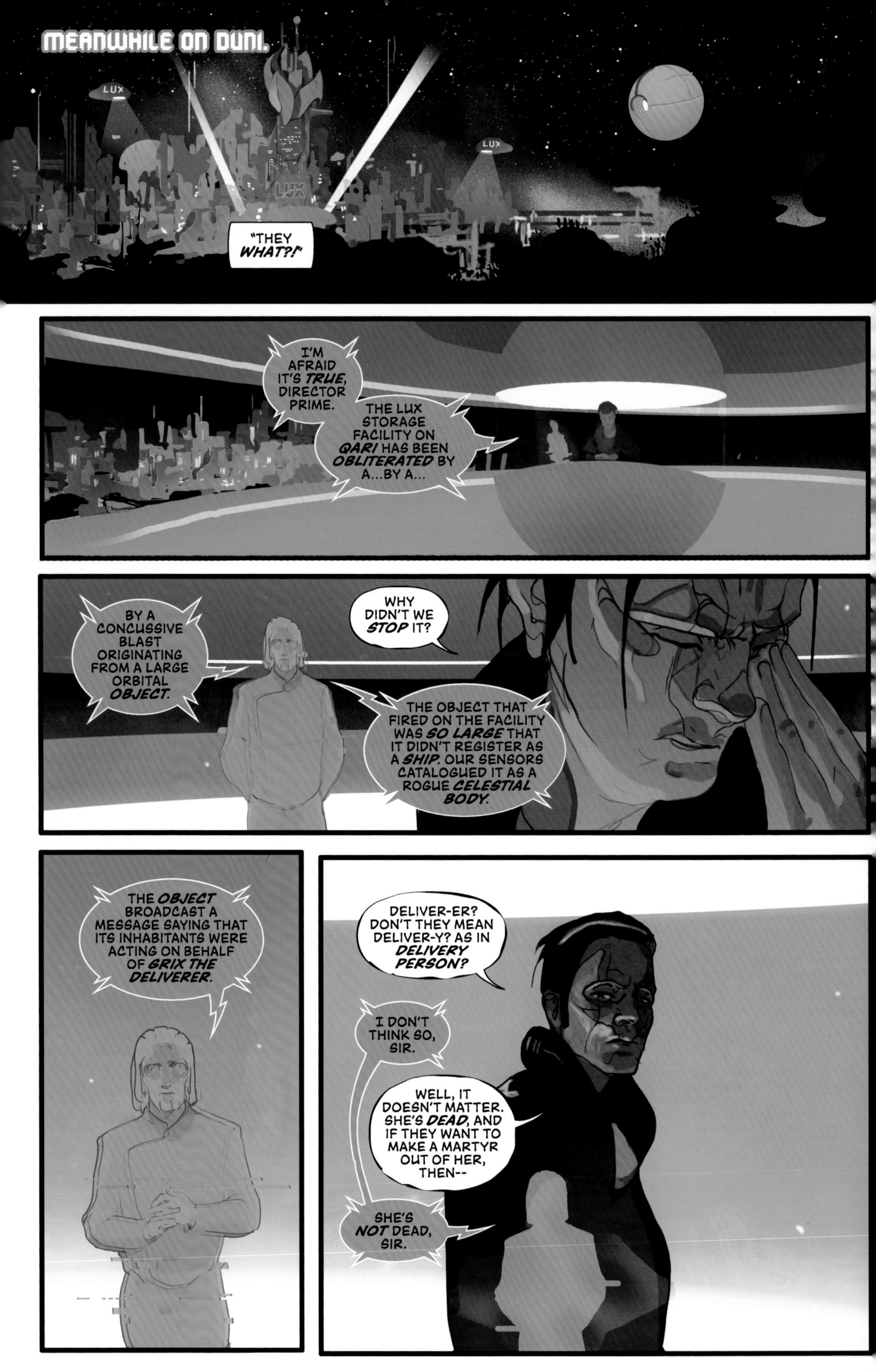
MEANWHILE ON DUNI.
LUX
LUX
LUX
"THEY WHAT?!"
I'M AFRAID IT'S TRUE, DIRECTOR PRIME.
THE LUX STORAGE FACILITY ON QARI HAS BEEN OBLITERATED BY A...BY A...
BY A CONCUSSIVE BLAST ORIGINATING FROM A LARGE ORBITAL OBJECT.
WHY DIDN'T WE STOP IT?
THE OBJECT THAT FIRED ON THE FACILITY WAS SO LARGE THAT IT DIDN'T REGISTER AS A SHIP. OUR SENSORS CATALOGUED IT AS A ROGUE CELESTIAL BODY.
THE OBJECT BROADCAST A MESSAGE SAYING THAT ITS INHABITANTS WERE ACTING ON BEHALF OF GRIX THE DELIVERER.
DELIVER-ER? DON'T THEY MEAN DELIVER-Y? AS IN DELIVERY PERSON?
I DON'T THINK SO, SIR.
WELL, IT DOESN'T MATTER. SHE'S DEAD, AND IF THEY WANT TO MAKE A MARTYR OUT OF HER, THEN--
SHE'S NOT DEAD, SIR.

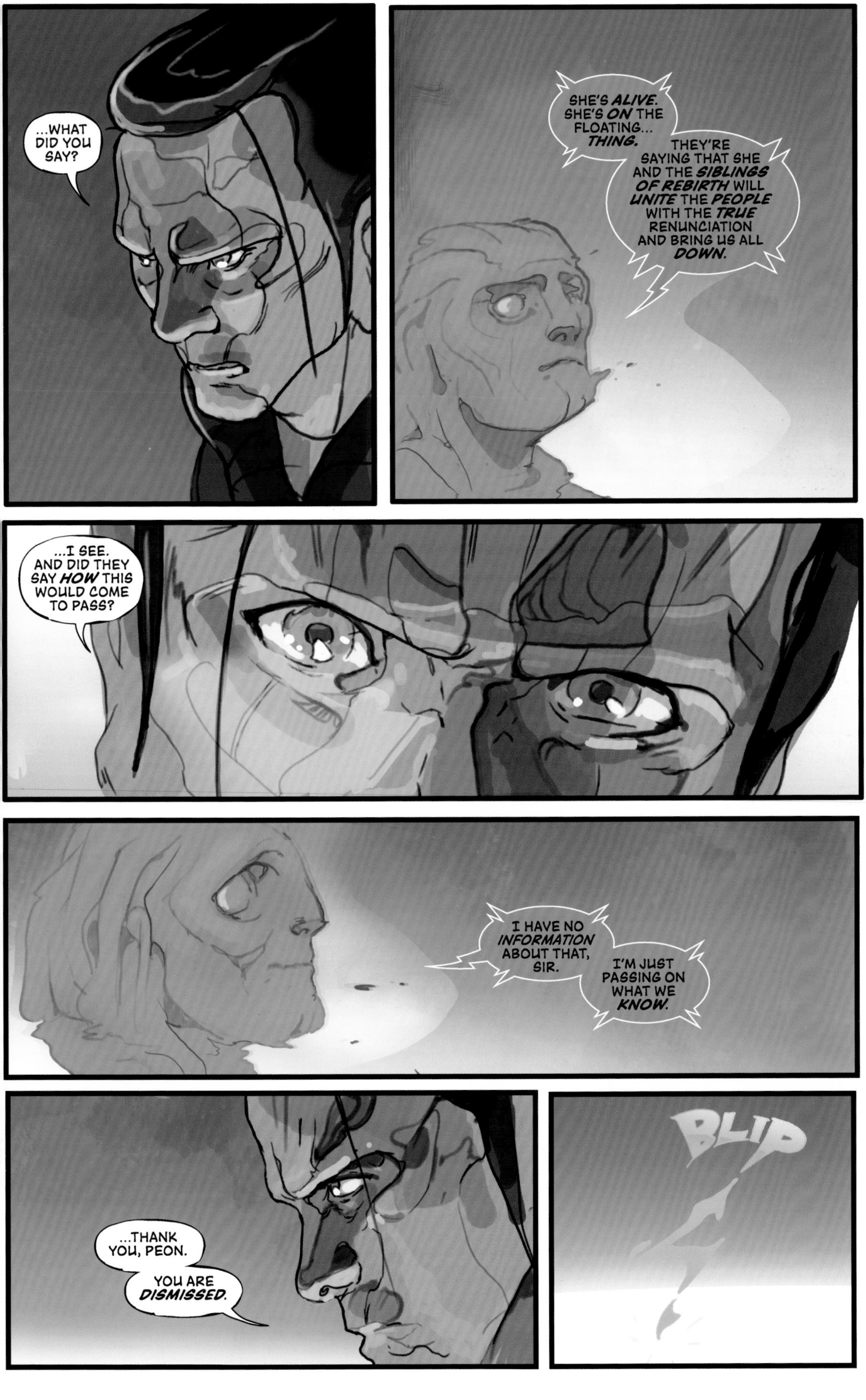
...WHAT DID YOU SAY?
SHE'S ALIVE. SHE'S ON THE FLOATING... THING.
THEY'RE SAYING THAT SHE AND THE SIBLINGS OF REBIRTH WILL UNITE THE PEOPLE WITH THE TRUE RENUNCIATION AND BRING US ALL DOWN.
...I SEE. AND DID THEY SAY HOW THIS WOULD COME TO PASS?
I HAVE NO INFORMATION ABOUT THAT, SIR.
I'M JUST PASSING ON WHAT WE KNOW.
...THANK YOU, PEON.
YOU ARE DISMISSED.
BLIP

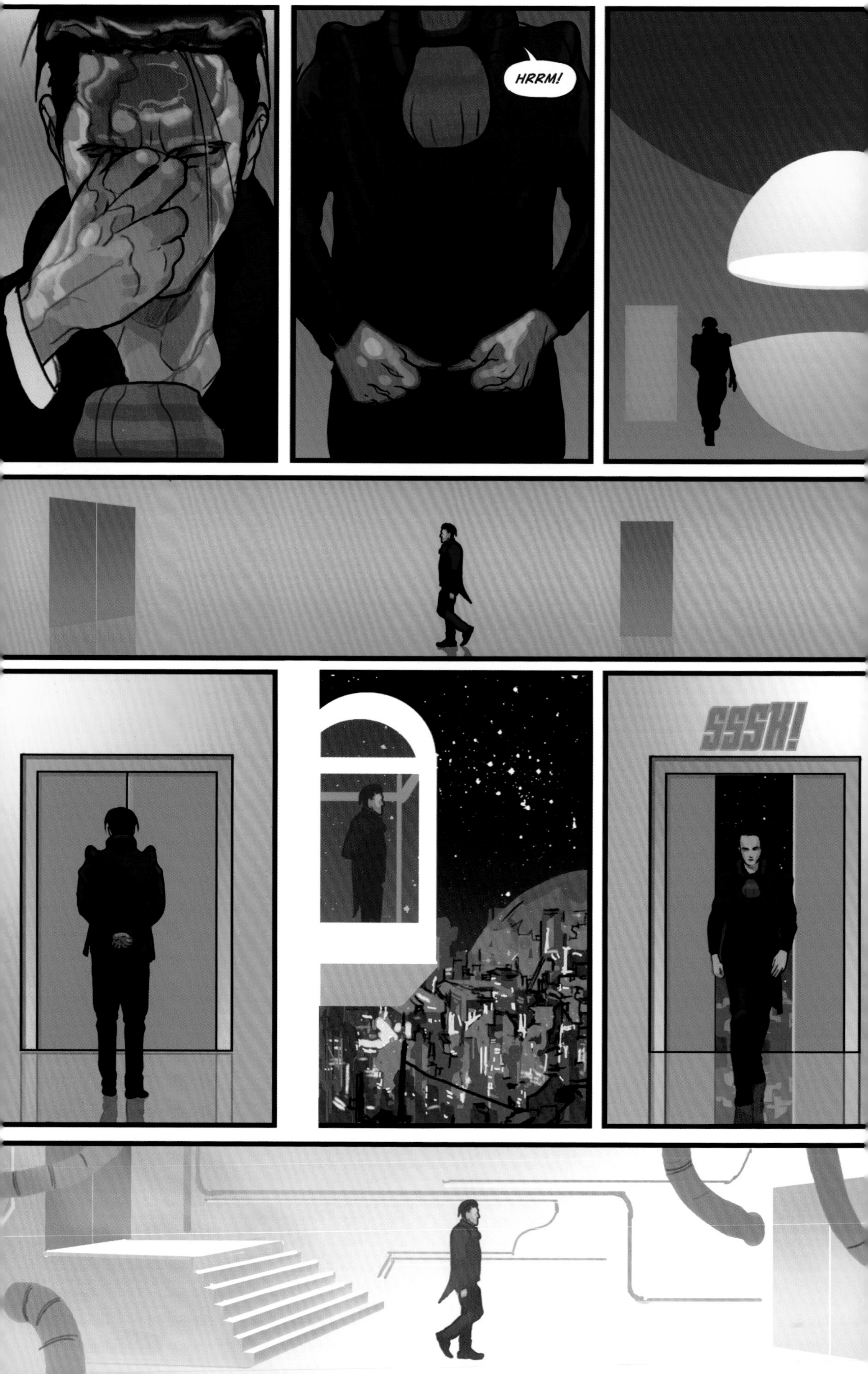
HRRM!
SSSK!

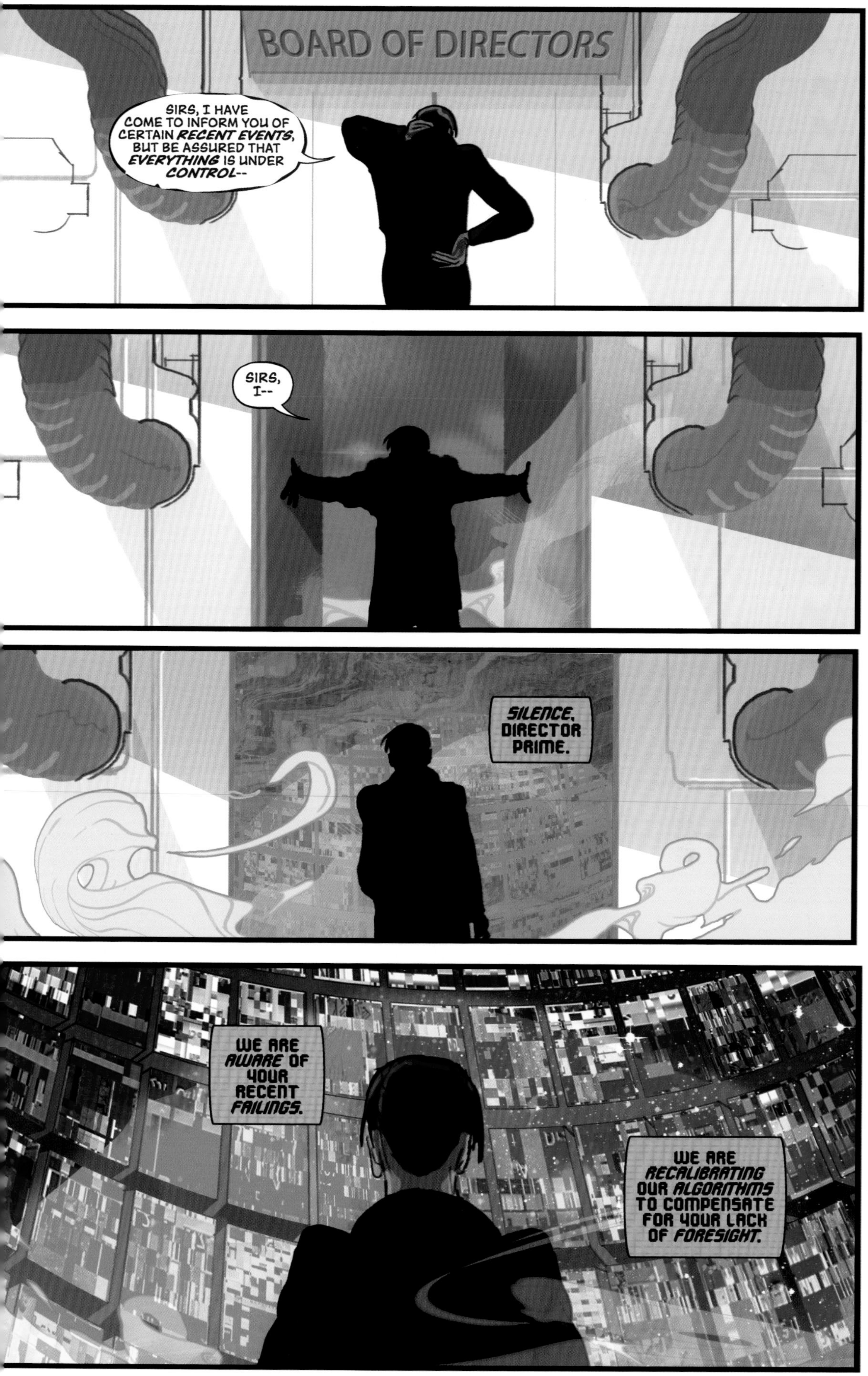
BOARD OF DIRECTORS
SIRS, I HAVE COME TO INFORM YOU OF CERTAIN RECENT EVENTS, BUT BE ASSURED THAT EVERYTHING IS UNDER CONTROL--
SIRS, I--
SILENCE, DIRECTOR PRIME.
WE ARE AWARE OF YOUR RECENT FAILINGS.
WE ARE RECALIBRATING OUR ALGORITHMS TO COMPENSATE FOR YOUR LACK OF FORESIGHT.

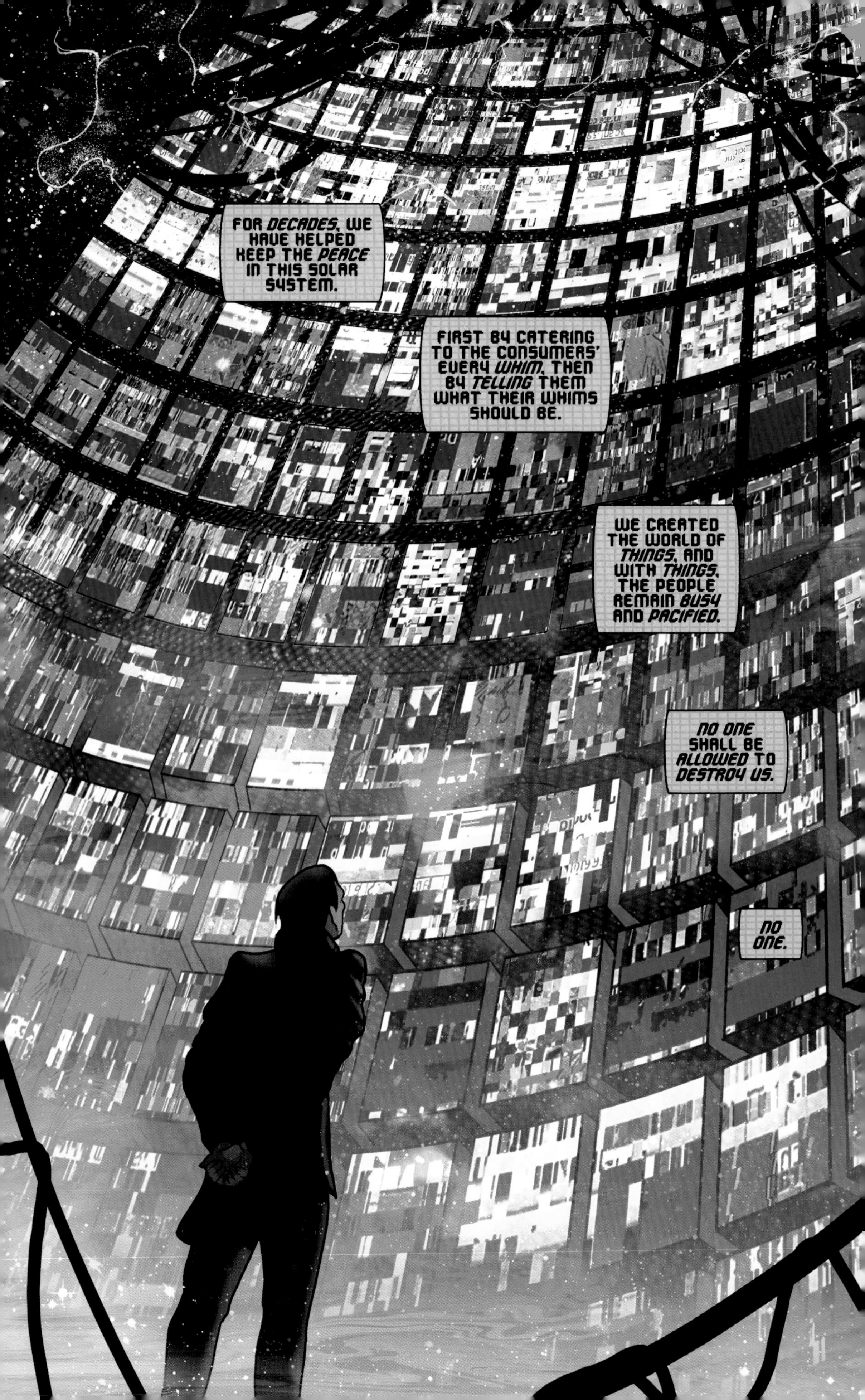
FOR *DECADES*, WE HAVE HELPED KEEP THE *PEACE* IN THIS SOLAR SYSTEM.
FIRST BY CATERING TO THE CONSUMERS' EVERY *WHIM*, THEN BY *TELLING* THEM WHAT THEIR WHIMS SHOULD BE.
WE CREATED THE WORLD OF *THINGS*, AND WITH *THINGS*, THE PEOPLE REMAIN *BUSY* AND *PACIFIED*.
*NO ONE* SHALL BE *ALLOWED* TO *DESTROY US*.
*NO ONE.*

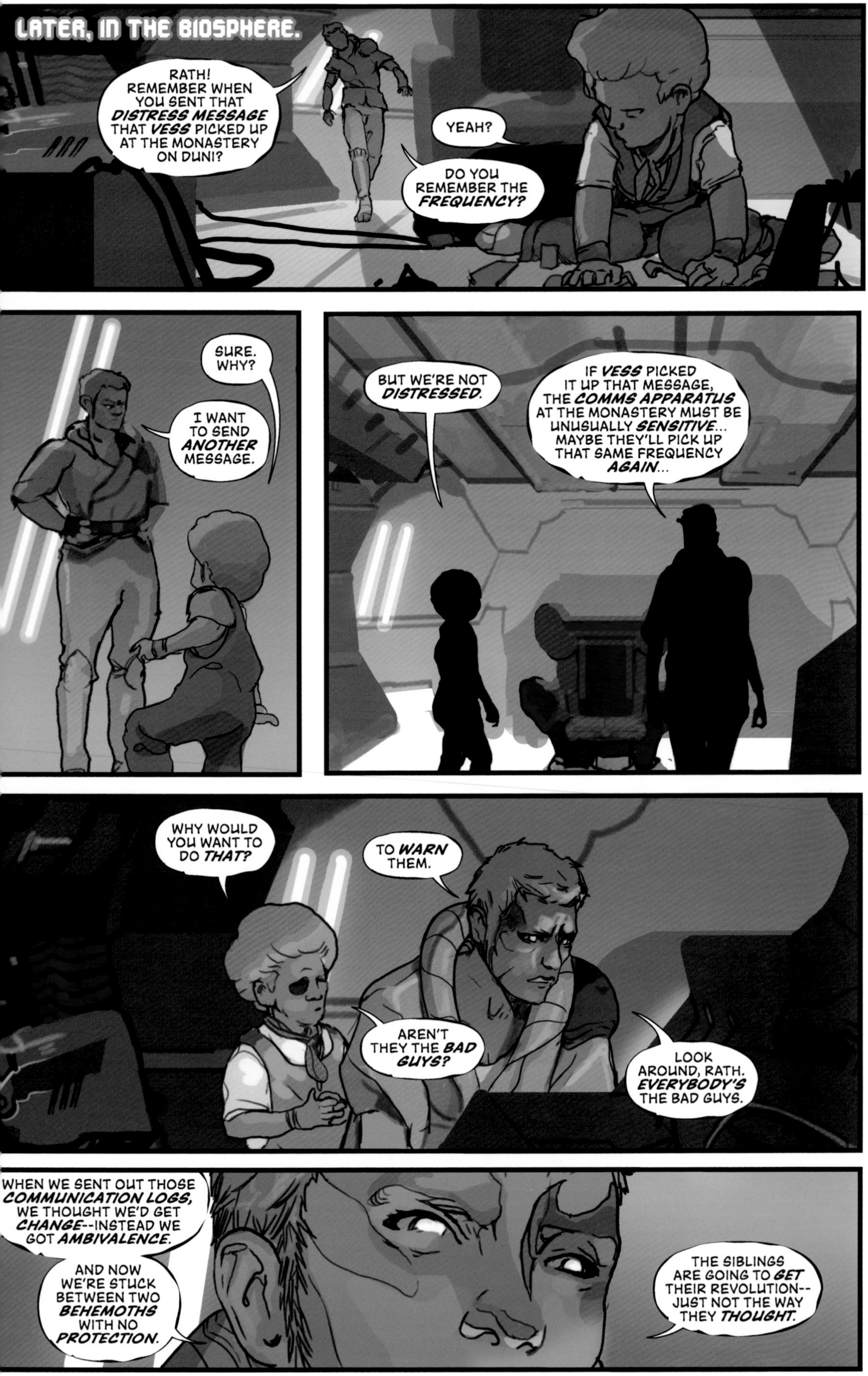
LATER, IN THE BIOSPHERE.
RATH! REMEMBER WHEN YOU SENT THAT DISTRESS MESSAGE THAT VESS PICKED UP AT THE MONASTERY ON DUNI?
YEAH?
DO YOU REMEMBER THE FREQUENCY?
SURE. WHY?
I WANT TO SEND ANOTHER MESSAGE.
BUT WE'RE NOT DISTRESSED.
IF VESS PICKED IT UP THAT MESSAGE, THE COMMS APPARATUS AT THE MONASTERY MUST BE UNUSUALLY SENSITIVE... MAYBE THEY'LL PICK UP THAT SAME FREQUENCY AGAIN...
WHY WOULD YOU WANT TO DO THAT?
TO WARN THEM.
AREN'T THEY THE BAD GUYS?
LOOK AROUND, RATH. EVERYBODY'S THE BAD GUYS.
WHEN WE SENT OUT THOSE COMMUNICATION LOGS, WE THOUGHT WE'D GET CHANGE--INSTEAD WE GOT AMBIVALENCE.
AND NOW WE'RE STUCK BETWEEN TWO BEHEMOTHS WITH NO PROTECTION.
THE SIBLINGS ARE GOING TO GET THEIR REVOLUTION-- JUST NOT THE WAY THEY THOUGHT.

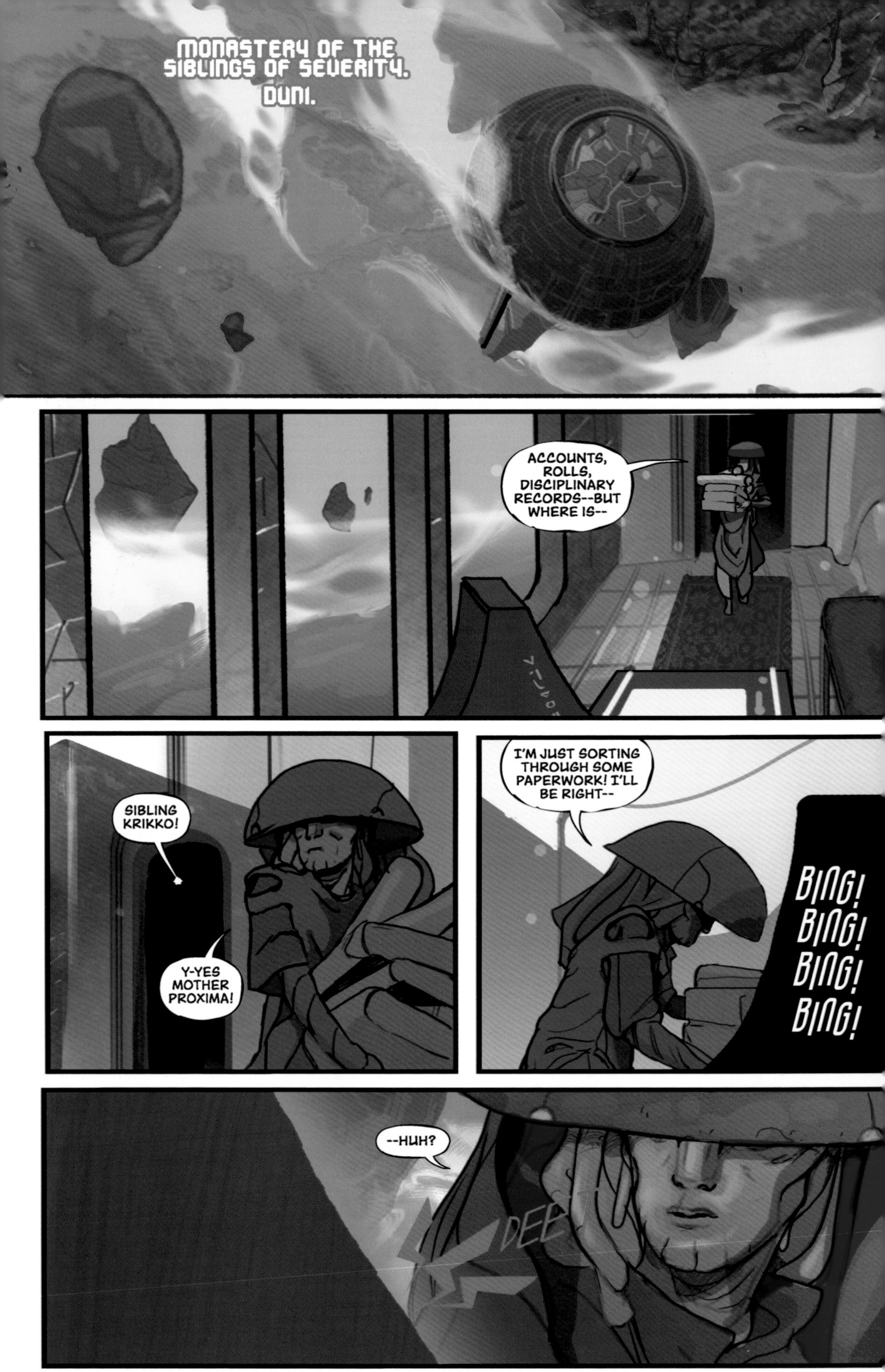
MONASTERY OF THE SIBLINGS OF SEVERITY. DUNI.
ACCOUNTS, ROLLS, DISCIPLINARY RECORDS--BUT WHERE IS--
SIBLING KRIKKO!
Y-YES MOTHER PROXIMA!
I'M JUST SORTING THROUGH SOME PAPERWORK! I'LL BE RIGHT--
BING! BING! BING! BING!
--HUH?
DEEET

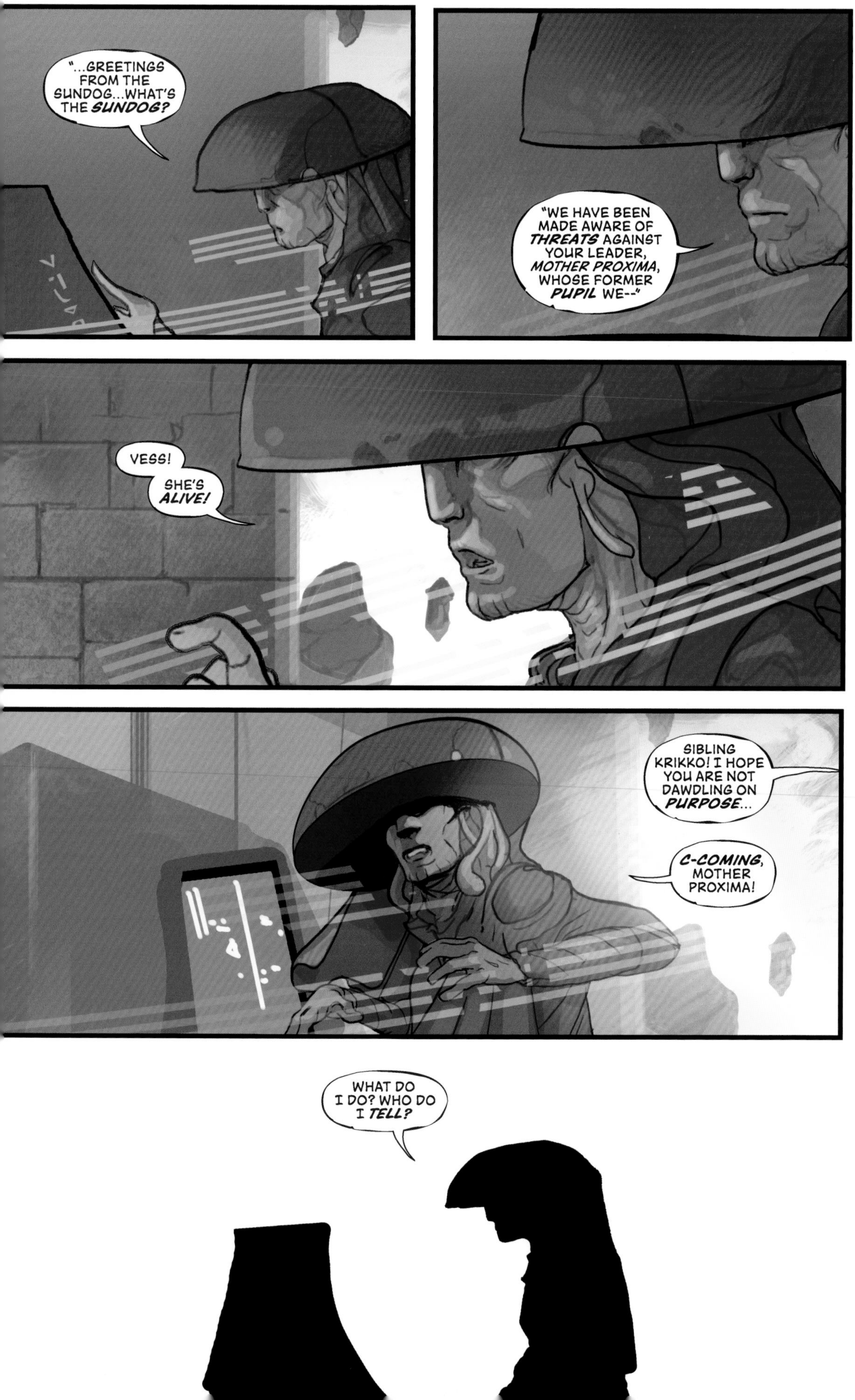
"...GREETINGS FROM THE SUNDOG...WHAT'S THE SUNDOG?
"WE HAVE BEEN MADE AWARE OF THREATS AGAINST YOUR LEADER, MOTHER PROXIMA, WHOSE FORMER PUPIL WE--"
VESS!
SHE'S ALIVE!
SIBLING KRIKKO! I HOPE YOU ARE NOT DAWDLING ON PURPOSE...
C-COMING, MOTHER PROXIMA!
WHAT DO I DO? WHO DO I TELL?

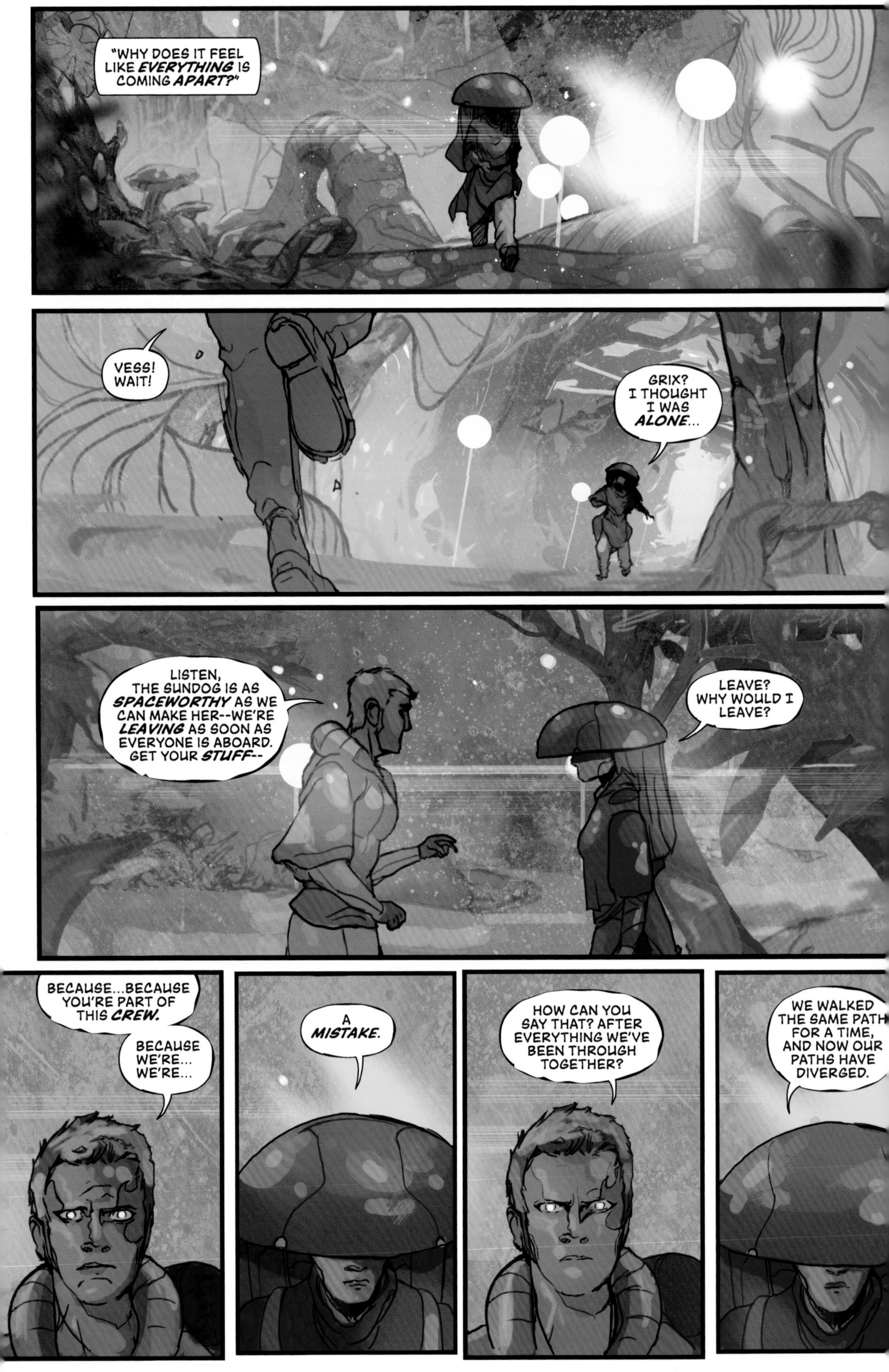
"WHY DOES IT FEEL LIKE EVERYTHING IS COMING APART?"
VESS! WAIT!
GRIX? I THOUGHT I WAS ALONE...
LISTEN, THE SUNDOG IS AS SPACEWORTHY AS WE CAN MAKE HER--WE'RE LEAVING AS SOON AS EVERYONE IS ABOARD. GET YOUR STUFF--
LEAVE? WHY WOULD I LEAVE?
BECAUSE...BECAUSE YOU'RE PART OF THIS CREW.
BECAUSE WE'RE... WE'RE...
A MISTAKE.
HOW CAN YOU SAY THAT? AFTER EVERYTHING WE'VE BEEN THROUGH TOGETHER?
WE WALKED THE SAME PATH FOR A TIME, AND NOW OUR PATHS HAVE DIVERGED.

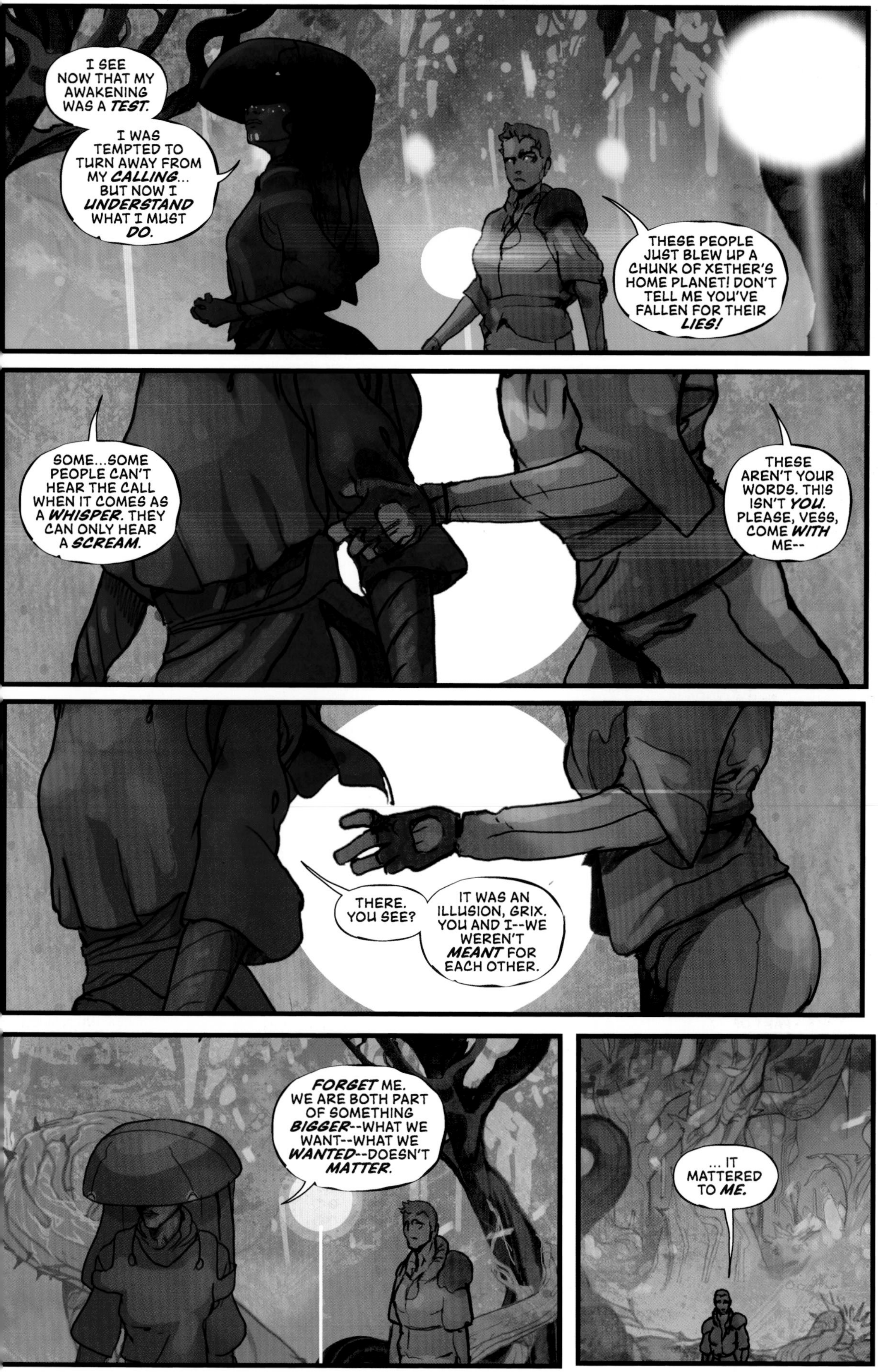
I SEE NOW THAT MY AWAKENING WAS A TEST.
I WAS TEMPTED TO TURN AWAY FROM MY CALLING... BUT NOW I UNDERSTAND WHAT I MUST DO.
THESE PEOPLE JUST BLEW UP A CHUNK OF XETHER'S HOME PLANET! DON'T TELL ME YOU'VE FALLEN FOR THEIR LIES!
SOME...SOME PEOPLE CAN'T HEAR THE CALL WHEN IT COMES AS A WHISPER. THEY CAN ONLY HEAR A SCREAM.
THESE AREN'T YOUR WORDS. THIS ISN'T YOU. PLEASE, VESS, COME WITH ME--
THERE. YOU SEE?
IT WAS AN ILLUSION, GRIX. YOU AND I--WE WEREN'T MEANT FOR EACH OTHER.
FORGET ME. WE ARE BOTH PART OF SOMETHING BIGGER--WHAT WE WANT--WHAT WE WANTED--DOESN'T MATTER.
... IT MATTERED TO ME.

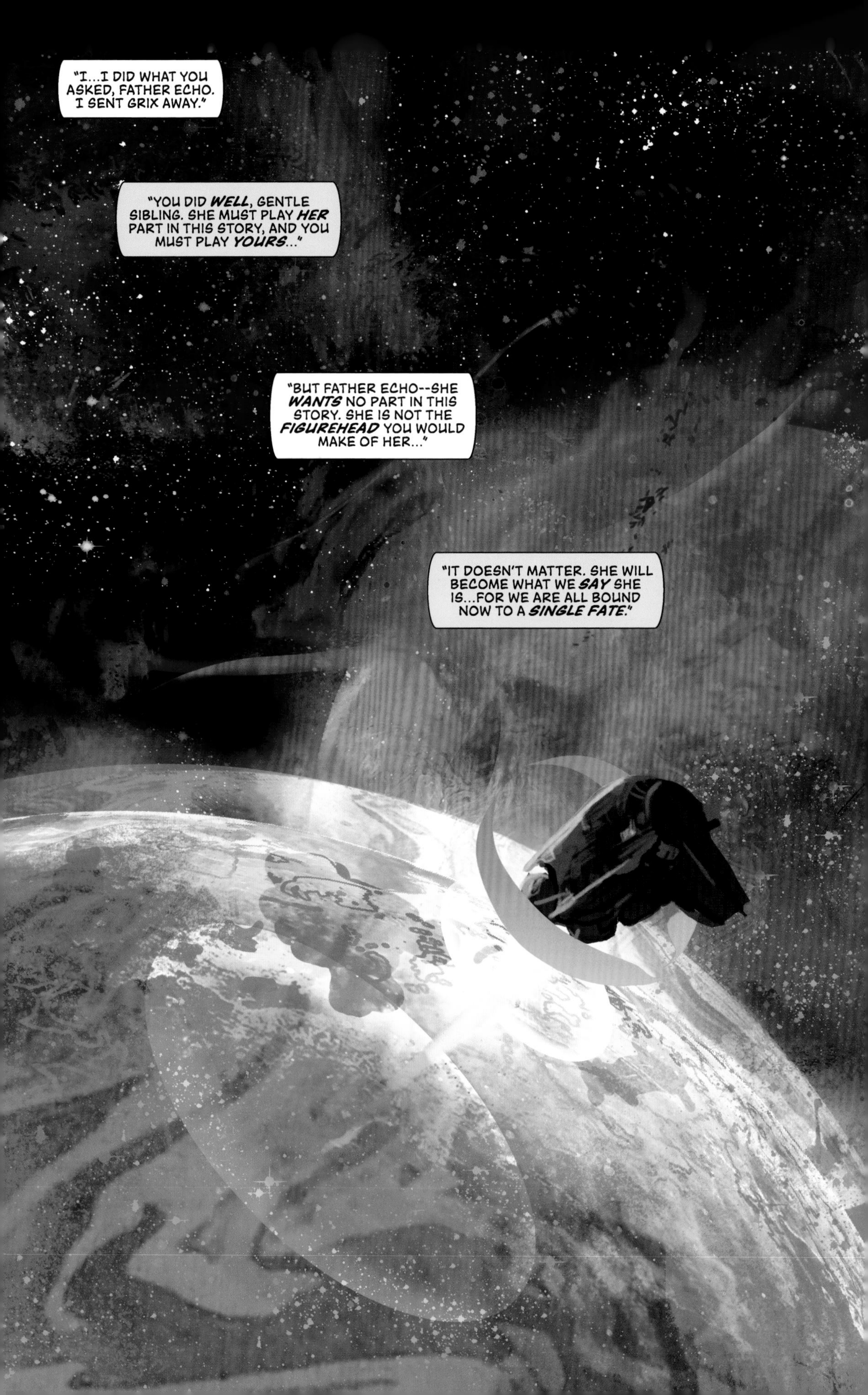
"I...I DID WHAT YOU ASKED, FATHER ECHO. I SENT GRIX AWAY."
"YOU DID WELL, GENTLE SIBLING. SHE MUST PLAY HER PART IN THIS STORY, AND YOU MUST PLAY YOURS..."
"BUT FATHER ECHO--SHE WANTS NO PART IN THIS STORY. SHE IS NOT THE FIGUREHEAD YOU WOULD MAKE OF HER..."
"IT DOESN'T MATTER. SHE WILL BECOME WHAT WE SAY SHE IS...FOR WE ARE ALL BOUND NOW TO A SINGLE FATE."

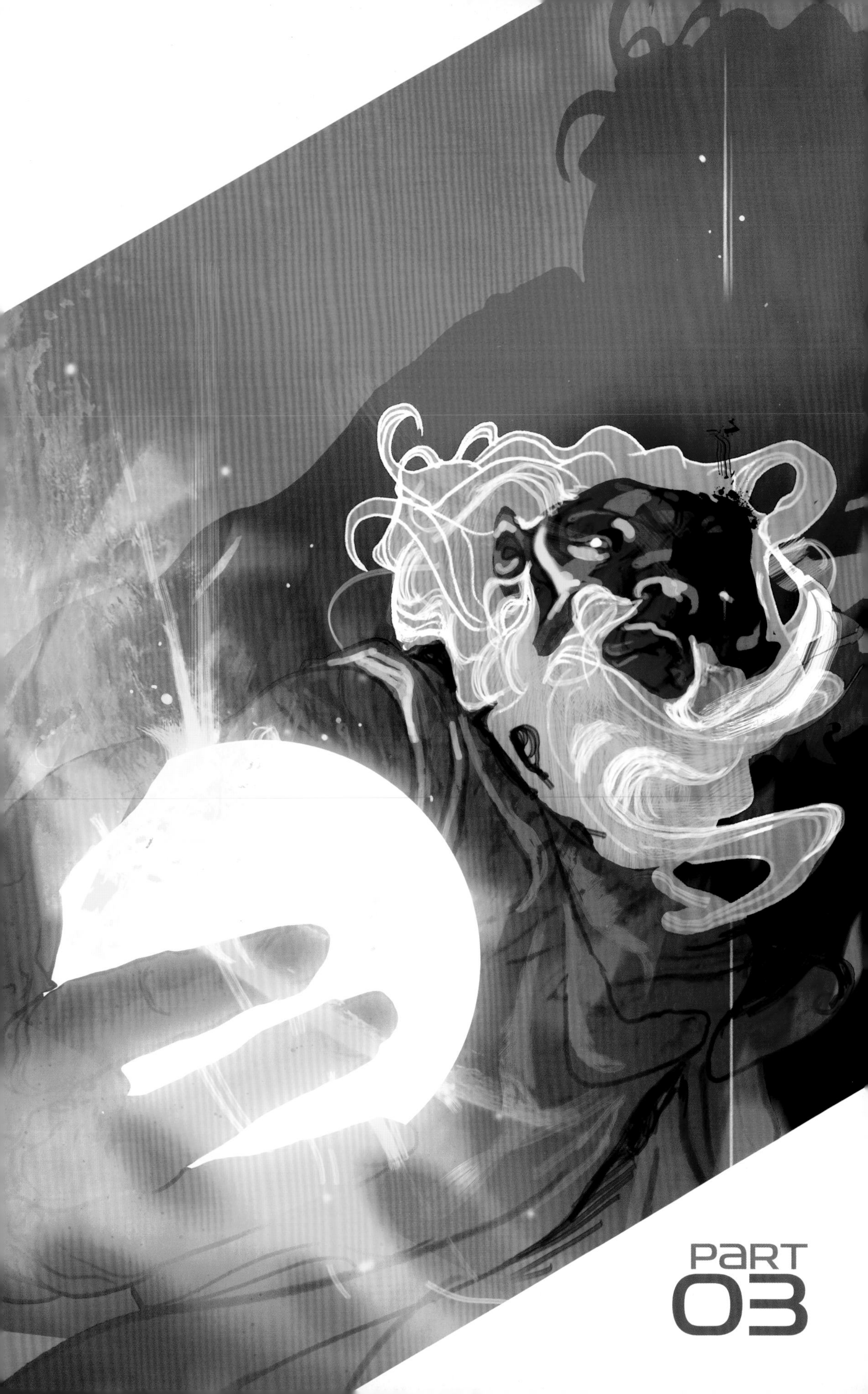

# PART 03

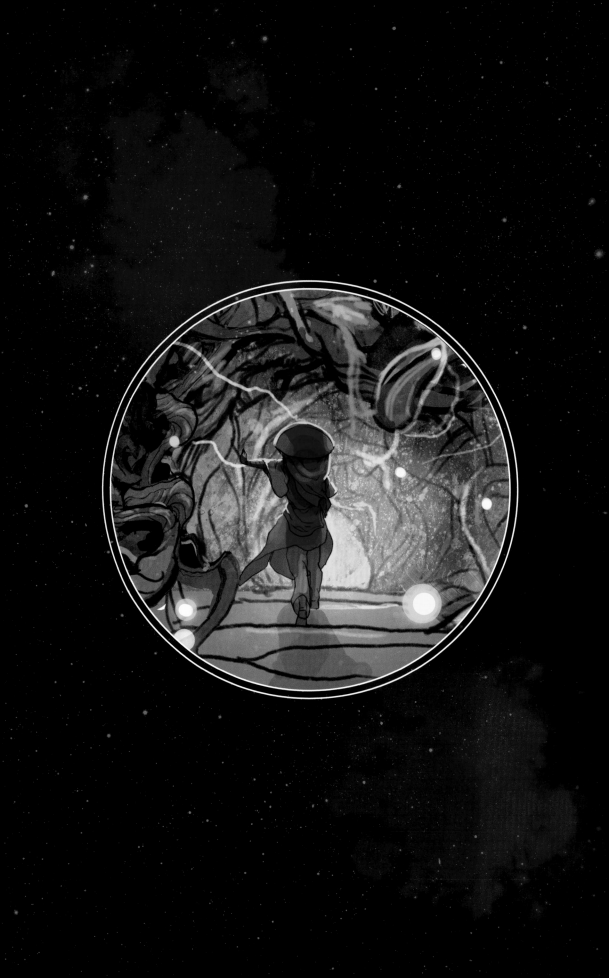

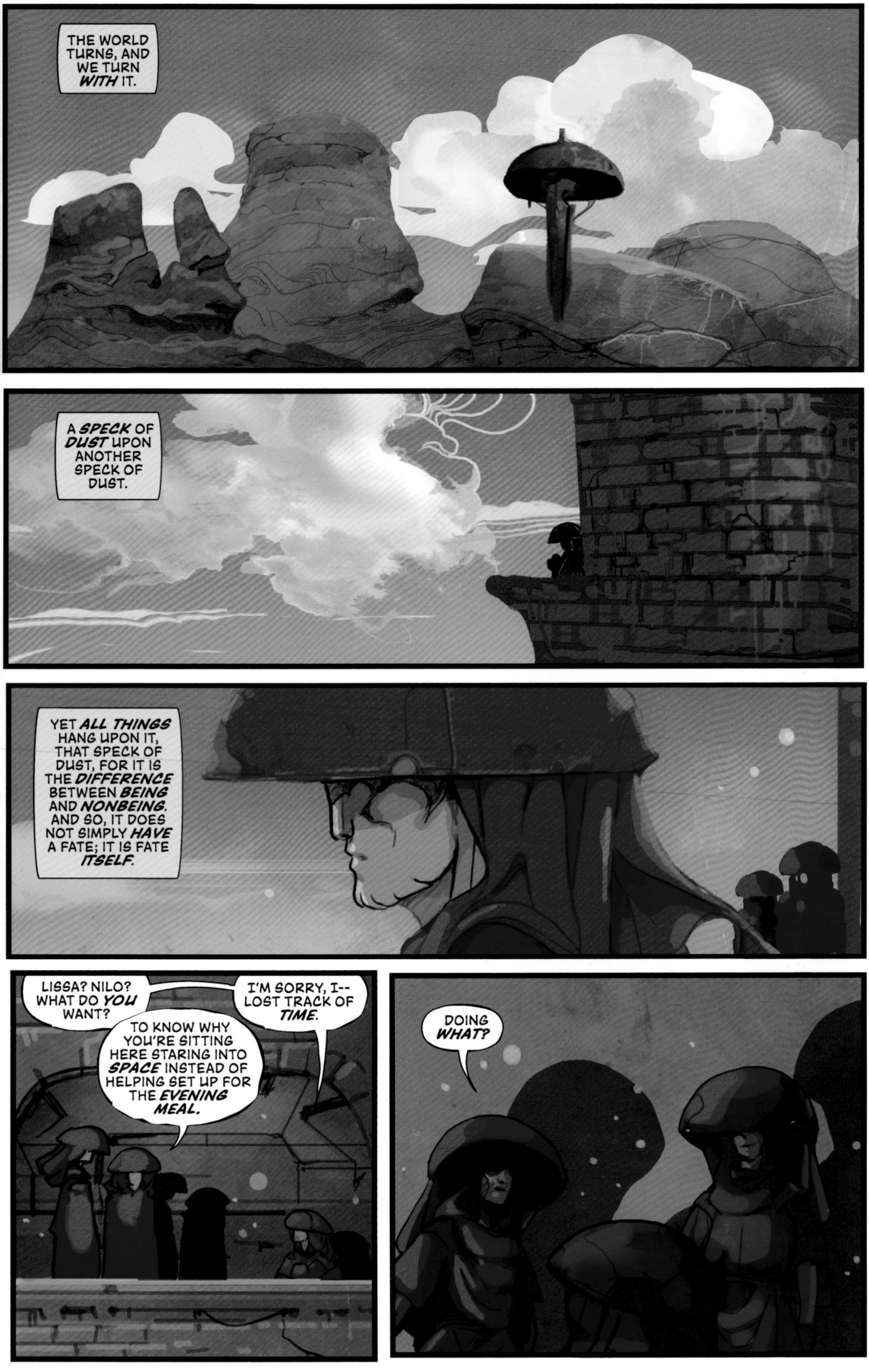
THE WORLD TURNS, AND WE TURN WITH IT.
A SPECK OF DUST UPON ANOTHER SPECK OF DUST.
YET ALL THINGS HANG UPON IT, THAT SPECK OF DUST, FOR IT IS THE DIFFERENCE BETWEEN BEING AND NONBEING. AND SO, IT DOES NOT SIMPLY HAVE A FATE; IT IS FATE ITSELF.
LISSA? NILO? WHAT DO YOU WANT?
TO KNOW WHY YOU'RE SITTING HERE STARING INTO SPACE INSTEAD OF HELPING SET UP FOR THE EVENING MEAL.
I'M SORRY, I-- LOST TRACK OF TIME.
DOING WHAT?

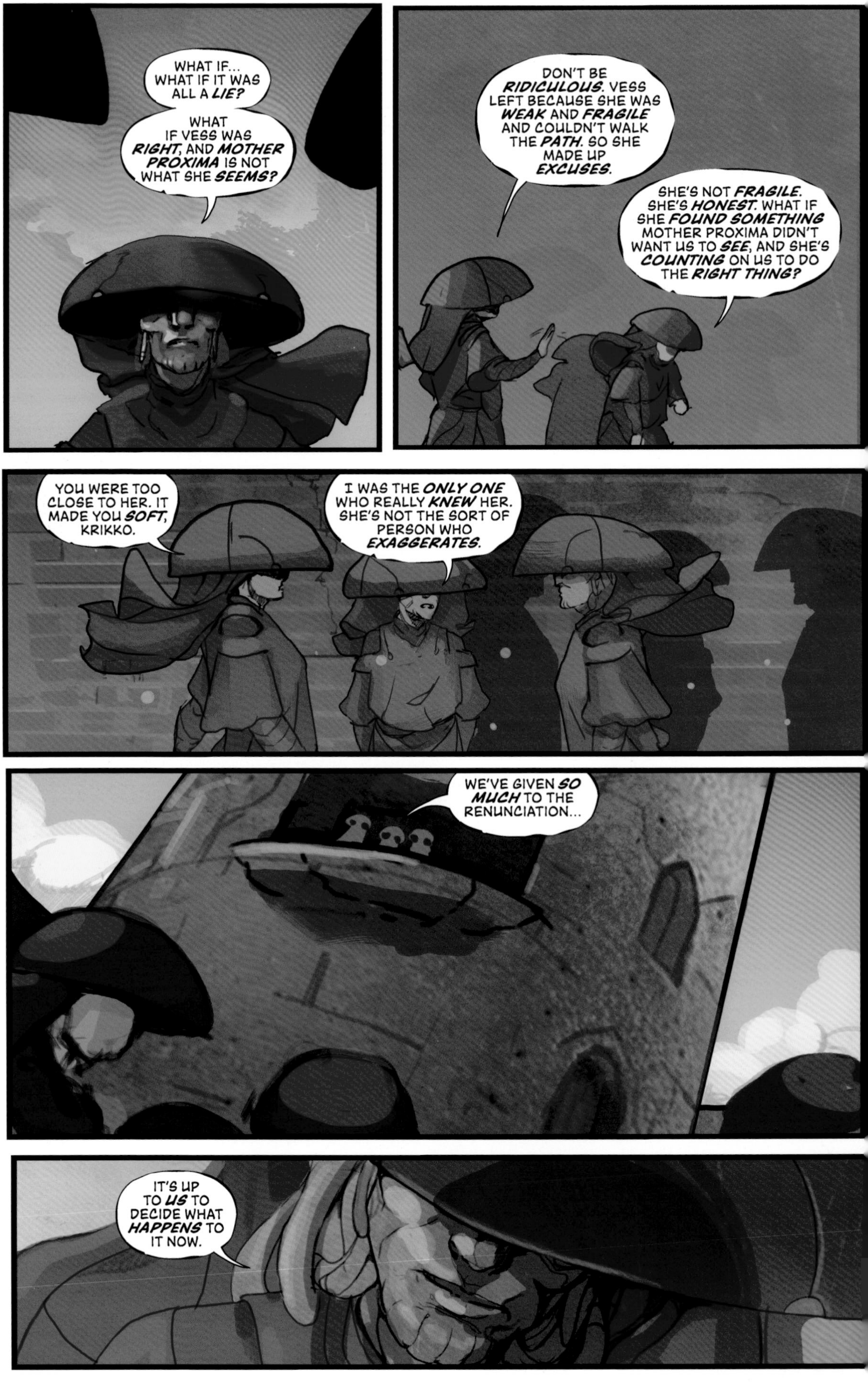
WHAT IF... WHAT IF IT WAS ALL A LIE?
WHAT IF VESS WAS RIGHT, AND MOTHER PROXIMA IS NOT WHAT SHE SEEMS?
DON'T BE RIDICULOUS. VESS LEFT BECAUSE SHE WAS WEAK AND FRAGILE AND COULDN'T WALK THE PATH. SO SHE MADE UP EXCUSES.
SHE'S NOT FRAGILE. SHE'S HONEST. WHAT IF SHE FOUND SOMETHING MOTHER PROXIMA DIDN'T WANT US TO SEE, AND SHE'S COUNTING ON US TO DO THE RIGHT THING?
YOU WERE TOO CLOSE TO HER. IT MADE YOU SOFT, KRIKKO.
I WAS THE ONLY ONE WHO REALLY KNEW HER. SHE'S NOT THE SORT OF PERSON WHO EXAGGERATES.
WE'VE GIVEN SO MUCH TO THE RENUNCIATION...
IT'S UP TO US TO DECIDE WHAT HAPPENS TO IT NOW.

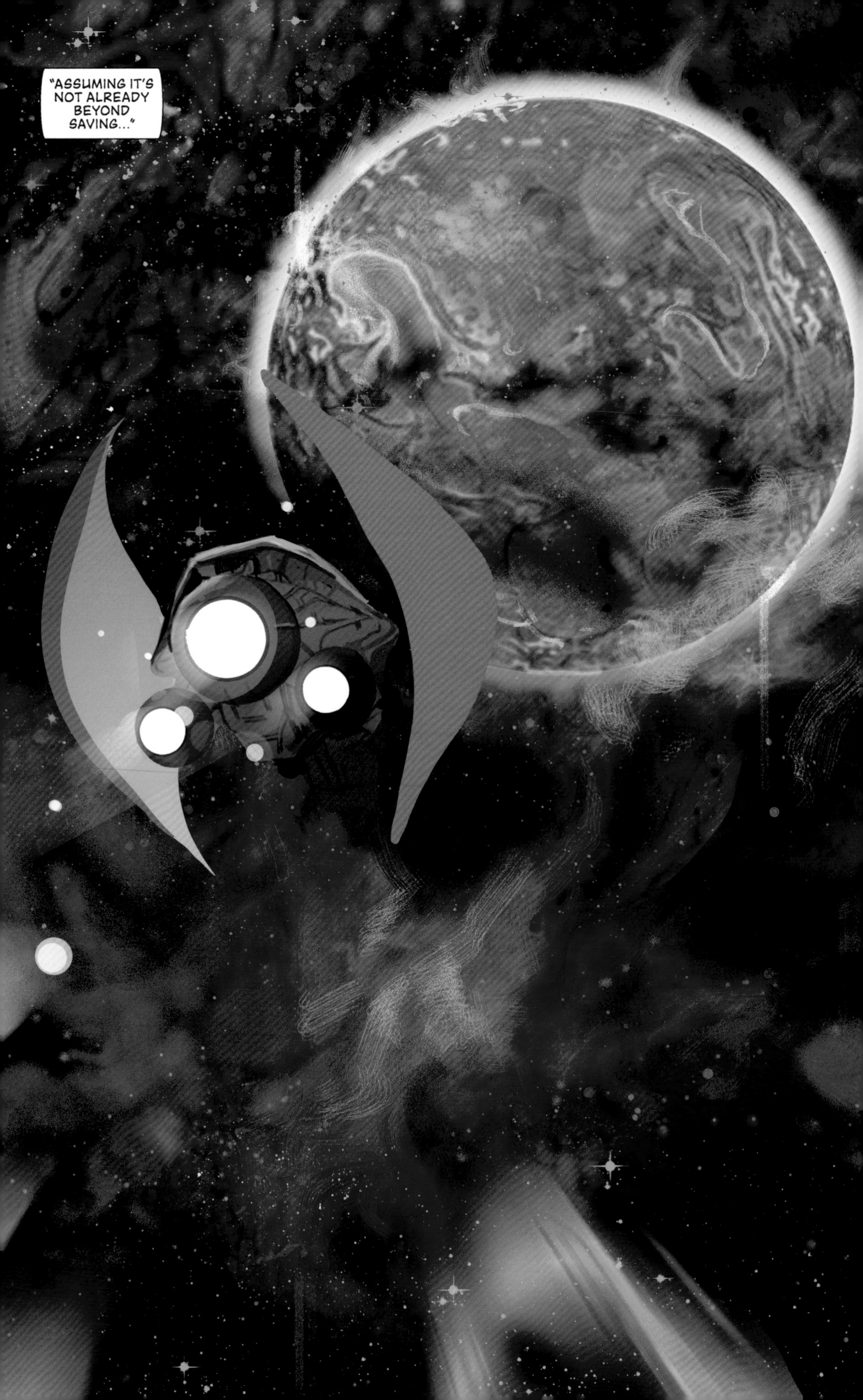
"ASSUMING IT'S NOT ALREADY BEYOND SAVING..."

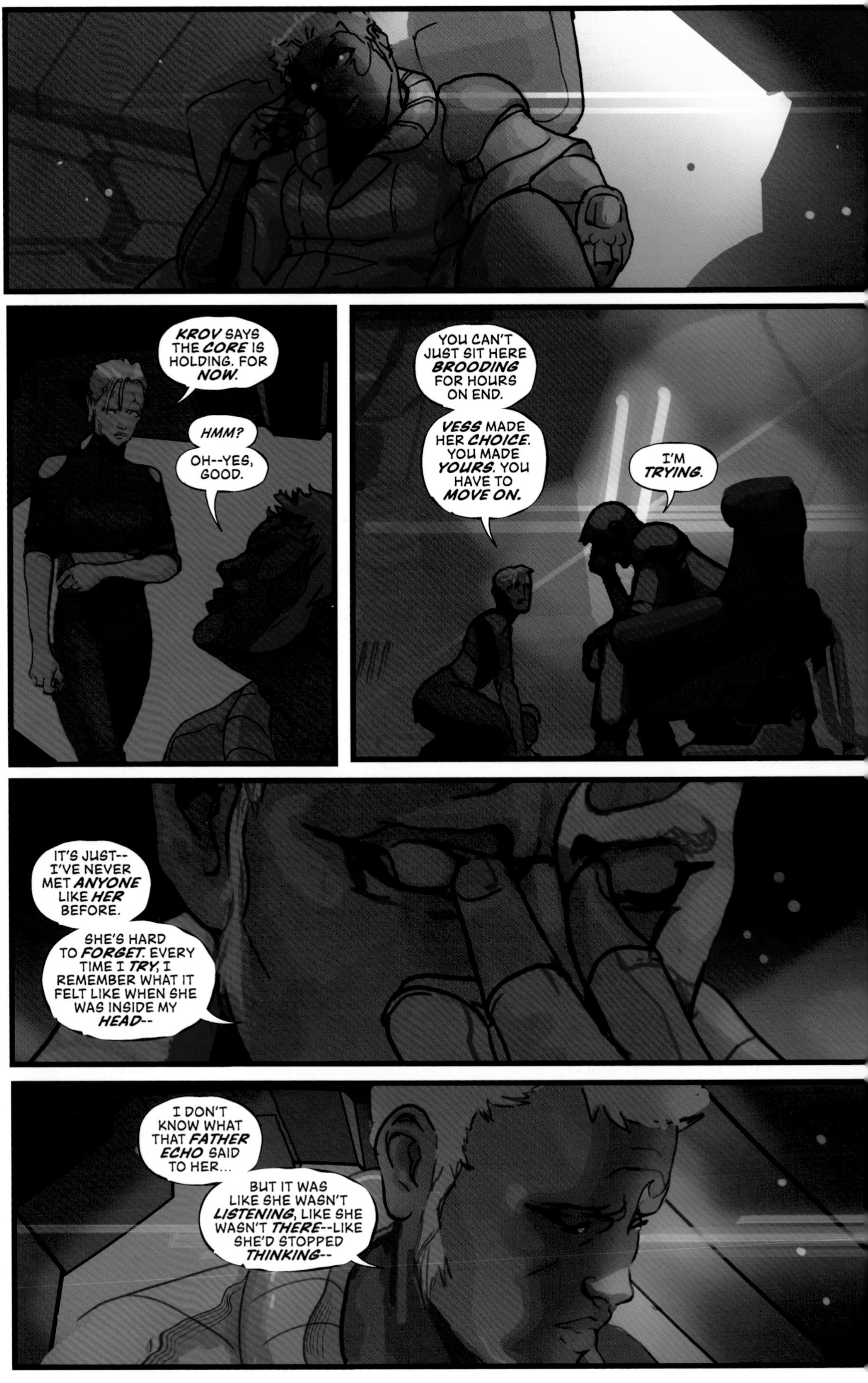
KROV SAYS THE CORE IS HOLDING. FOR NOW.
HMM?
OH--YES, GOOD.
YOU CAN'T JUST SIT HERE BROODING FOR HOURS ON END.
VESS MADE HER CHOICE. YOU MADE YOURS. YOU HAVE TO MOVE ON.
I'M TRYING.
IT'S JUST-- I'VE NEVER MET ANYONE LIKE HER BEFORE.
SHE'S HARD TO FORGET. EVERY TIME I TRY, I REMEMBER WHAT IT FELT LIKE WHEN SHE WAS INSIDE MY HEAD--
I DON'T KNOW WHAT THAT FATHER ECHO SAID TO HER...
BUT IT WAS LIKE SHE WASN'T LISTENING, LIKE SHE WASN'T THERE--LIKE SHE'D STOPPED THINKING--

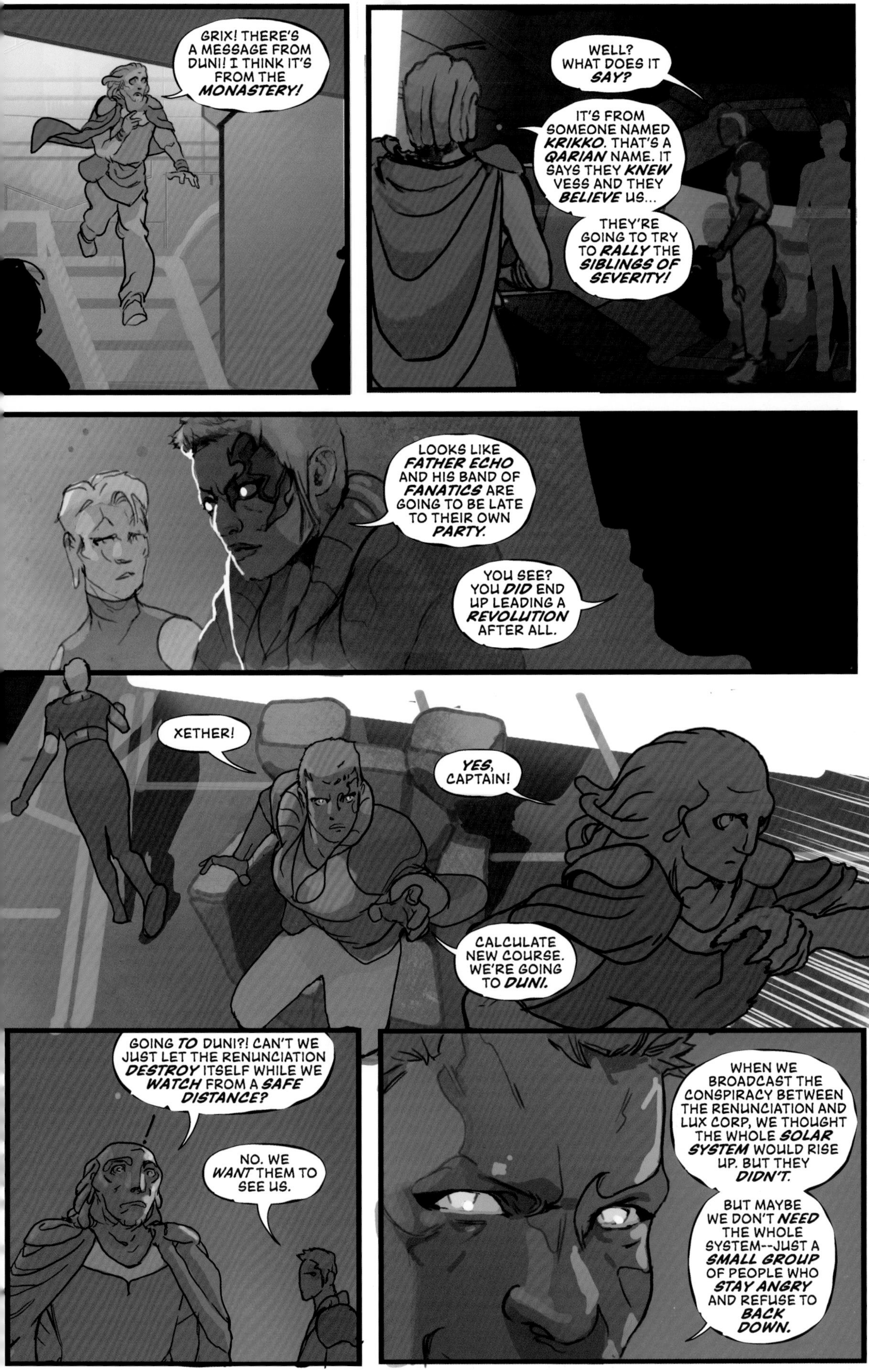
GRIX! THERE'S A MESSAGE FROM DUNI! I THINK IT'S FROM THE *MONASTERY!*
WELL? WHAT DOES IT *SAY?*
IT'S FROM SOMEONE NAMED *KRIKKO*. THAT'S A *QARIAN* NAME. IT SAYS THEY *KNEW* VESS AND THEY *BELIEVE* US...
THEY'RE GOING TO TRY TO *RALLY* THE *SIBLINGS OF SEVERITY!*
LOOKS LIKE *FATHER ECHO* AND HIS BAND OF *FANATICS* ARE GOING TO BE LATE TO THEIR OWN *PARTY*.
YOU SEE? YOU *DID* END UP LEADING A *REVOLUTION* AFTER ALL.
XETHER!
*YES*, CAPTAIN!
CALCULATE NEW COURSE. WE'RE GOING TO *DUNI*.
GOING *TO* DUNI?! CAN'T WE JUST LET THE RENUNCIATION *DESTROY* ITSELF WHILE WE *WATCH* FROM A *SAFE DISTANCE?*
!
NO. WE *WANT* THEM TO SEE US.
WHEN WE BROADCAST THE CONSPIRACY BETWEEN THE RENUNCIATION AND LUX CORP, WE THOUGHT THE WHOLE *SOLAR SYSTEM* WOULD RISE UP. BUT THEY *DIDN'T*.
BUT MAYBE WE DON'T *NEED* THE WHOLE SYSTEM--JUST A *SMALL GROUP* OF PEOPLE WHO *STAY ANGRY* AND REFUSE TO *BACK DOWN*.

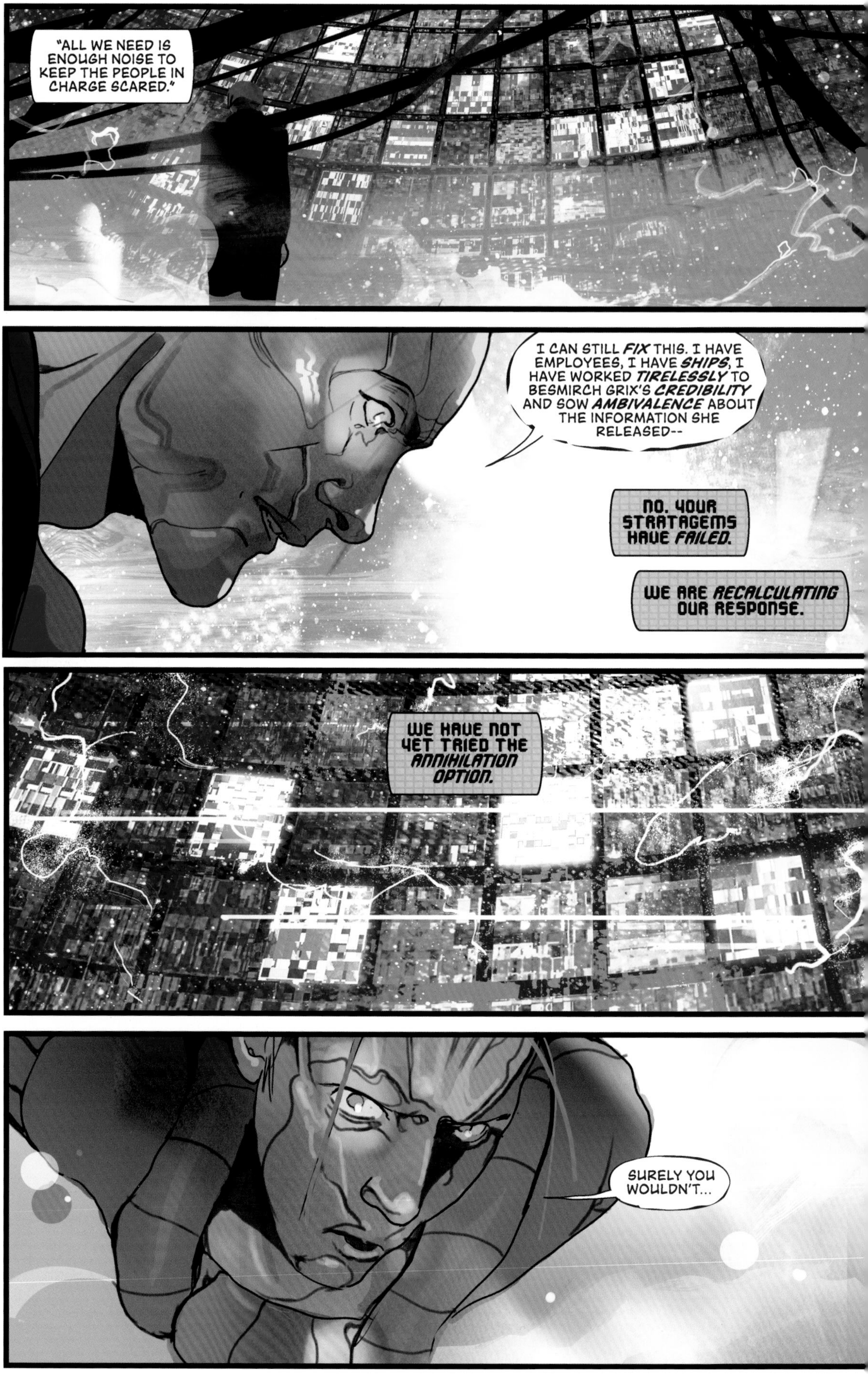
"ALL WE NEED IS ENOUGH NOISE TO KEEP THE PEOPLE IN CHARGE SCARED."
I CAN STILL FIX THIS. I HAVE EMPLOYEES, I HAVE SHIPS, I HAVE WORKED TIRELESSLY TO BESMIRCH GRIX'S CREDIBILITY AND SOW AMBIVALENCE ABOUT THE INFORMATION SHE RELEASED--
NO. YOUR STRATAGEMS HAVE FAILED.
WE ARE RECALCULATING OUR RESPONSE.
WE HAVE NOT YET TRIED THE ANNIHILATION OPTION.
SURELY YOU WOULDN'T...

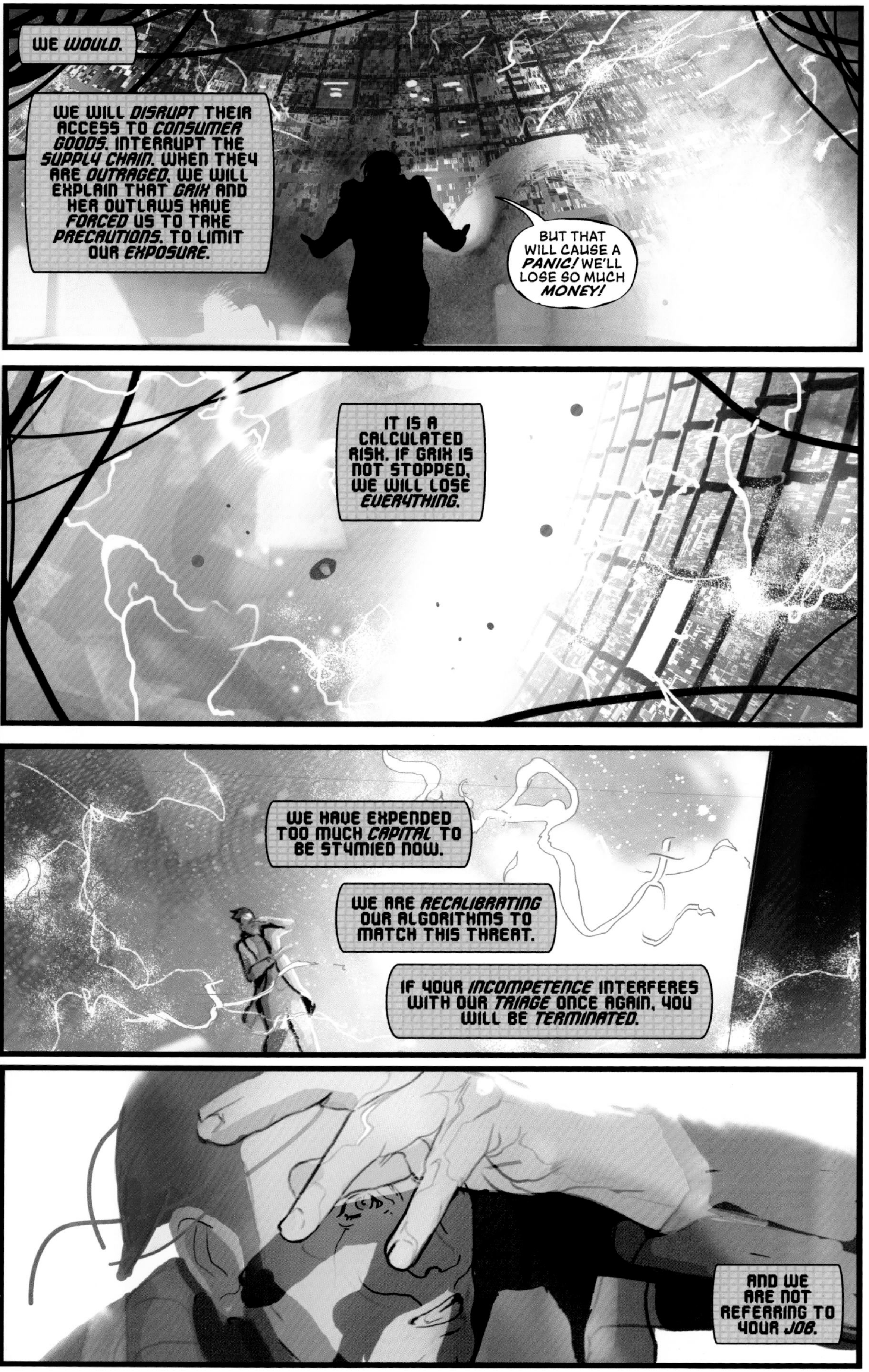
WE WOULD.
WE WILL DISRUPT THEIR ACCESS TO CONSUMER GOODS. INTERRUPT THE SUPPLY CHAIN. WHEN THEY ARE OUTRAGED, WE WILL EXPLAIN THAT GRIX AND HER OUTLAWS HAVE FORCED US TO TAKE PRECAUTIONS. TO LIMIT OUR EXPOSURE.
BUT THAT WILL CAUSE A PANIC! WE'LL LOSE SO MUCH MONEY!
IT IS A CALCULATED RISK. IF GRIX IS NOT STOPPED, WE WILL LOSE EVERYTHING.
WE HAVE EXPENDED TOO MUCH CAPITAL TO BE STYMIED NOW.
WE ARE RECALIBRATING OUR ALGORITHMS TO MATCH THIS THREAT.
IF YOUR INCOMPETENCE INTERFERES WITH OUR TRIAGE ONCE AGAIN, YOU WILL BE TERMINATED.
AND WE ARE NOT REFERRING TO YOUR JOB.

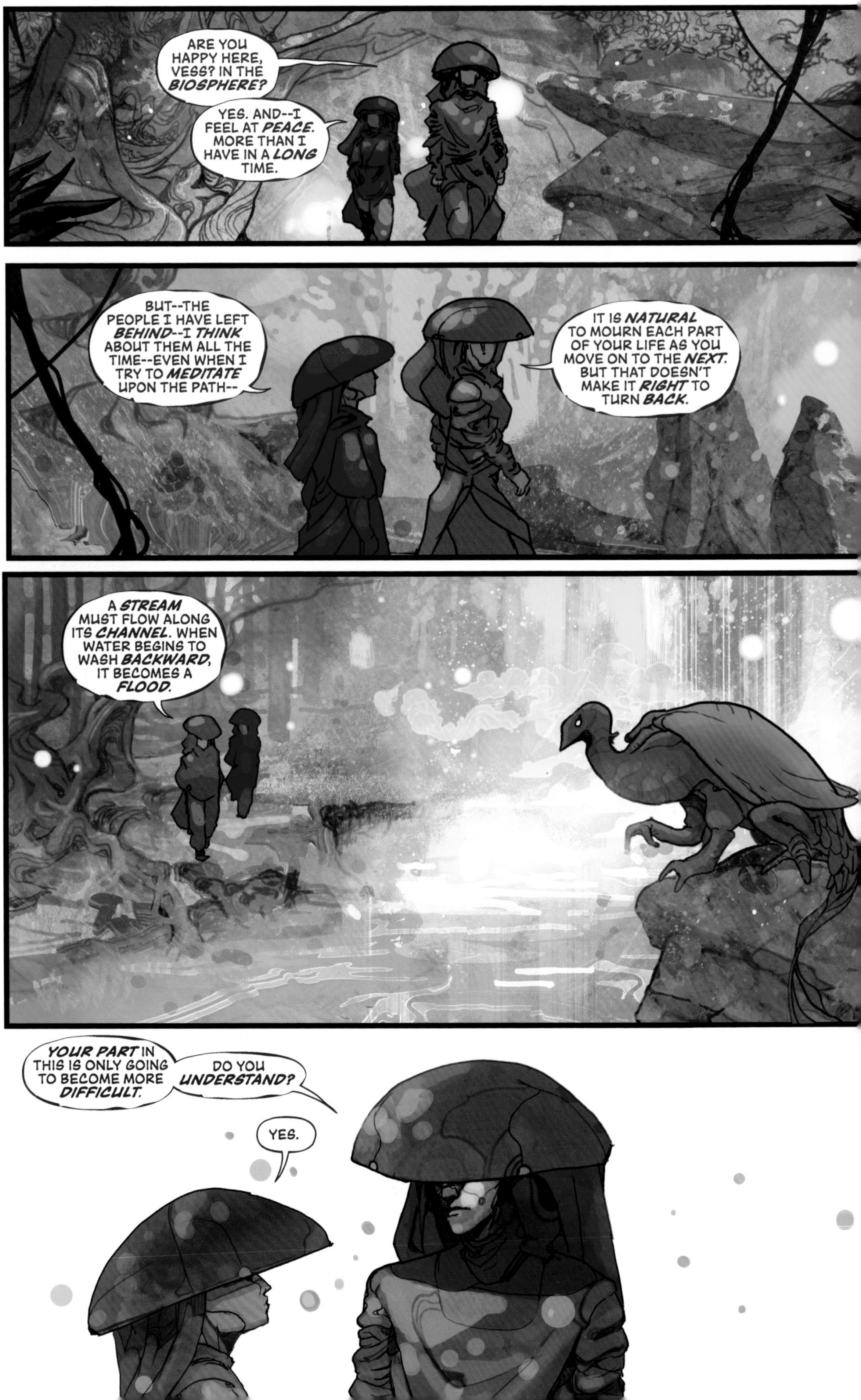
ARE YOU HAPPY HERE, VESS? IN THE BIOSPHERE?
YES. AND--I FEEL AT PEACE. MORE THAN I HAVE IN A LONG TIME.
BUT--THE PEOPLE I HAVE LEFT BEHIND--I THINK ABOUT THEM ALL THE TIME--EVEN WHEN I TRY TO MEDITATE UPON THE PATH--
IT IS NATURAL TO MOURN EACH PART OF YOUR LIFE AS YOU MOVE ON TO THE NEXT. BUT THAT DOESN'T MAKE IT RIGHT TO TURN BACK.
A STREAM MUST FLOW ALONG ITS CHANNEL. WHEN WATER BEGINS TO WASH BACKWARD, IT BECOMES A FLOOD.
YOUR PART IN THIS IS ONLY GOING TO BECOME MORE DIFFICULT.
DO YOU UNDERSTAND?
YES.

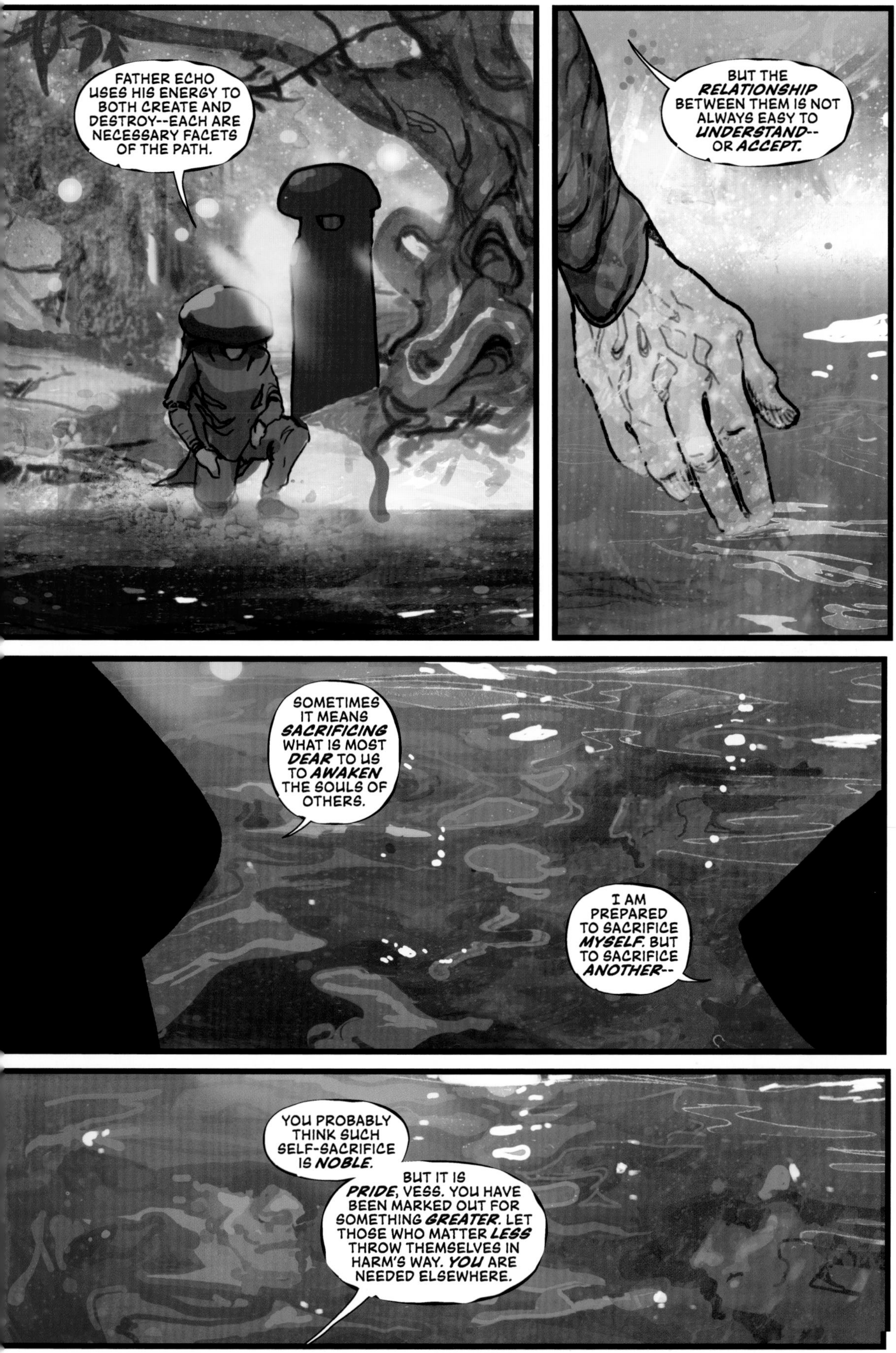
FATHER ECHO USES HIS ENERGY TO BOTH CREATE AND DESTROY--EACH ARE NECESSARY FACETS OF THE PATH.
BUT THE *RELATIONSHIP* BETWEEN THEM IS NOT ALWAYS EASY TO *UNDERSTAND*-- OR *ACCEPT.*
SOMETIMES IT MEANS *SACRIFICING* WHAT IS MOST *DEAR* TO US TO *AWAKEN* THE SOULS OF OTHERS.
I AM PREPARED TO SACRIFICE *MYSELF*. BUT TO SACRIFICE *ANOTHER*--
YOU PROBABLY THINK SUCH SELF-SACRIFICE IS *NOBLE*.
BUT IT IS *PRIDE*, VESS. YOU HAVE BEEN MARKED OUT FOR SOMETHING *GREATER*. LET THOSE WHO MATTER *LESS* THROW THEMSELVES IN HARM'S WAY. *YOU* ARE NEEDED ELSEWHERE.

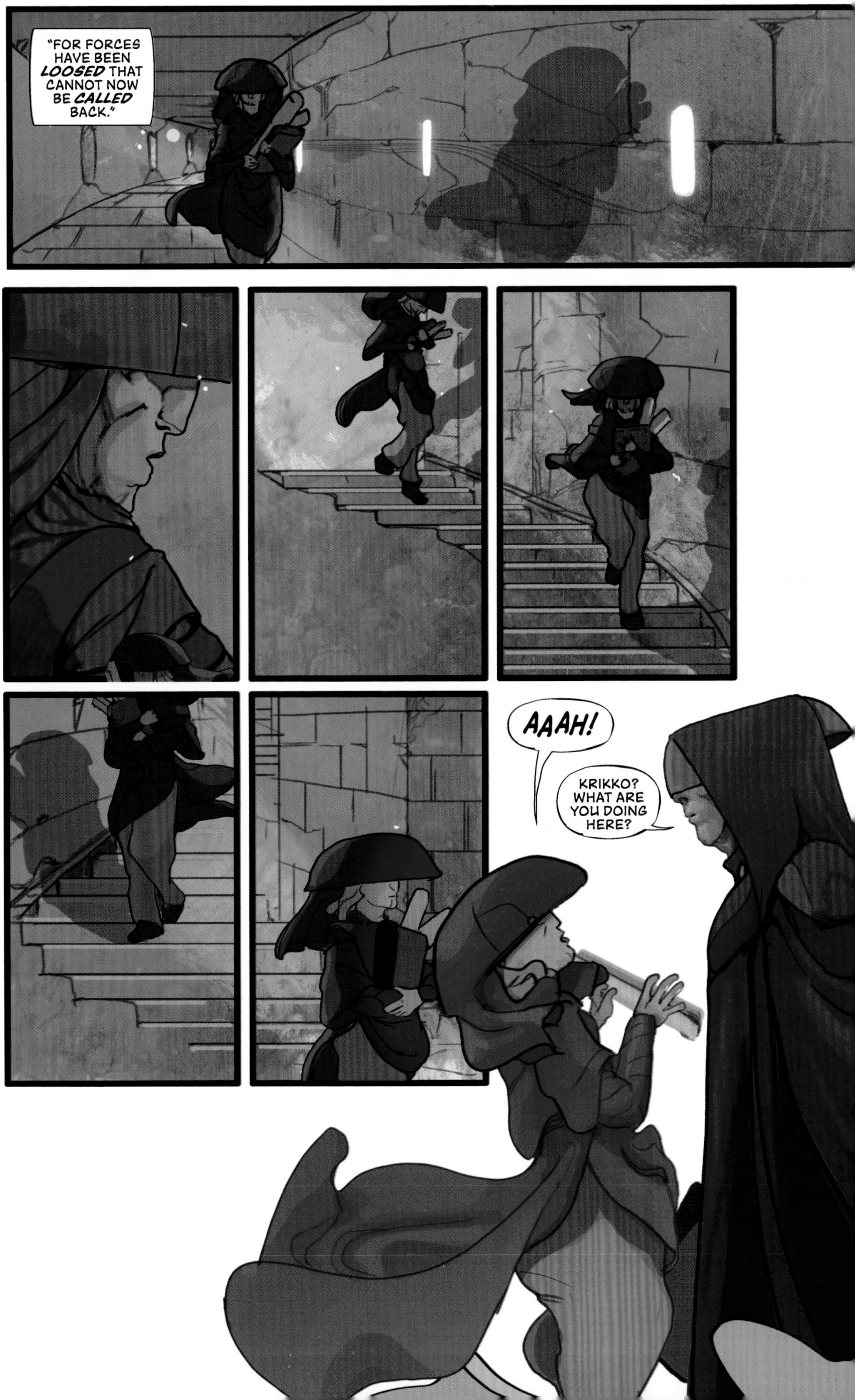
"FOR FORCES HAVE BEEN LOOSED THAT CANNOT NOW BE CALLED BACK."
AAAH!
KRIKKO? WHAT ARE YOU DOING HERE?

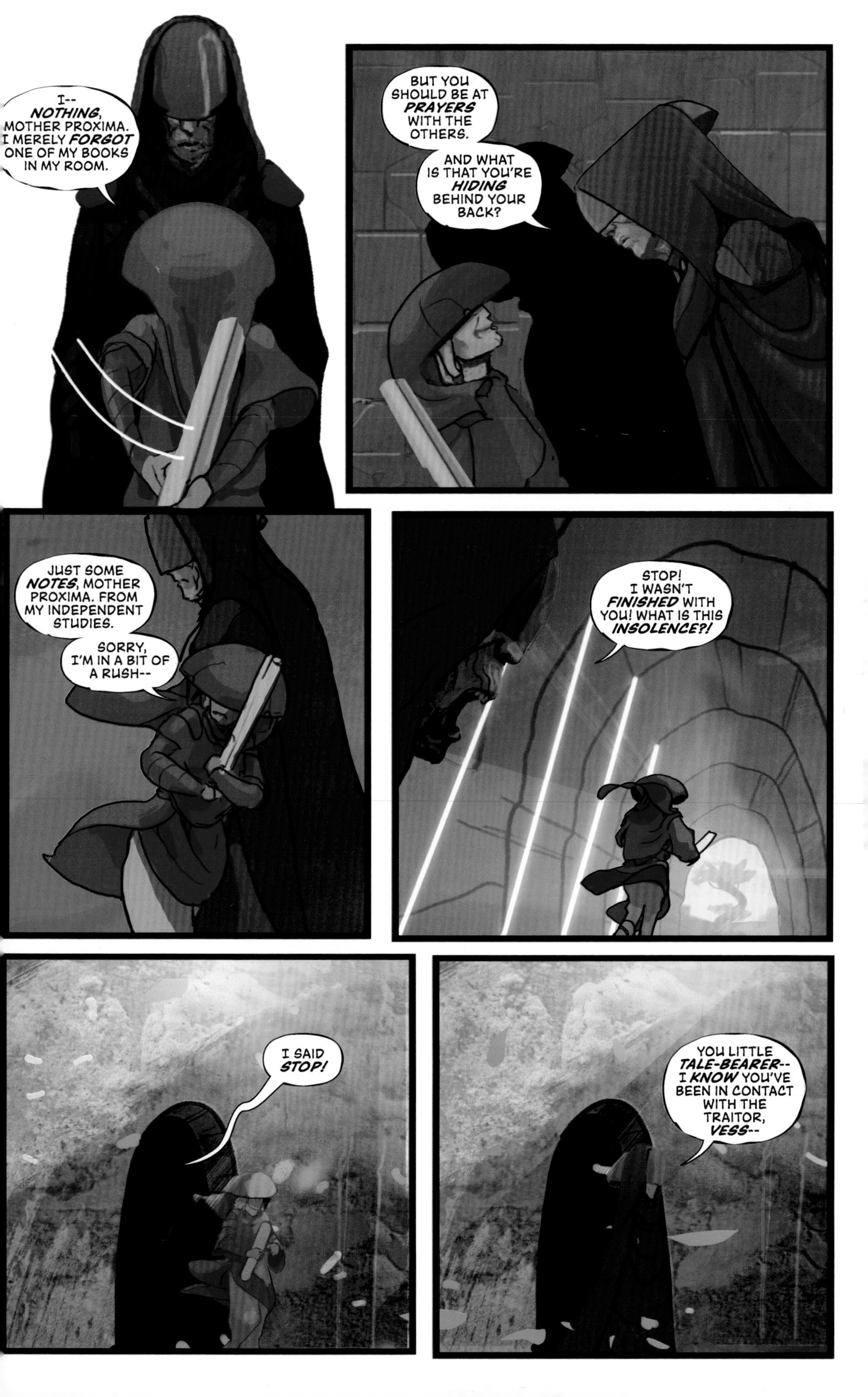
I-- NOTHING, MOTHER PROXIMA. I MERELY FORGOT ONE OF MY BOOKS IN MY ROOM.
BUT YOU SHOULD BE AT PRAYERS WITH THE OTHERS.
AND WHAT IS THAT YOU'RE HIDING BEHIND YOUR BACK?
JUST SOME NOTES, MOTHER PROXIMA. FROM MY INDEPENDENT STUDIES.
SORRY, I'M IN A BIT OF A RUSH--
STOP! I WASN'T FINISHED WITH YOU! WHAT IS THIS INSOLENCE?!
I SAID STOP!
YOU LITTLE TALE-BEARER-- I KNOW YOU'VE BEEN IN CONTACT WITH THE TRAITOR, VESS--

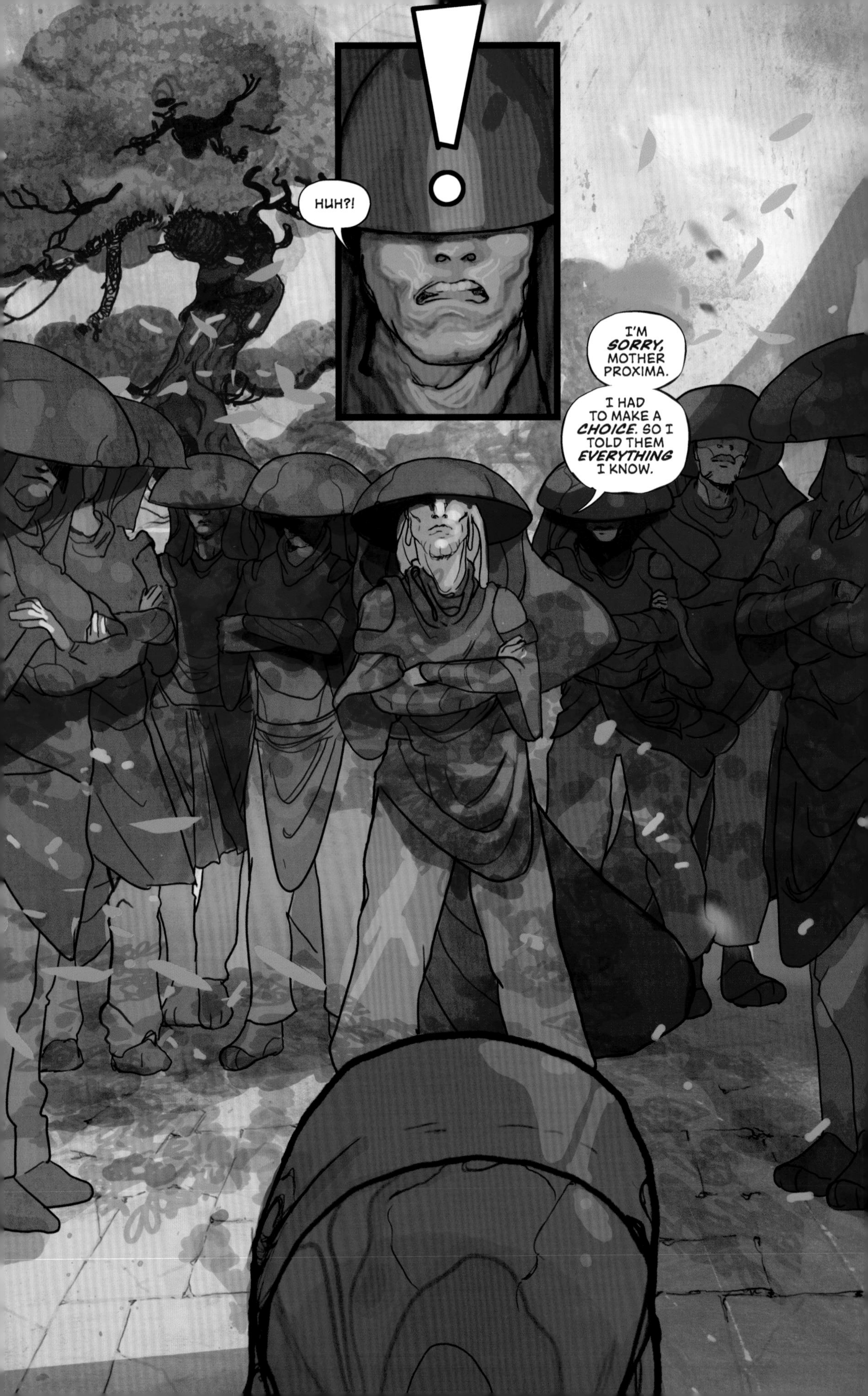
HUH?!
I'M SORRY, MOTHER PROXIMA.
I HAD TO MAKE A CHOICE. SO I TOLD THEM EVERYTHING I KNOW.

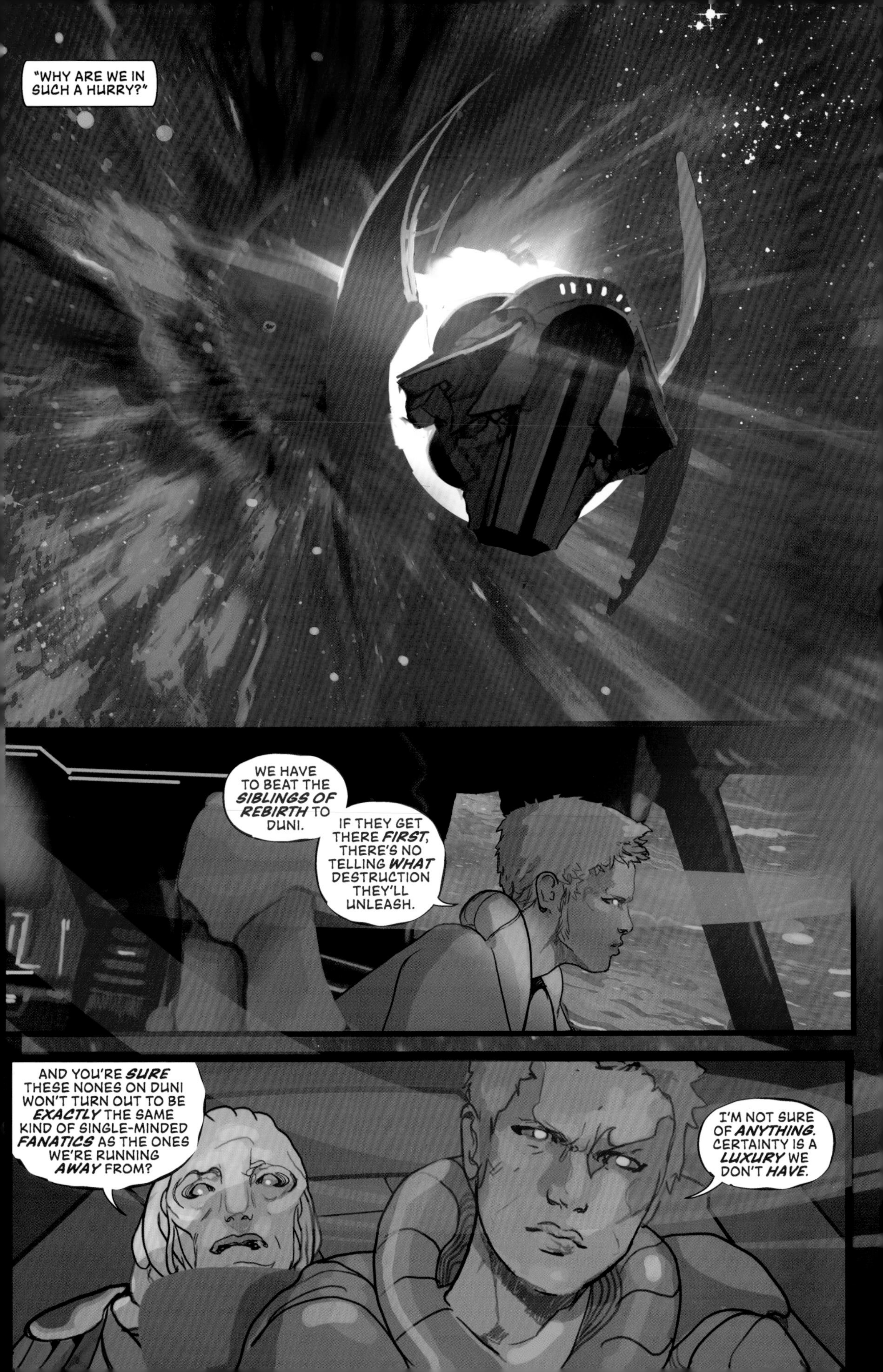
"WHY ARE WE IN SUCH A HURRY?"
WE HAVE TO BEAT THE SIBLINGS OF REBIRTH TO DUNI.
IF THEY GET THERE FIRST, THERE'S NO TELLING WHAT DESTRUCTION THEY'LL UNLEASH.
AND YOU'RE SURE THESE NONES ON DUNI WON'T TURN OUT TO BE EXACTLY THE SAME KIND OF SINGLE-MINDED FANATICS AS THE ONES WE'RE RUNNING AWAY FROM?
I'M NOT SURE OF ANYTHING. CERTAINTY IS A LUXURY WE DON'T HAVE.

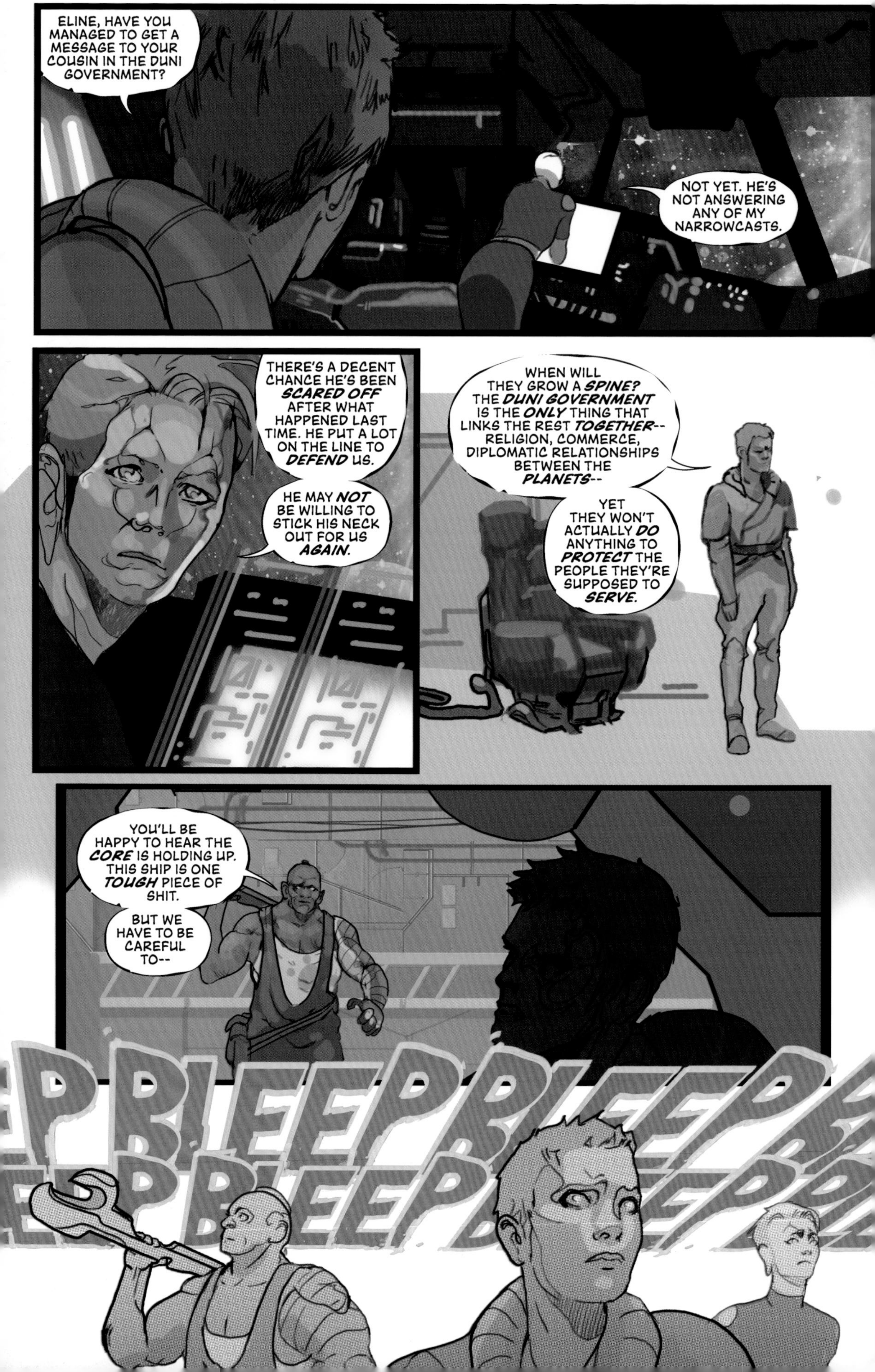
ELINE, HAVE YOU MANAGED TO GET A MESSAGE TO YOUR COUSIN IN THE DUNI GOVERNMENT?
NOT YET. HE'S NOT ANSWERING ANY OF MY NARROWCASTS.
THERE'S A DECENT CHANCE HE'S BEEN SCARED OFF AFTER WHAT HAPPENED LAST TIME. HE PUT A LOT ON THE LINE TO DEFEND US.
HE MAY NOT BE WILLING TO STICK HIS NECK OUT FOR US AGAIN.
WHEN WILL THEY GROW A SPINE? THE DUNI GOVERNMENT IS THE ONLY THING THAT LINKS THE REST TOGETHER-- RELIGION, COMMERCE, DIPLOMATIC RELATIONSHIPS BETWEEN THE PLANETS--
YET THEY WON'T ACTUALLY DO ANYTHING TO PROTECT THE PEOPLE THEY'RE SUPPOSED TO SERVE.
YOU'LL BE HAPPY TO HEAR THE CORE IS HOLDING UP. THIS SHIP IS ONE TOUGH PIECE OF SHIT.
BUT WE HAVE TO BE CAREFUL TO--
BLEEP BLEEP BLEEP
BLEEP BLEEP BLEEP

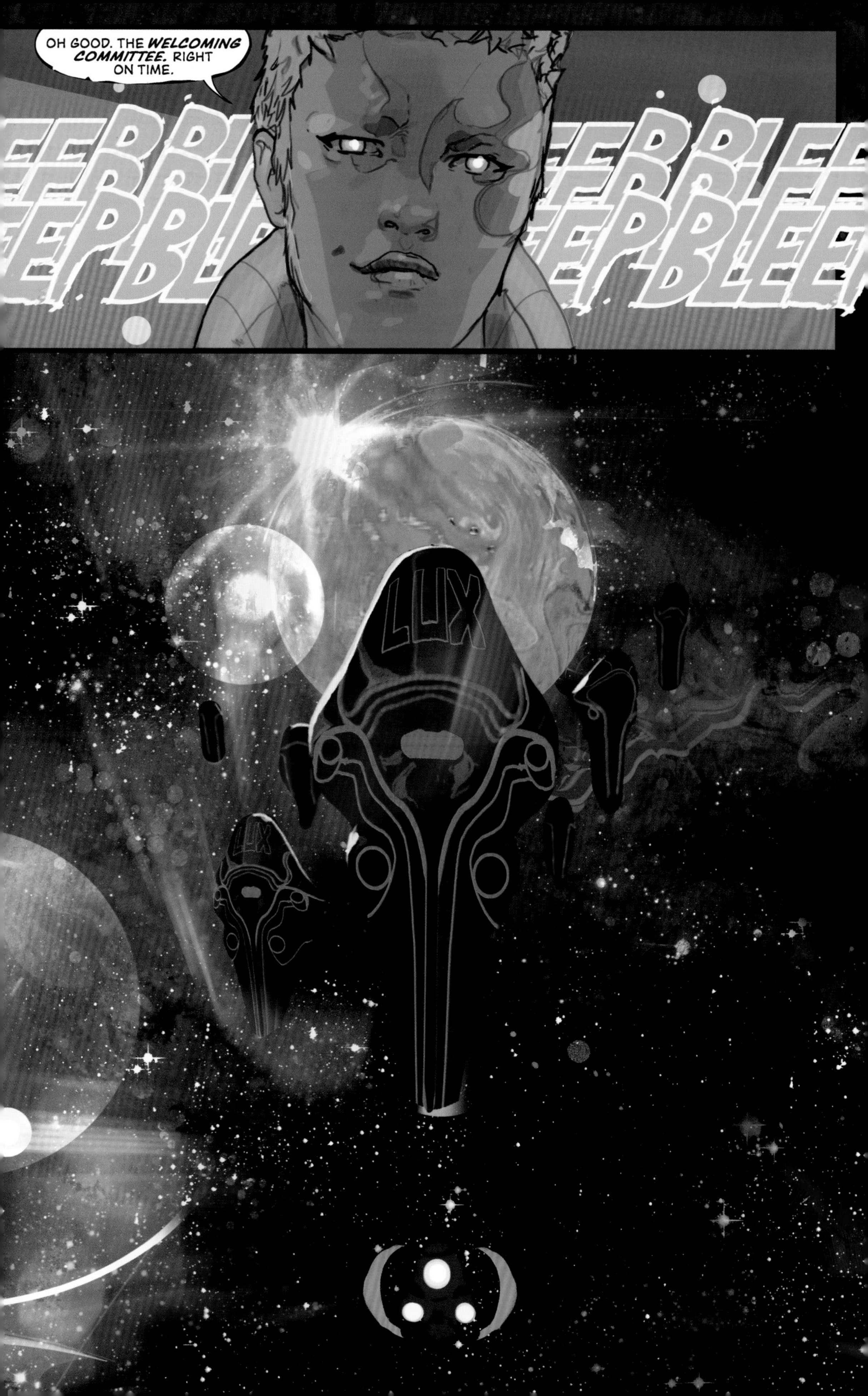
OH GOOD. THE *WELCOMING COMMITTEE.* RIGHT ON TIME.
BLEEP
LUX
LUX

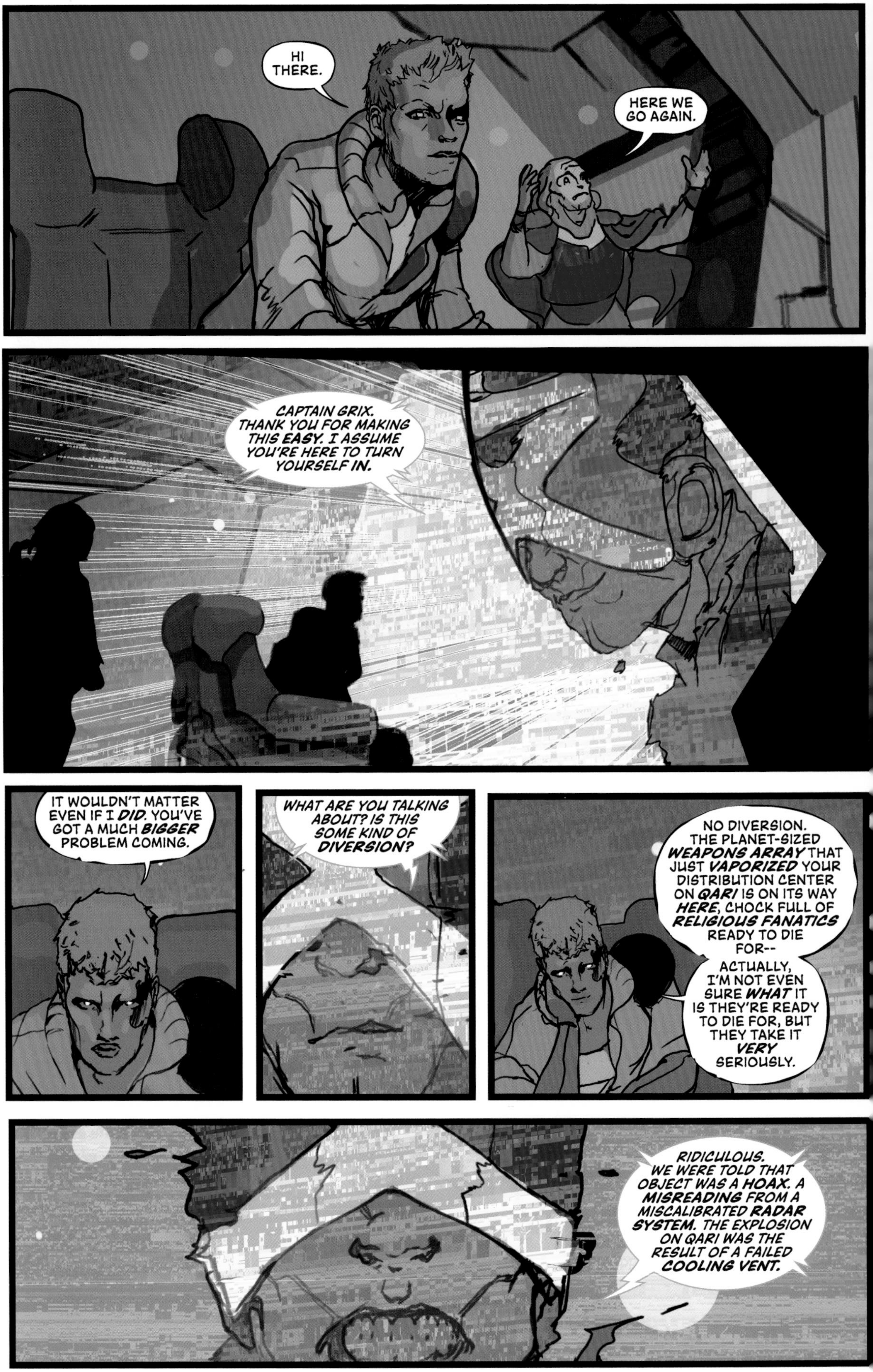
HI THERE.
HERE WE GO AGAIN.
CAPTAIN GRIX. THANK YOU FOR MAKING THIS EASY. I ASSUME YOU'RE HERE TO TURN YOURSELF IN.
IT WOULDN'T MATTER EVEN IF I DID. YOU'VE GOT A MUCH BIGGER PROBLEM COMING.
WHAT ARE YOU TALKING ABOUT? IS THIS SOME KIND OF DIVERSION?
NO DIVERSION. THE PLANET-SIZED WEAPONS ARRAY THAT JUST VAPORIZED YOUR DISTRIBUTION CENTER ON QARI IS ON ITS WAY HERE, CHOCK FULL OF RELIGIOUS FANATICS READY TO DIE FOR--
ACTUALLY, I'M NOT EVEN SURE WHAT IT IS THEY'RE READY TO DIE FOR, BUT THEY TAKE IT VERY SERIOUSLY.
RIDICULOUS. WE WERE TOLD THAT OBJECT WAS A HOAX. A MISREADING FROM A MISCALIBRATED RADAR SYSTEM. THE EXPLOSION ON QARI WAS THE RESULT OF A FAILED COOLING VENT.

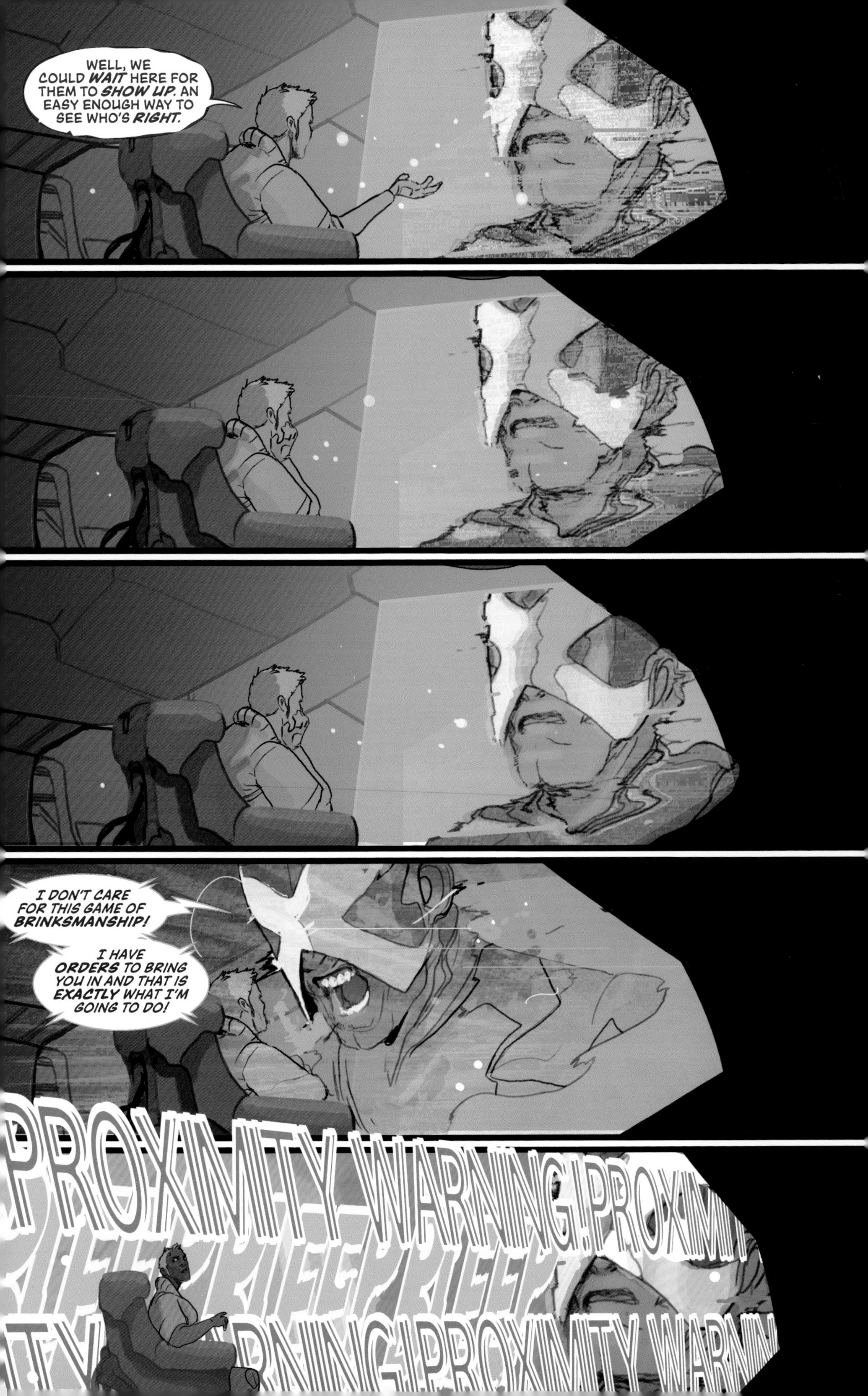

WELL, WE COULD WAIT HERE FOR THEM TO SHOW UP. AN EASY ENOUGH WAY TO SEE WHO'S RIGHT.
I DON'T CARE FOR THIS GAME OF BRINKSMANSHIP!
I HAVE ORDERS TO BRING YOU IN AND THAT IS EXACTLY WHAT I'M GOING TO DO!
PROXIMITY WARNING! PROXIMI
PROXIMITY WARN

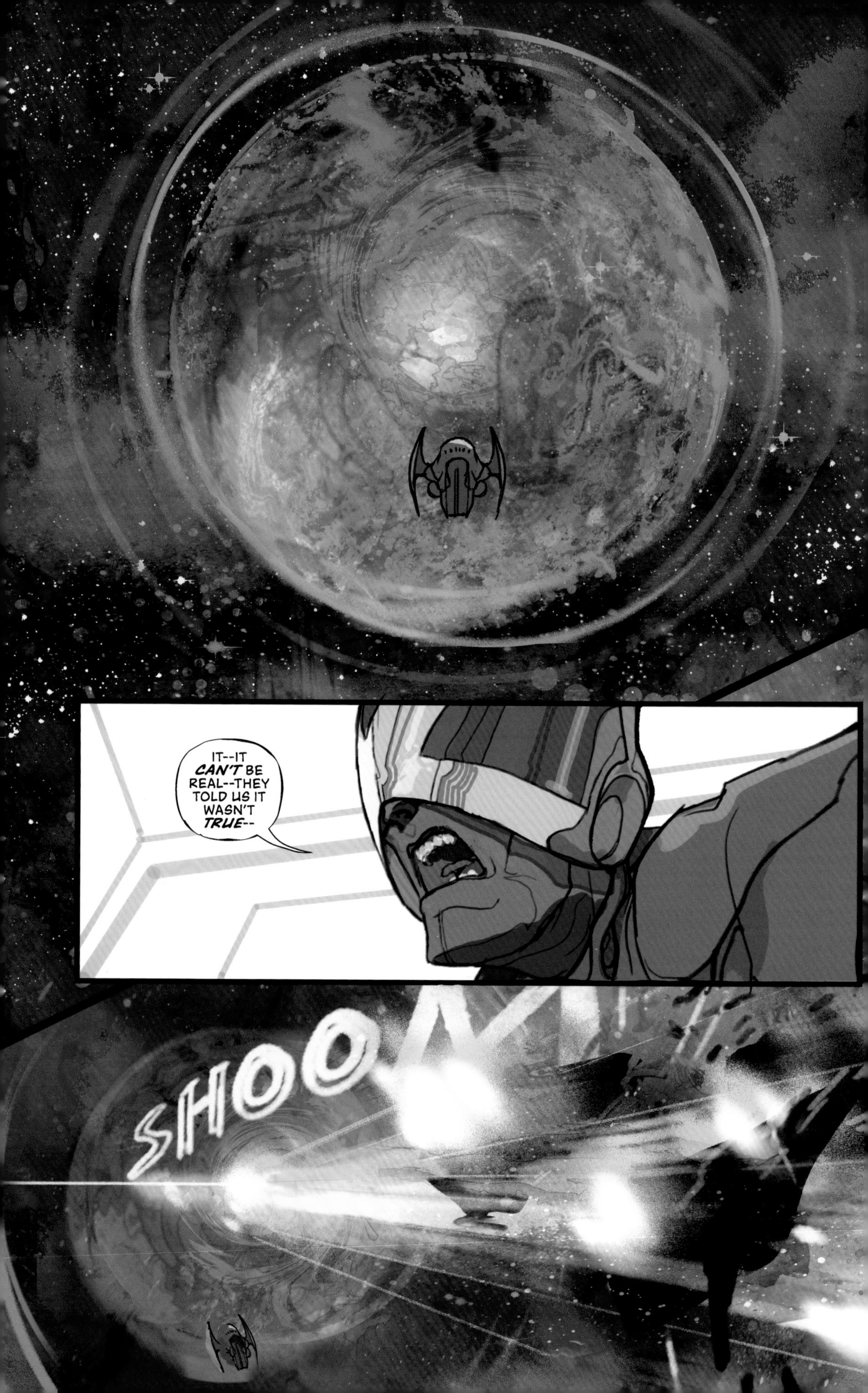
IT--IT *CAN'T* BE REAL--THEY TOLD US IT WASN'T *TRUE*--
SHOOM

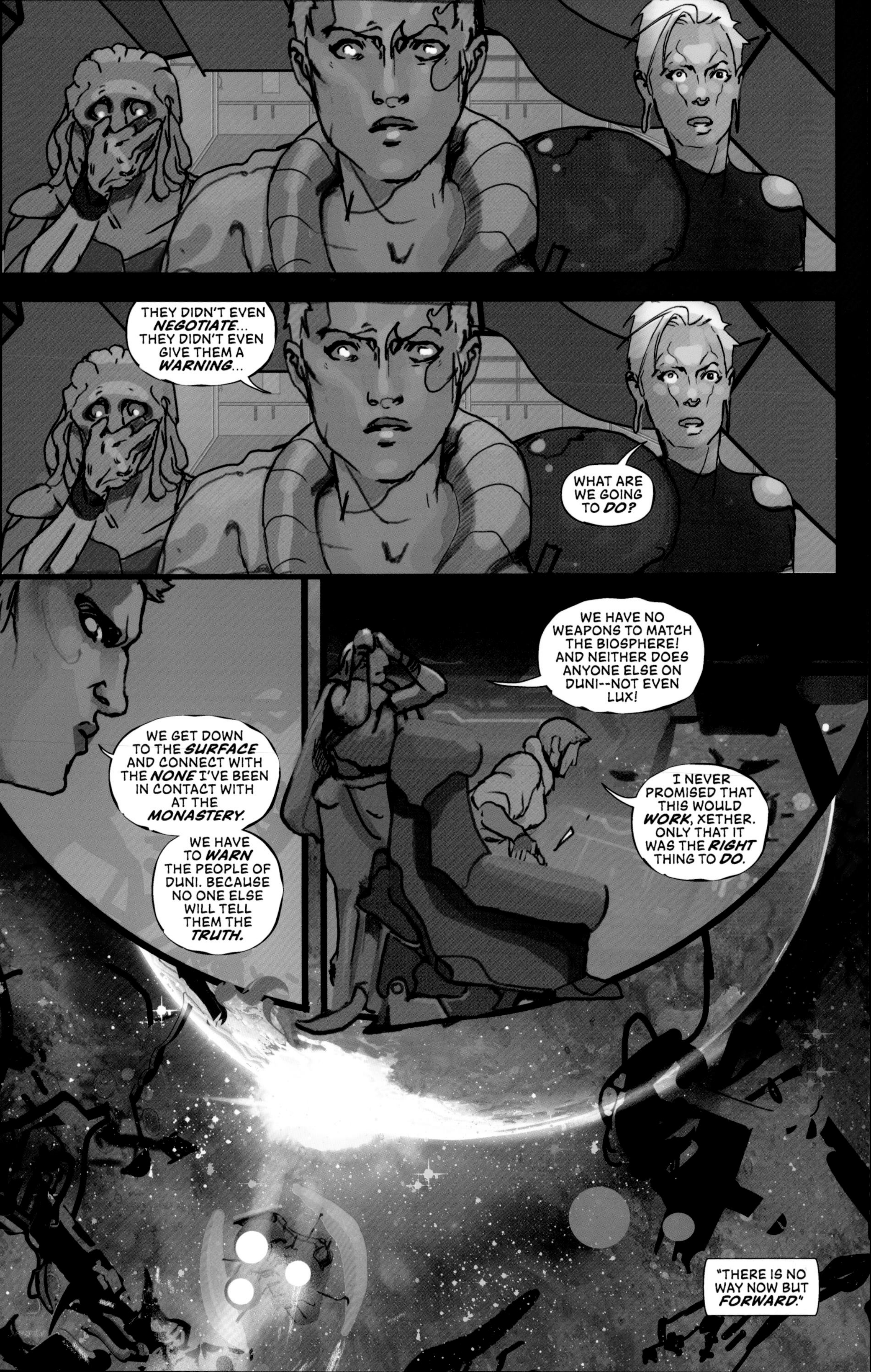
THEY DIDN'T EVEN *NEGOTIATE*... THEY DIDN'T EVEN GIVE THEM A *WARNING*...
WHAT ARE WE GOING TO *DO?*
WE HAVE NO WEAPONS TO MATCH THE BIOSPHERE! AND NEITHER DOES ANYONE ELSE ON DUNI--NOT EVEN LUX!
WE GET DOWN TO THE *SURFACE* AND CONNECT WITH THE *NONE* I'VE BEEN IN CONTACT WITH AT THE *MONASTERY*.
WE HAVE TO *WARN* THE PEOPLE OF DUNI. BECAUSE NO ONE ELSE WILL TELL THEM THE *TRUTH.*
I NEVER PROMISED THAT THIS WOULD *WORK*, XETHER. ONLY THAT IT WAS THE *RIGHT* THING TO *DO*.
"THERE IS NO WAY NOW BUT *FORWARD*."

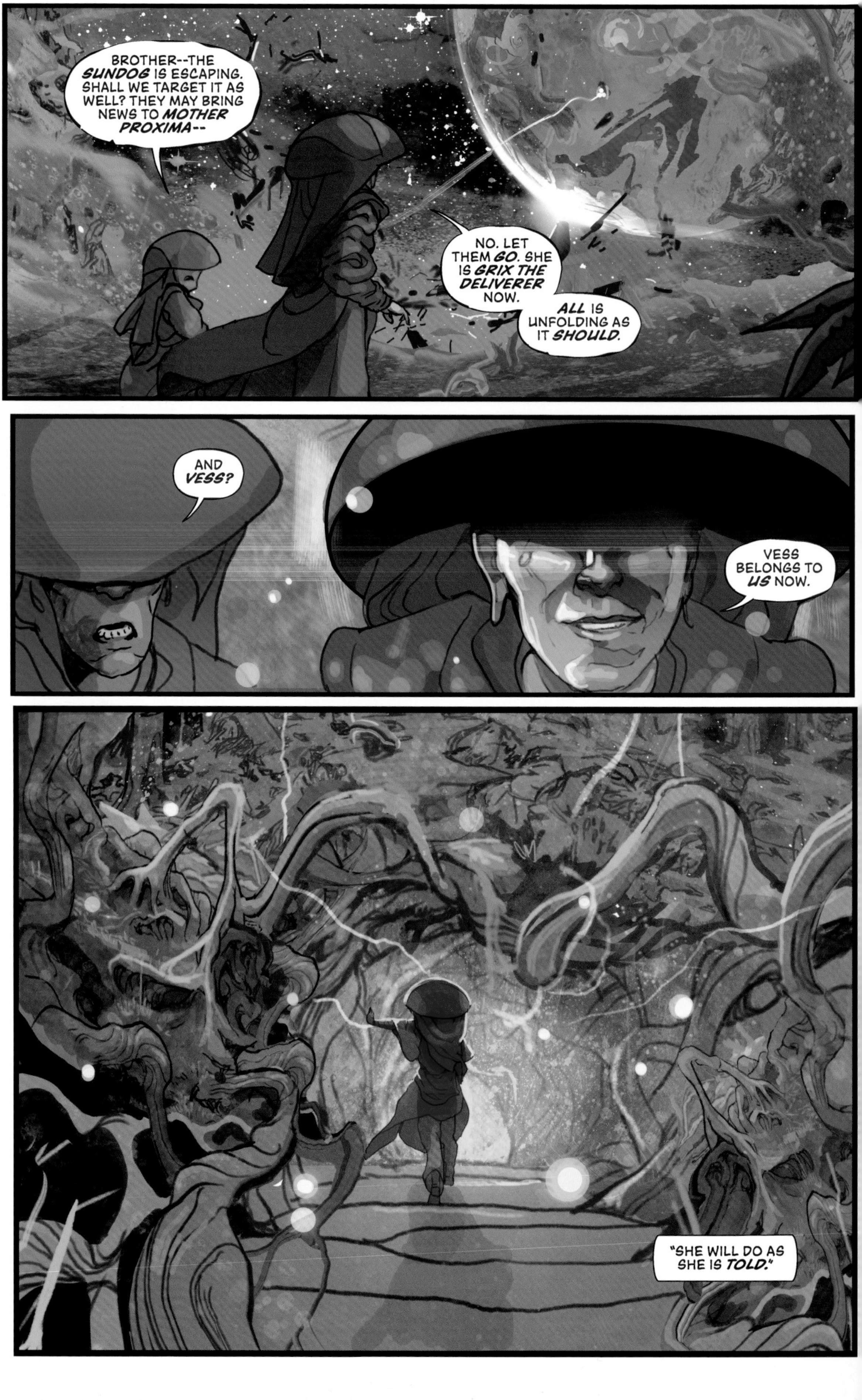
BROTHER--THE SUNDOG IS ESCAPING. SHALL WE TARGET IT AS WELL? THEY MAY BRING NEWS TO MOTHER PROXIMA--
NO. LET THEM GO. SHE IS GRIX THE DELIVERER NOW.
ALL IS UNFOLDING AS IT SHOULD.
AND VESS?
VESS BELONGS TO US NOW.
"SHE WILL DO AS SHE IS TOLD."

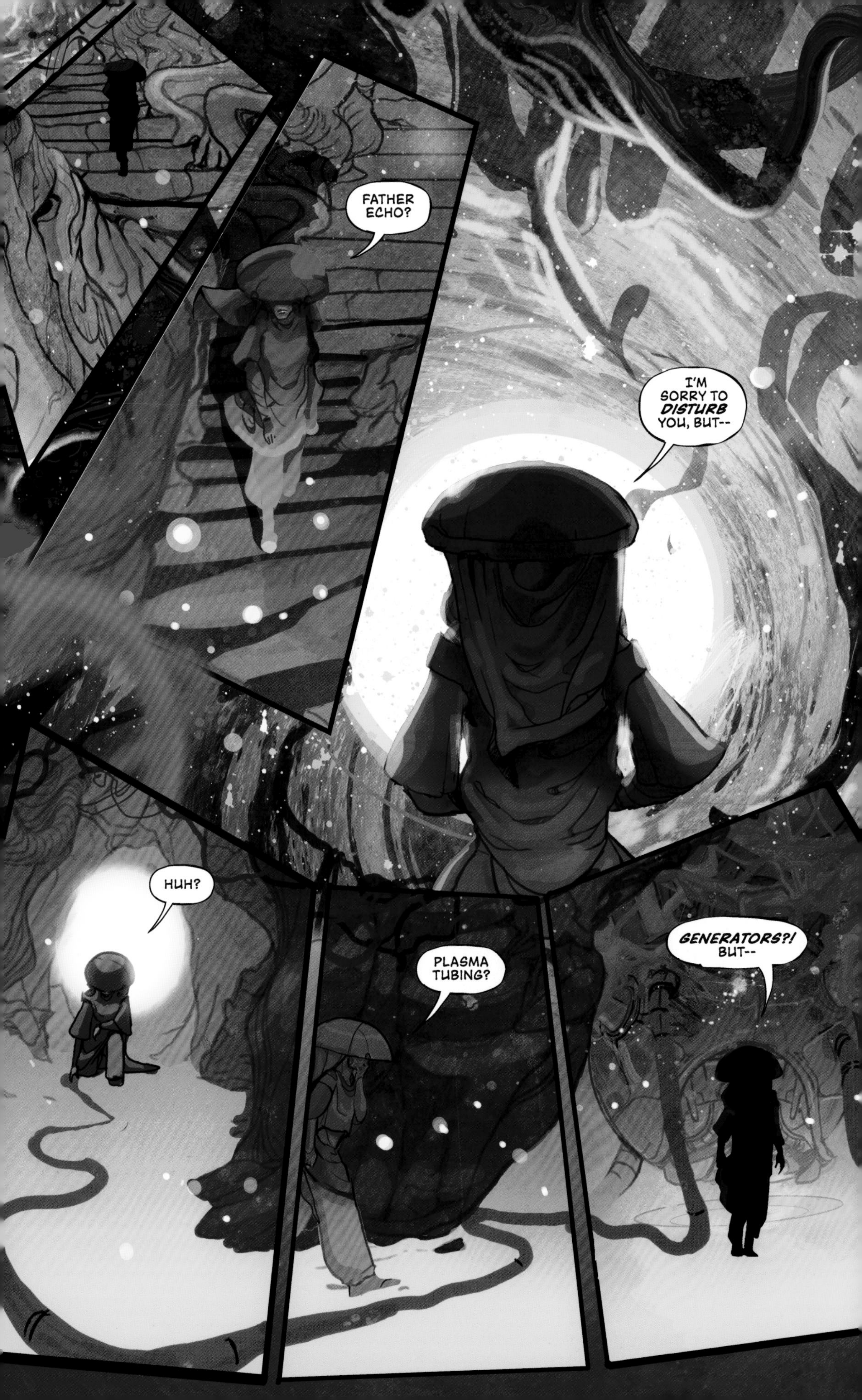
FATHER ECHO?
I'M SORRY TO DISTURB YOU, BUT--
HUH?
PLASMA TUBING?
GENERATORS?! BUT--

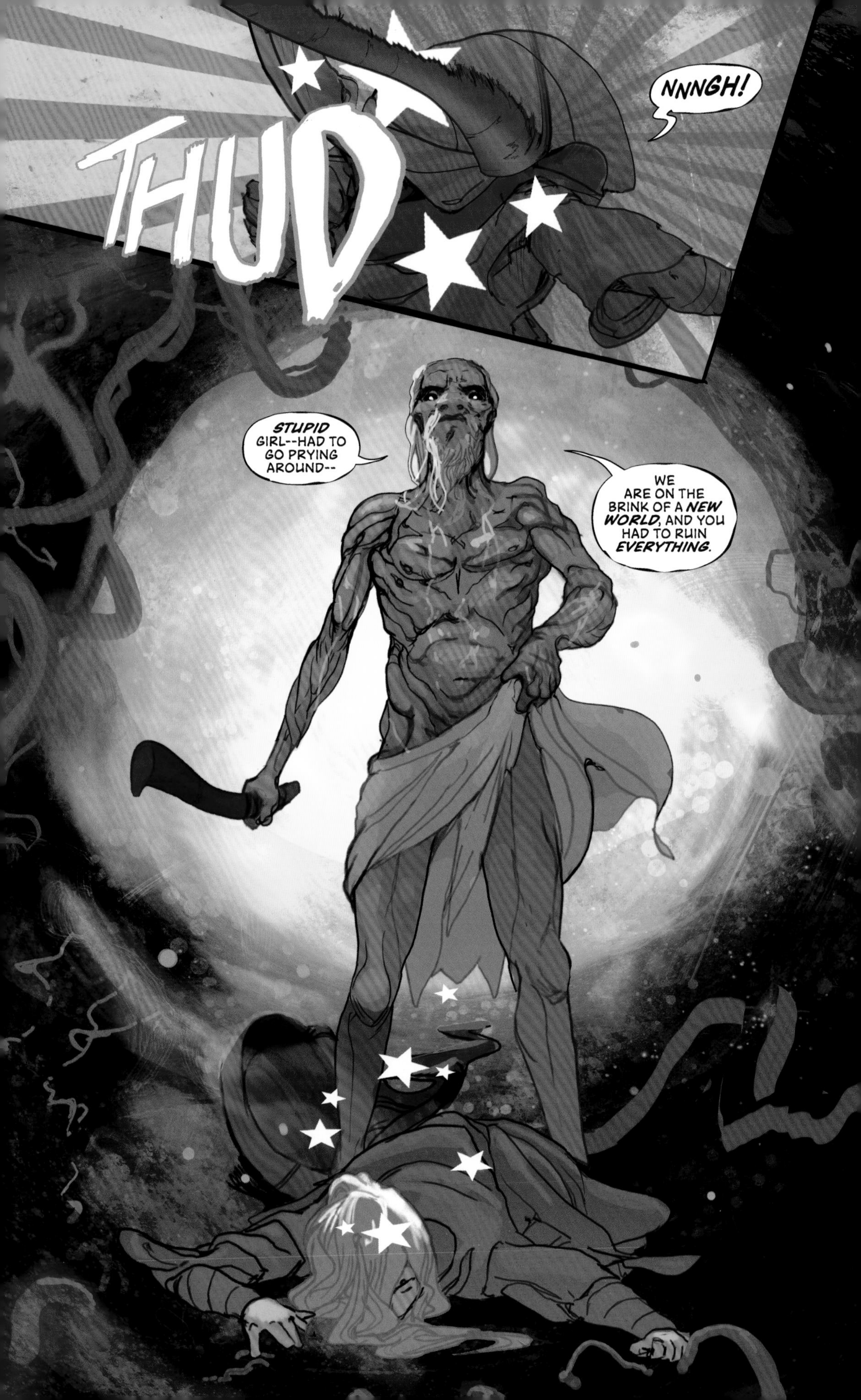
THUD
NNNGH!
STUPID GIRL--HAD TO GO PRYING AROUND--
WE ARE ON THE BRINK OF A NEW WORLD, AND YOU HAD TO RUIN EVERYTHING.

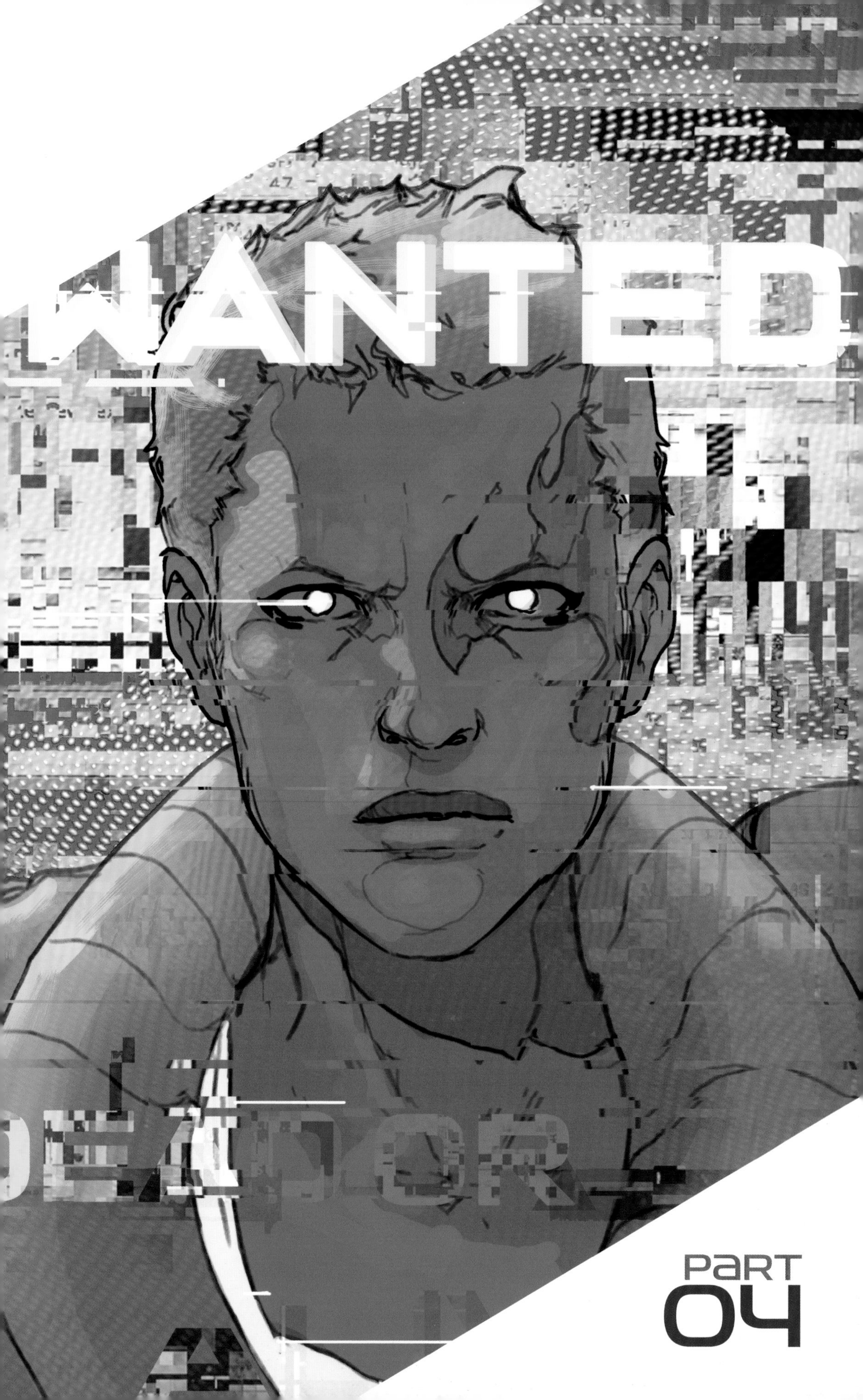
WANTED

# PART 04

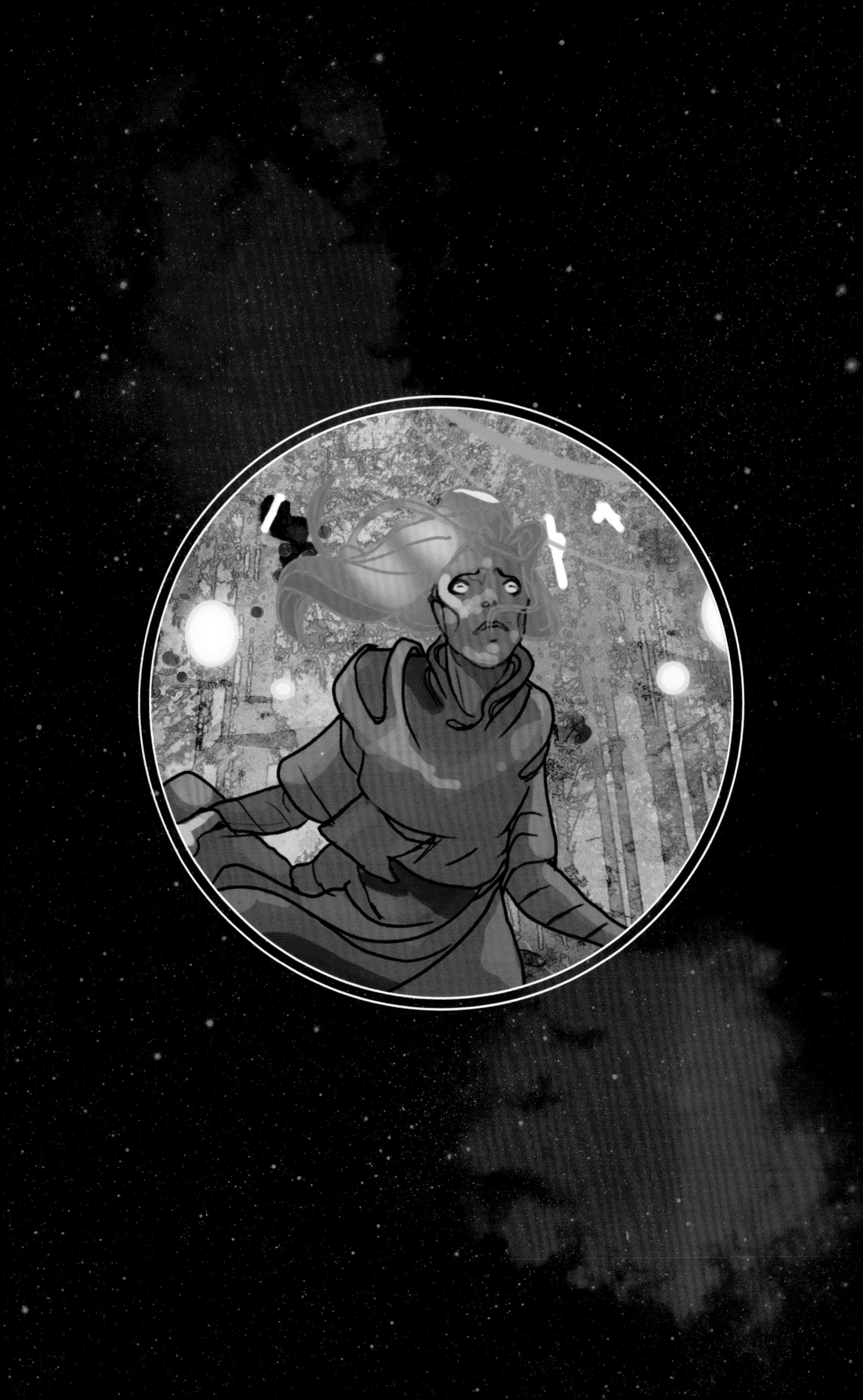

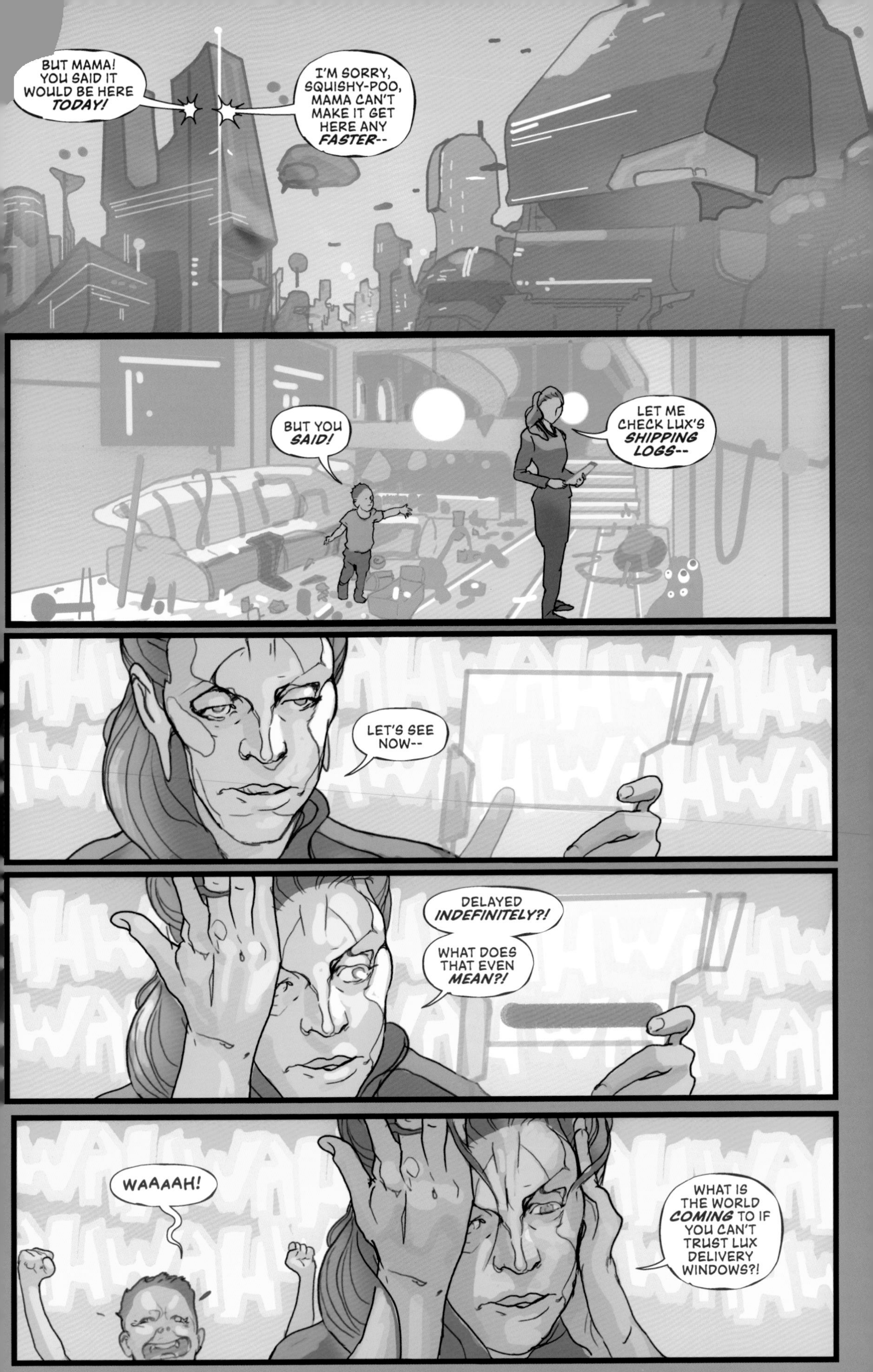
BUT MAMA! YOU SAID IT WOULD BE HERE TODAY!
I'M SORRY, SQUISHY-POO, MAMA CAN'T MAKE IT GET HERE ANY FASTER--
BUT YOU SAID!
LET ME CHECK LUX'S SHIPPING LOGS--
LET'S SEE NOW--
DELAYED INDEFINITELY?!
WHAT DOES THAT EVEN MEAN?!
WAAAAH!
WHAT IS THE WORLD COMING TO IF YOU CAN'T TRUST LUX DELIVERY WINDOWS?!

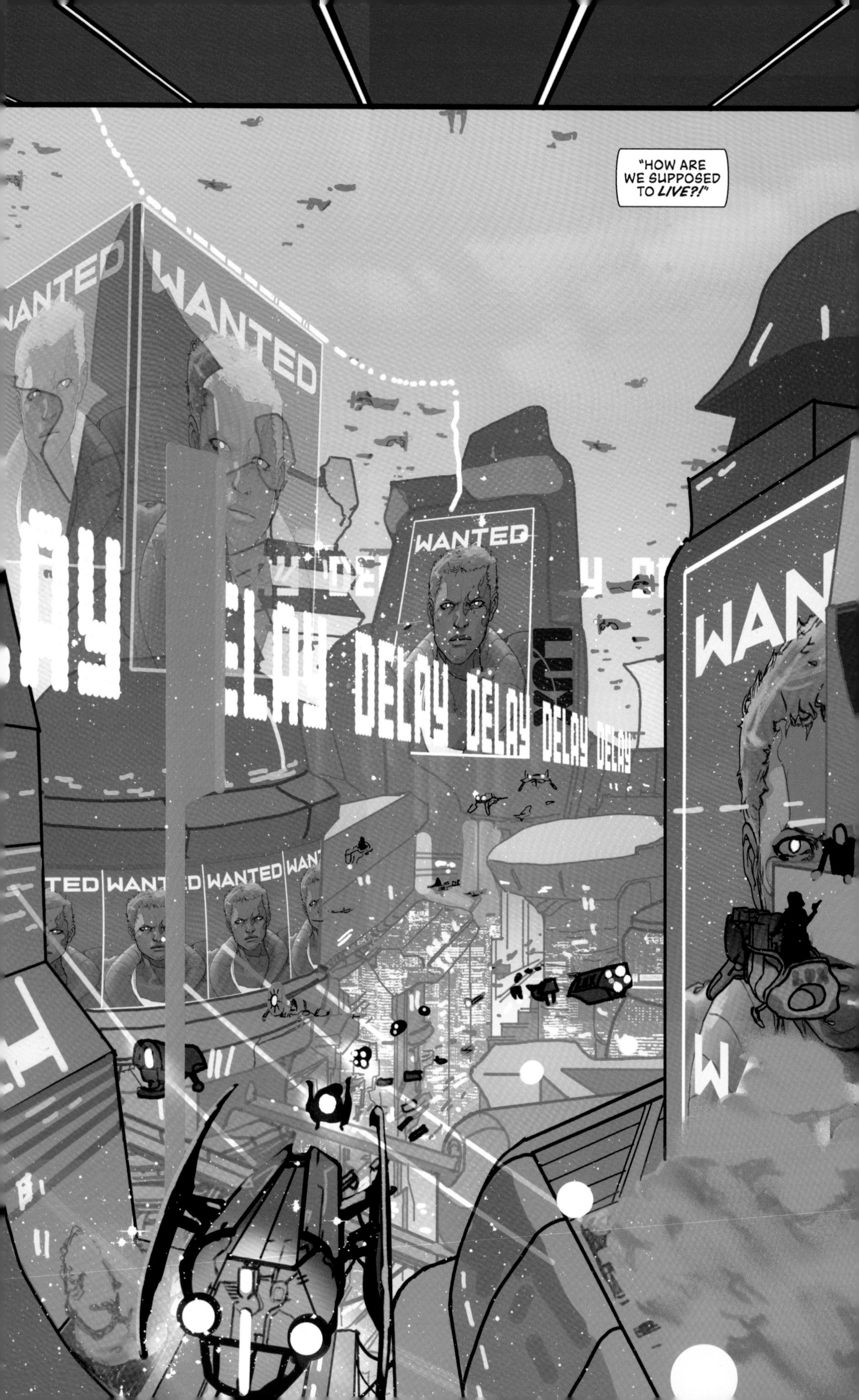
"HOW ARE WE SUPPOSED TO *LIVE?!*"
WANTED
WANTED
WANTED
DELAY DELAY DELAY DELAY
WANTED WANTED WANTED

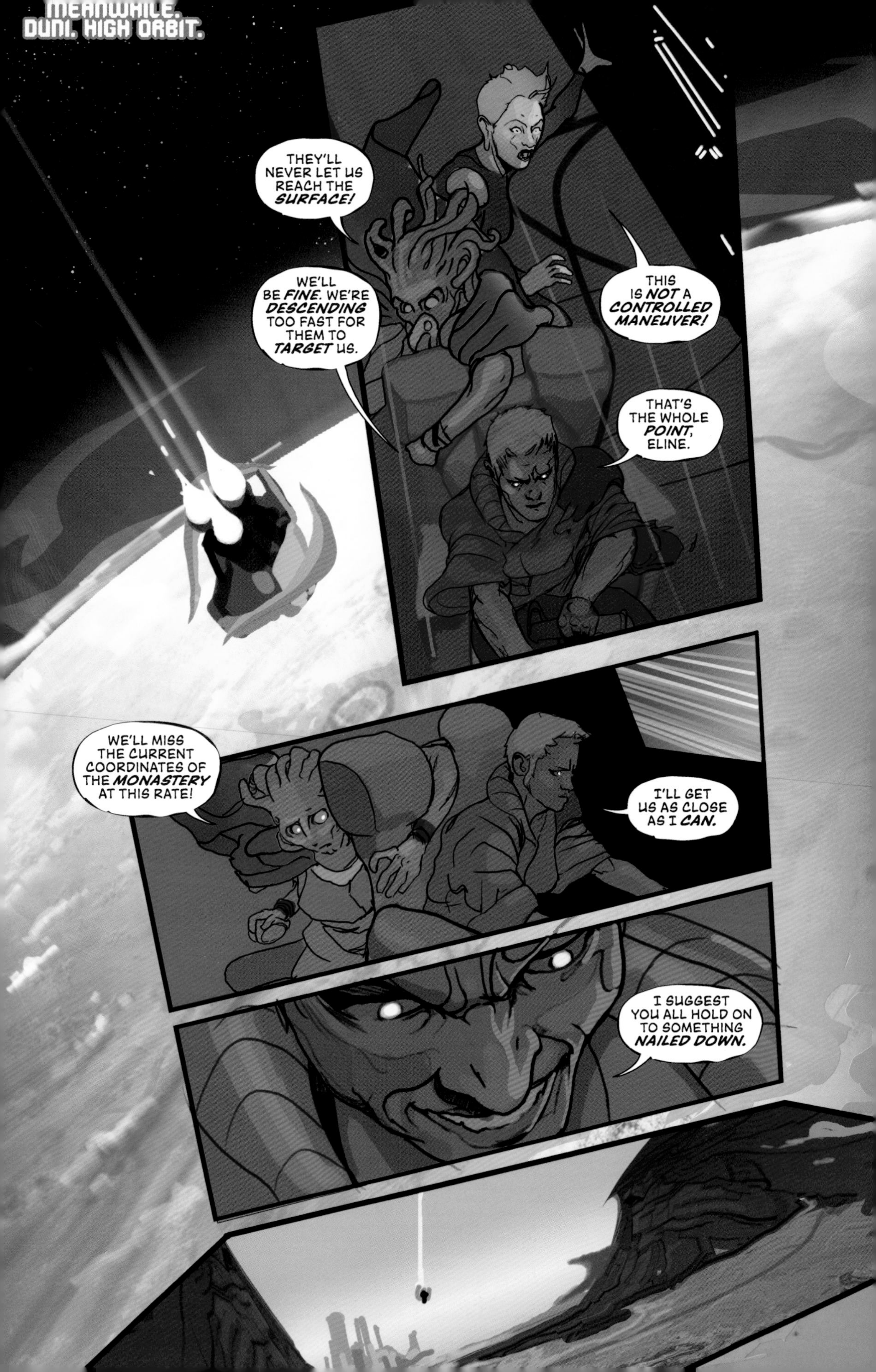
MEANWHILE.
DUNI. HIGH ORBIT.
THEY'LL NEVER LET US REACH THE SURFACE!
WE'LL BE FINE. WE'RE DESCENDING TOO FAST FOR THEM TO TARGET US.
THIS IS NOT A CONTROLLED MANEUVER!
THAT'S THE WHOLE POINT, ELINE.
WE'LL MISS THE CURRENT COORDINATES OF THE MONASTERY AT THIS RATE!
I'LL GET US AS CLOSE AS I CAN.
I SUGGEST YOU ALL HOLD ON TO SOMETHING NAILED DOWN.

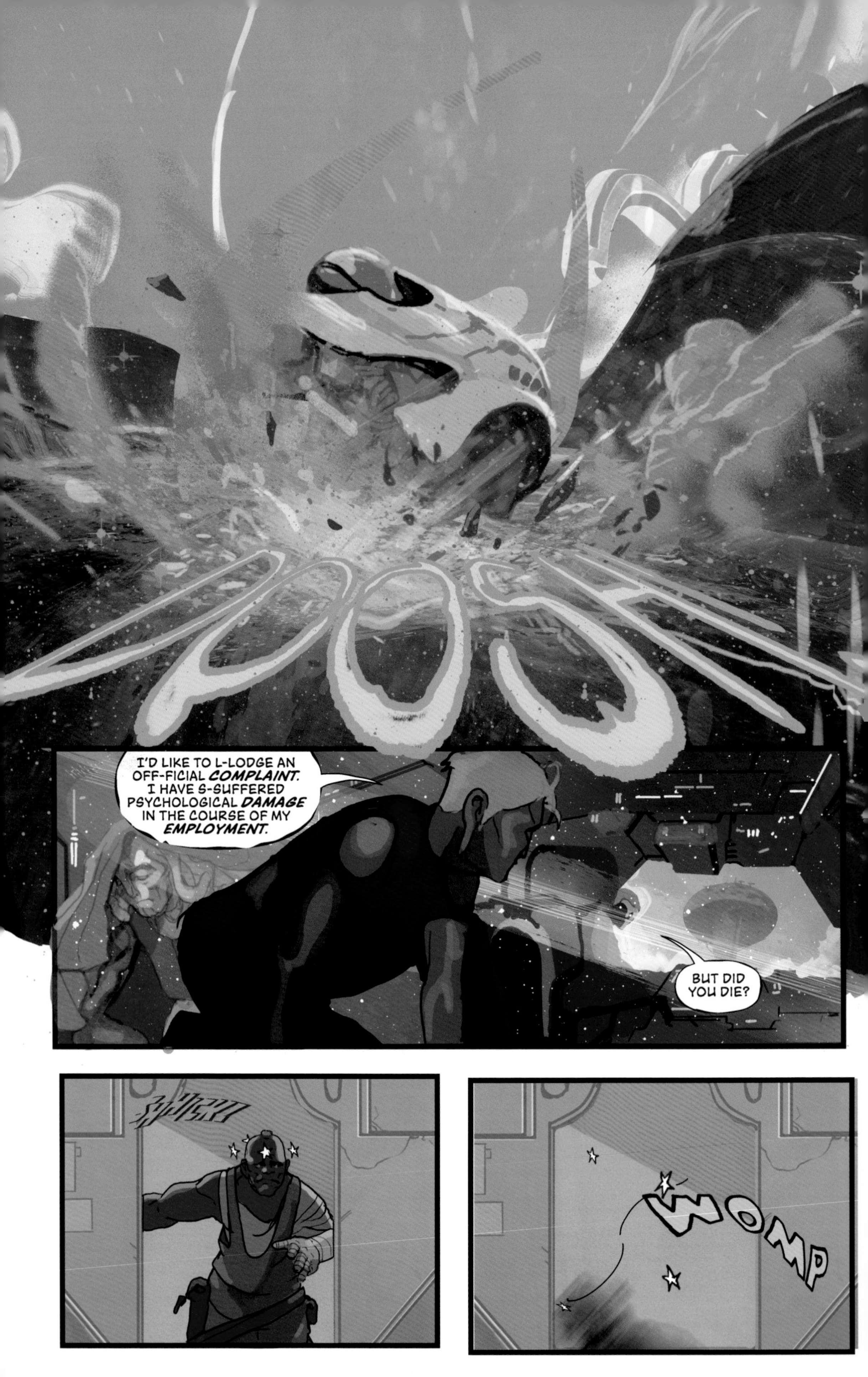
WOOSH
I'D LIKE TO L-LODGE AN OFF-FICIAL COMPLAINT. I HAVE S-SUFFERED PSYCHOLOGICAL DAMAGE IN THE COURSE OF MY EMPLOYMENT.
BUT DID YOU DIE?
WOMP

THE REST OF YOU STAY WITH THE *SUNDOG*. I'LL DEAL WITH THE *NONES*.

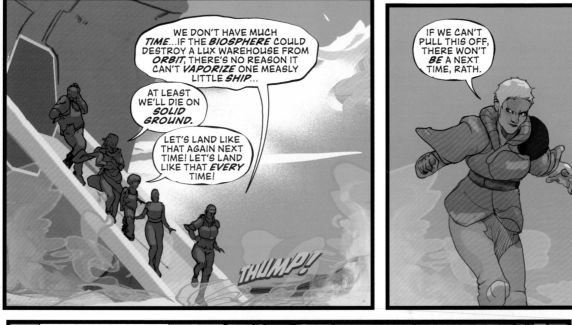

WE DON'T HAVE MUCH *TIME*...IF THE *BIOSPHERE* COULD DESTROY A LUX WAREHOUSE FROM *ORBIT*, THERE'S NO REASON IT CAN'T *VAPORIZE* ONE MEASLY LITTLE *SHIP*...

AT LEAST WE'LL DIE ON *SOLID GROUND*.

LET'S LAND LIKE THAT AGAIN NEXT TIME! LET'S LAND LIKE THAT *EVERY* TIME!

THUMP!

IF WE CAN'T PULL THIS OFF, THERE WON'T *BE* A NEXT TIME, RATH.

HAVE TO MAKE *MOTHER PROXIMA* SEE THE *BIGGER PICTURE*, EVEN IF SHE IS A CORRUPT, SCHEMING OLD *MEGALOMANIAC*...

THE ENEMY OF OUR ENEMY IS *NOT* OUR FRIEND.

I DIDN'T EXPOSE *LUX* AND THE *RENUNCIATION* ONLY TO SEE THEM *BOTH* REPLACED BY A BUNCH OF DANGEROUS *FANATICS*.

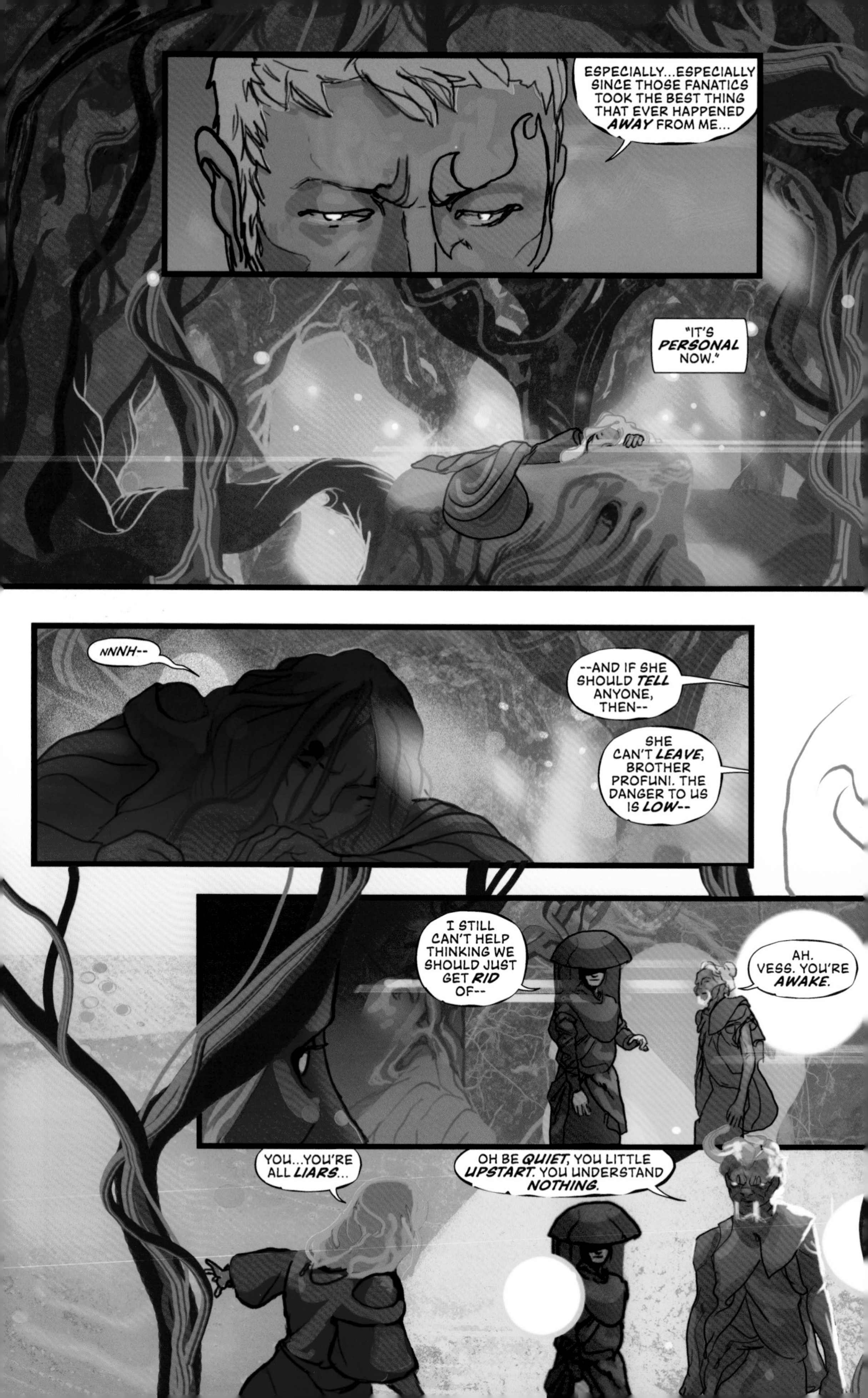
ESPECIALLY...ESPECIALLY SINCE THOSE FANATICS TOOK THE BEST THING THAT EVER HAPPENED AWAY FROM ME...
"IT'S PERSONAL NOW."
NNNH--
--AND IF SHE SHOULD TELL ANYONE, THEN--
SHE CAN'T LEAVE, BROTHER PROFUNI. THE DANGER TO US IS LOW--
I STILL CAN'T HELP THINKING WE SHOULD JUST GET RID OF--
AH. VESS. YOU'RE AWAKE.
YOU...YOU'RE ALL LIARS...
OH BE QUIET, YOU LITTLE UPSTART. YOU UNDERSTAND NOTHING.

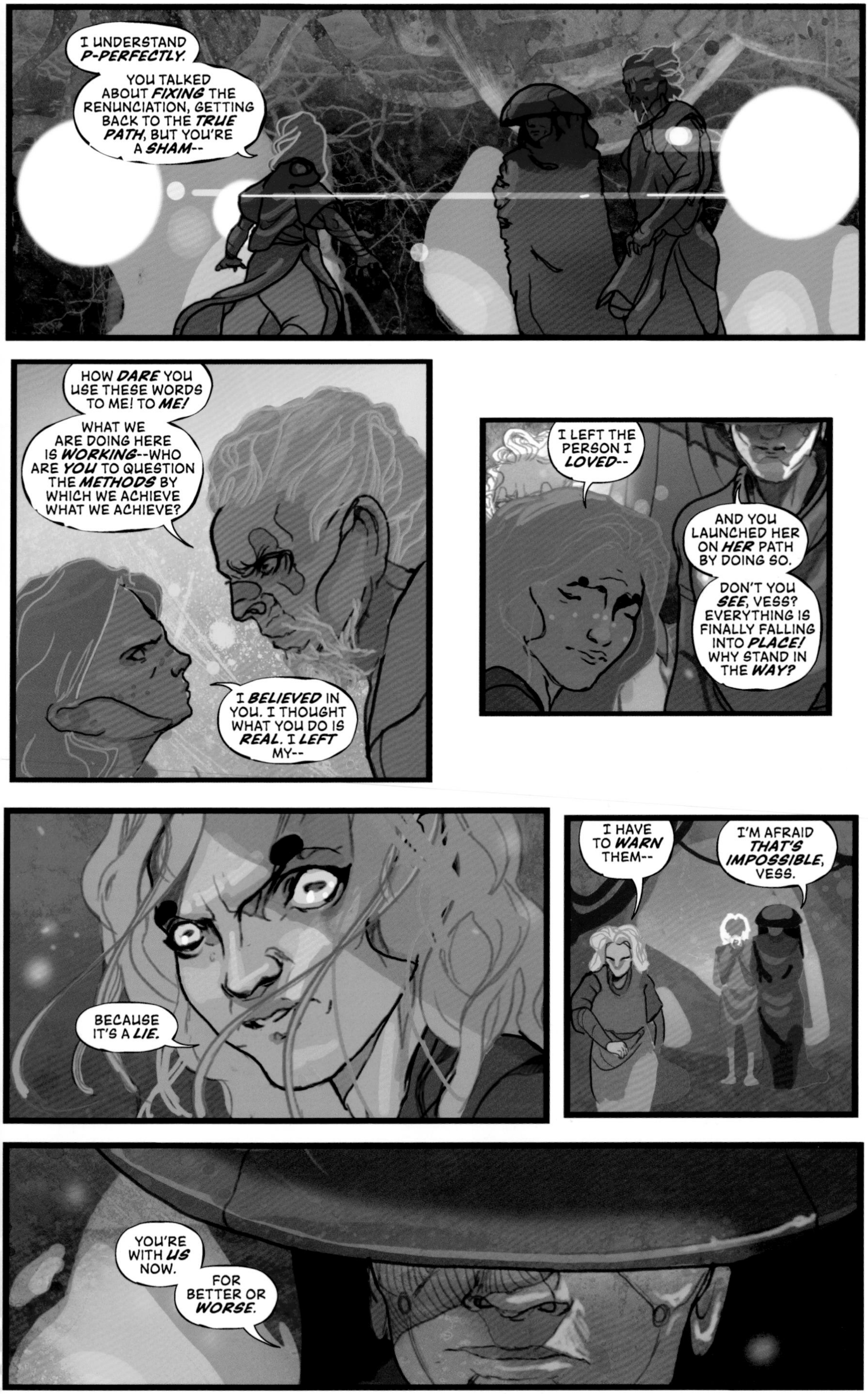
I UNDERSTAND P-PERFECTLY.
YOU TALKED ABOUT FIXING THE RENUNCIATION, GETTING BACK TO THE TRUE PATH, BUT YOU'RE A SHAM--
HOW DARE YOU USE THESE WORDS TO ME! TO ME!
WHAT WE ARE DOING HERE IS WORKING--WHO ARE YOU TO QUESTION THE METHODS BY WHICH WE ACHIEVE WHAT WE ACHIEVE?
I BELIEVED IN YOU. I THOUGHT WHAT YOU DO IS REAL. I LEFT MY--
I LEFT THE PERSON I LOVED--
AND YOU LAUNCHED HER ON HER PATH BY DOING SO.
DON'T YOU SEE, VESS? EVERYTHING IS FINALLY FALLING INTO PLACE! WHY STAND IN THE WAY?
BECAUSE IT'S A LIE.
I HAVE TO WARN THEM--
I'M AFRAID THAT'S IMPOSSIBLE, VESS.
YOU'RE WITH US NOW.
FOR BETTER OR WORSE.

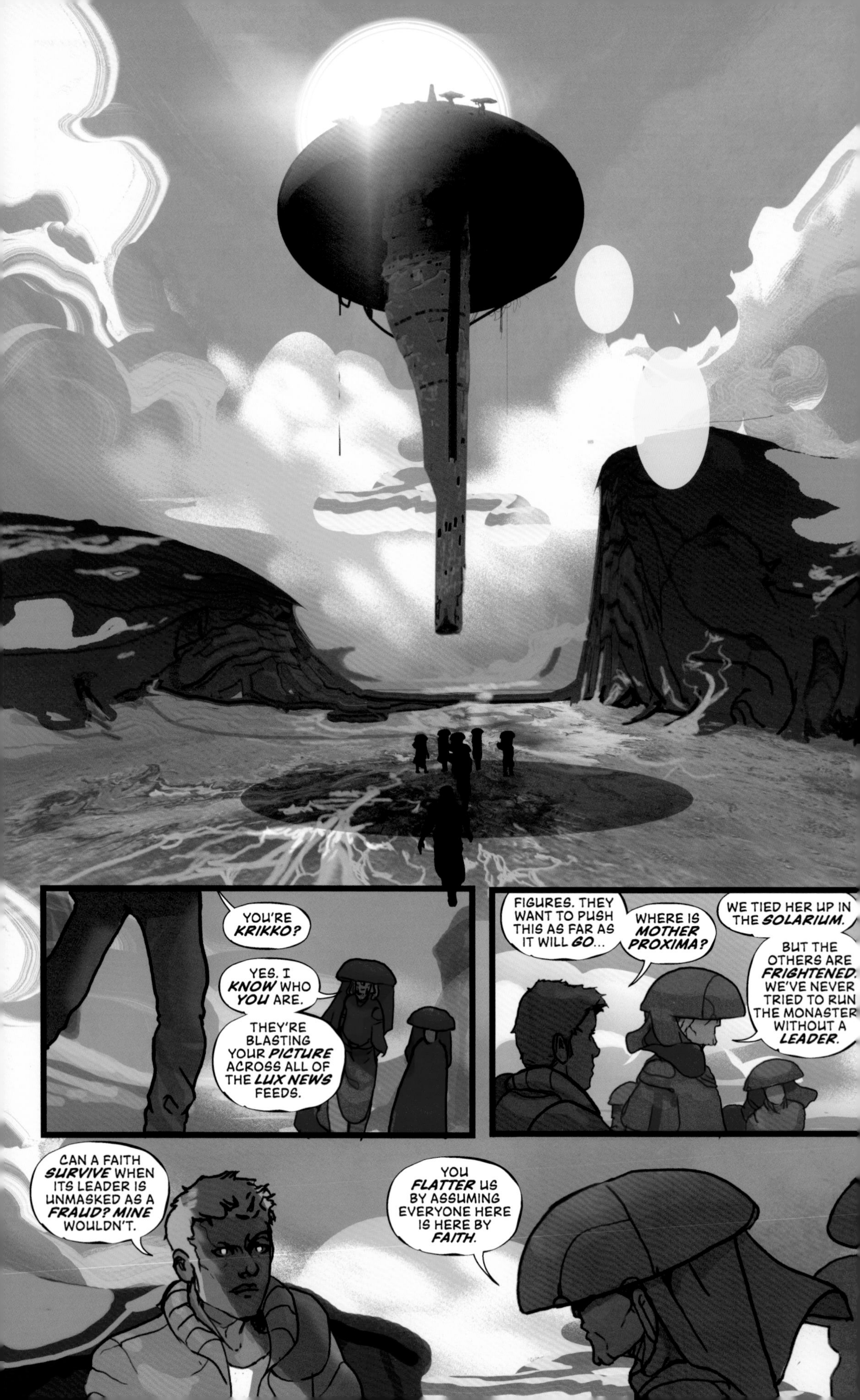

YOU'RE KRIKKO?
YES. I KNOW WHO YOU ARE.
THEY'RE BLASTING YOUR PICTURE ACROSS ALL OF THE LUX NEWS FEEDS.
FIGURES. THEY WANT TO PUSH THIS AS FAR AS IT WILL GO...
WHERE IS MOTHER PROXIMA?
WE TIED HER UP IN THE SOLARIUM.
BUT THE OTHERS ARE FRIGHTENED. WE'VE NEVER TRIED TO RUN THE MONASTER WITHOUT A LEADER.
CAN A FAITH SURVIVE WHEN ITS LEADER IS UNMASKED AS A FRAUD? MINE WOULDN'T.
YOU FLATTER US BY ASSUMING EVERYONE HERE IS HERE BY FAITH.

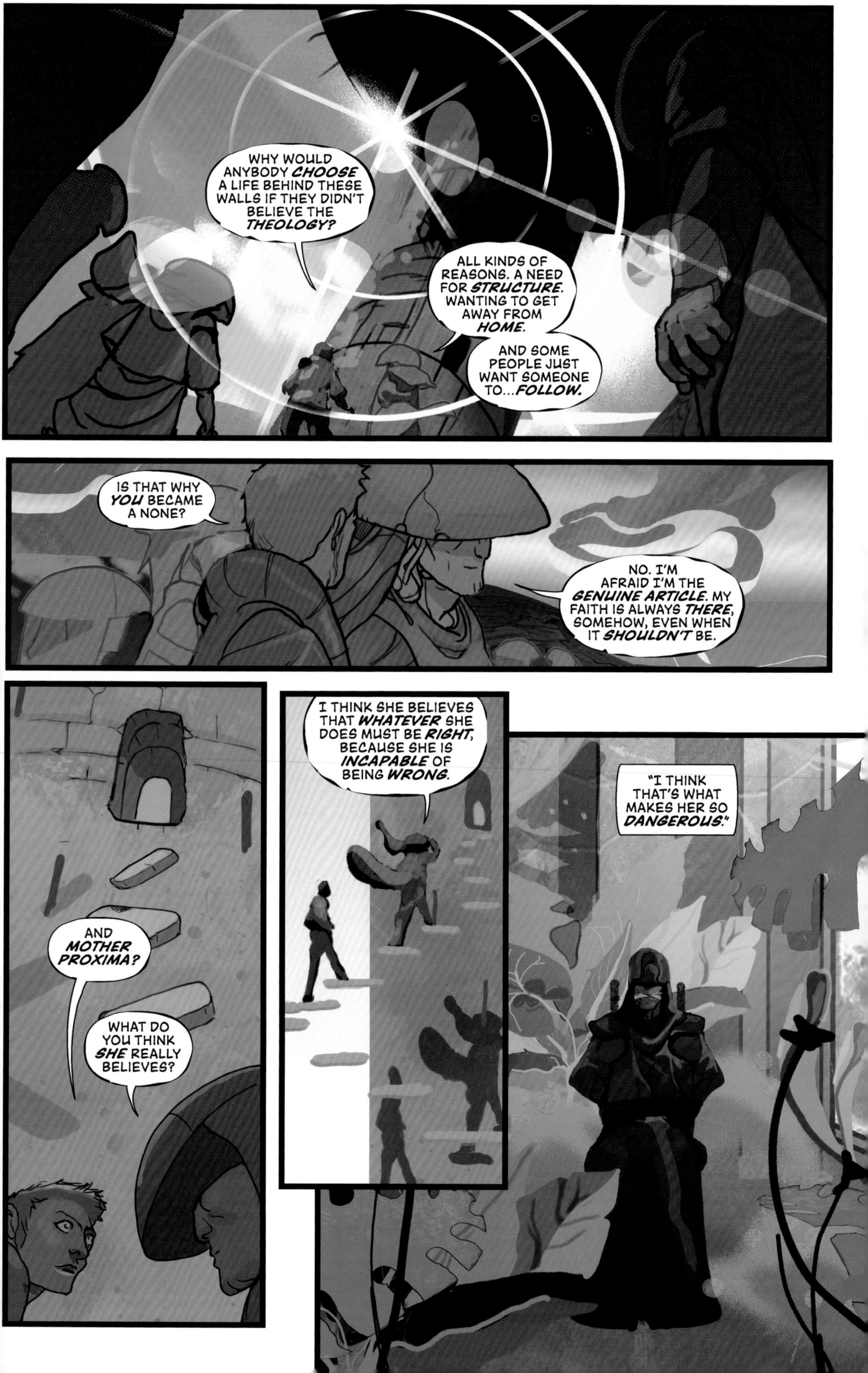
WHY WOULD ANYBODY CHOOSE A LIFE BEHIND THESE WALLS IF THEY DIDN'T BELIEVE THE THEOLOGY?
ALL KINDS OF REASONS. A NEED FOR STRUCTURE. WANTING TO GET AWAY FROM HOME.
AND SOME PEOPLE JUST WANT SOMEONE TO...FOLLOW.
IS THAT WHY YOU BECAME A NONE?
NO. I'M AFRAID I'M THE GENUINE ARTICLE. MY FAITH IS ALWAYS THERE, SOMEHOW, EVEN WHEN IT SHOULDN'T BE.
AND MOTHER PROXIMA?
WHAT DO YOU THINK SHE REALLY BELIEVES?
I THINK SHE BELIEVES THAT WHATEVER SHE DOES MUST BE RIGHT, BECAUSE SHE IS INCAPABLE OF BEING WRONG.
"I THINK THAT'S WHAT MAKES HER SO DANGEROUS."

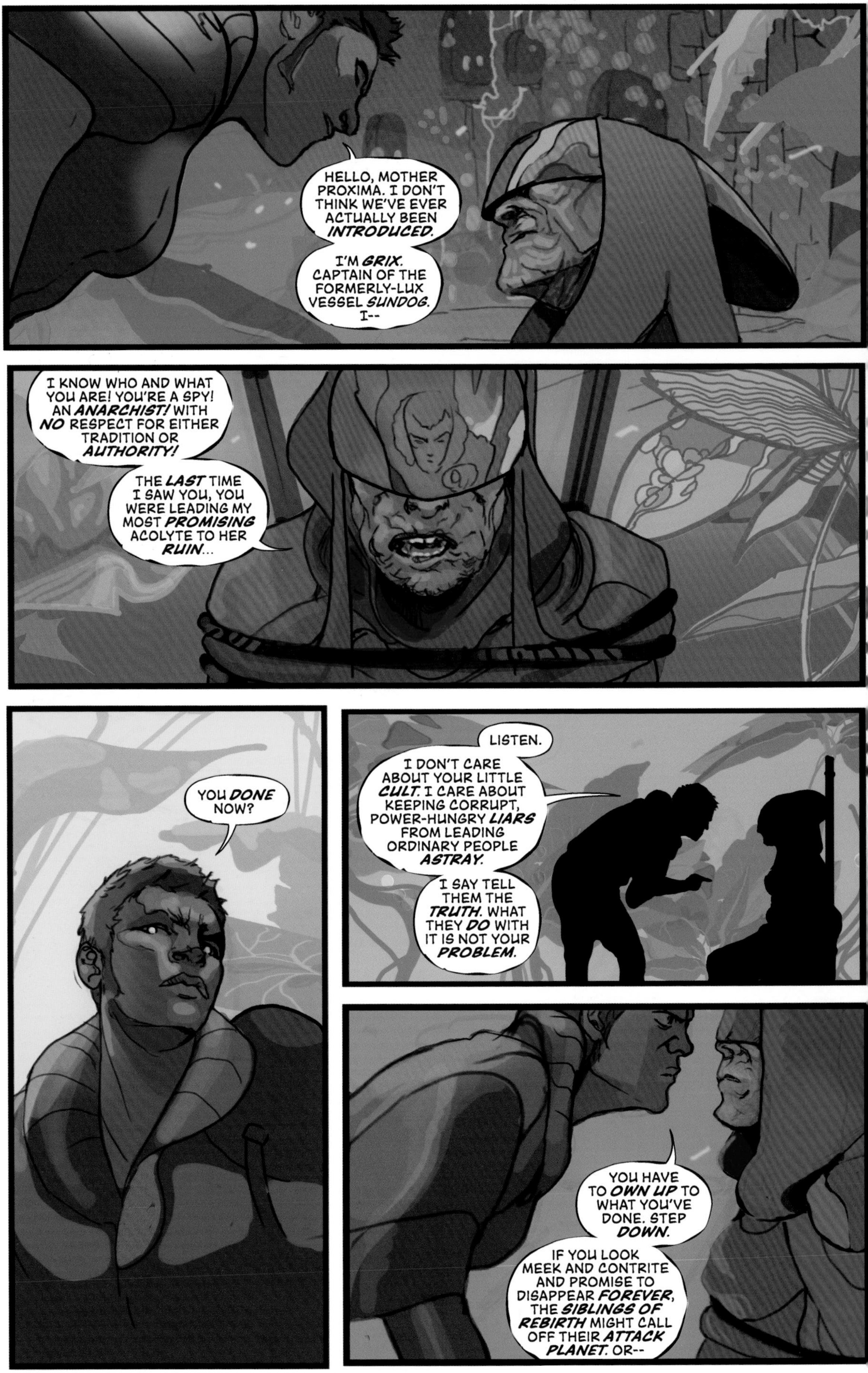
HELLO, MOTHER PROXIMA. I DON'T THINK WE'VE EVER ACTUALLY BEEN INTRODUCED.
I'M GRIX. CAPTAIN OF THE FORMERLY-LUX VESSEL SUNDOG. I--
I KNOW WHO AND WHAT YOU ARE! YOU'RE A SPY! AN ANARCHIST! WITH NO RESPECT FOR EITHER TRADITION OR AUTHORITY!
THE LAST TIME I SAW YOU, YOU WERE LEADING MY MOST PROMISING ACOLYTE TO HER RUIN...
YOU DONE NOW?
LISTEN.
I DON'T CARE ABOUT YOUR LITTLE CULT. I CARE ABOUT KEEPING CORRUPT, POWER-HUNGRY LIARS FROM LEADING ORDINARY PEOPLE ASTRAY.
I SAY TELL THEM THE TRUTH. WHAT THEY DO WITH IT IS NOT YOUR PROBLEM.
YOU HAVE TO OWN UP TO WHAT YOU'VE DONE. STEP DOWN.
IF YOU LOOK MEEK AND CONTRITE AND PROMISE TO DISAPPEAR FOREVER, THE SIBLINGS OF REBIRTH MIGHT CALL OFF THEIR ATTACK PLANET. OR--

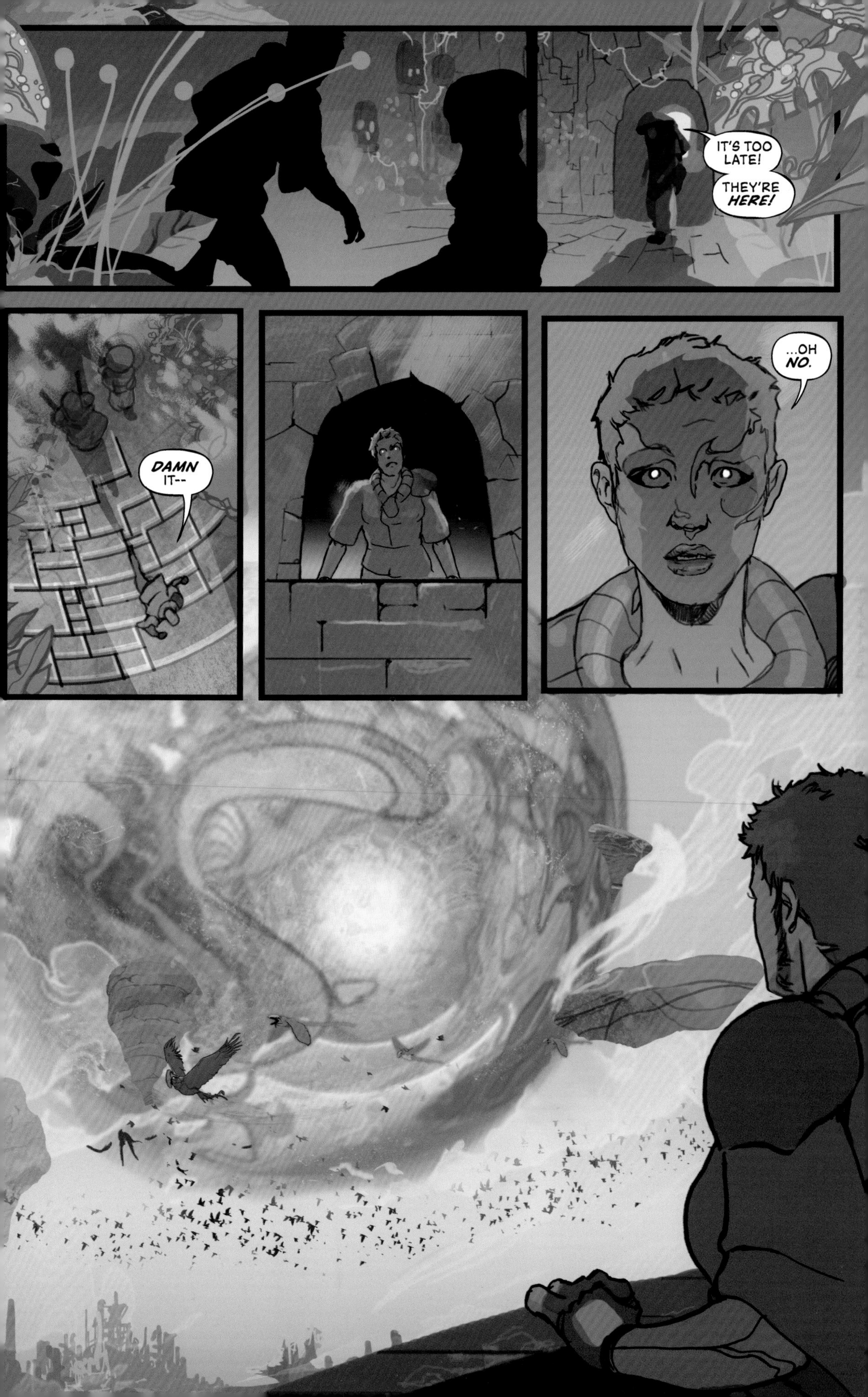
IT'S TOO LATE!
THEY'RE **HERE!**
**DAMN** IT--
...OH **NO.**

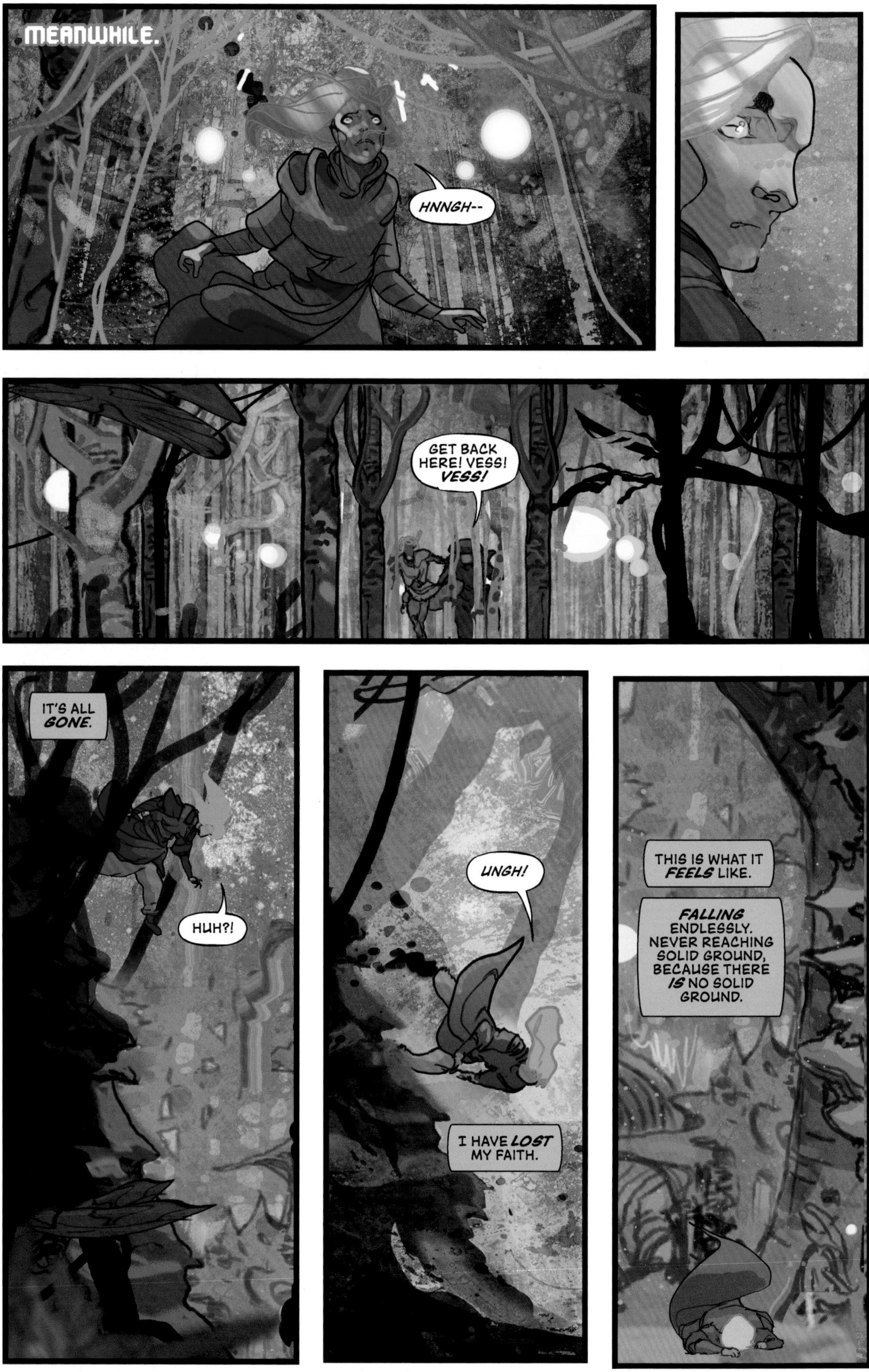
MEANWHILE.
HNNGH--
GET BACK HERE! VESS! VESS!
IT'S ALL GONE.
HUH?!
UNGH!
I HAVE LOST MY FAITH.
THIS IS WHAT IT FEELS LIKE.
FALLING ENDLESSLY. NEVER REACHING SOLID GROUND, BECAUSE THERE IS NO SOLID GROUND.

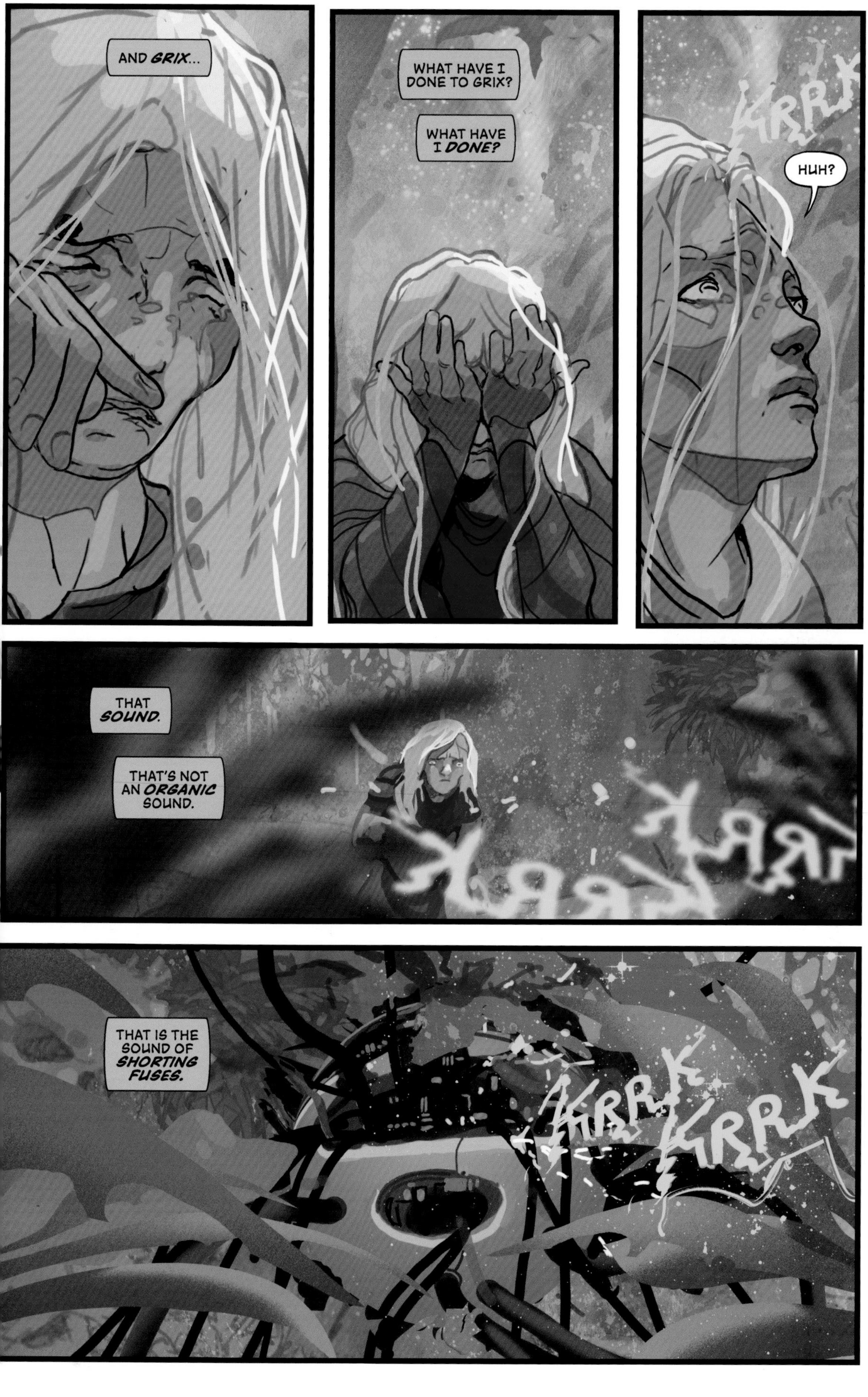
AND GRIX...
WHAT HAVE I DONE TO GRIX?
WHAT HAVE I DONE?
KRRK
HUH?
THAT SOUND.
THAT'S NOT AN ORGANIC SOUND.
KRRK
KRRK
THAT IS THE SOUND OF SHORTING FUSES.
KRRK
KRRK

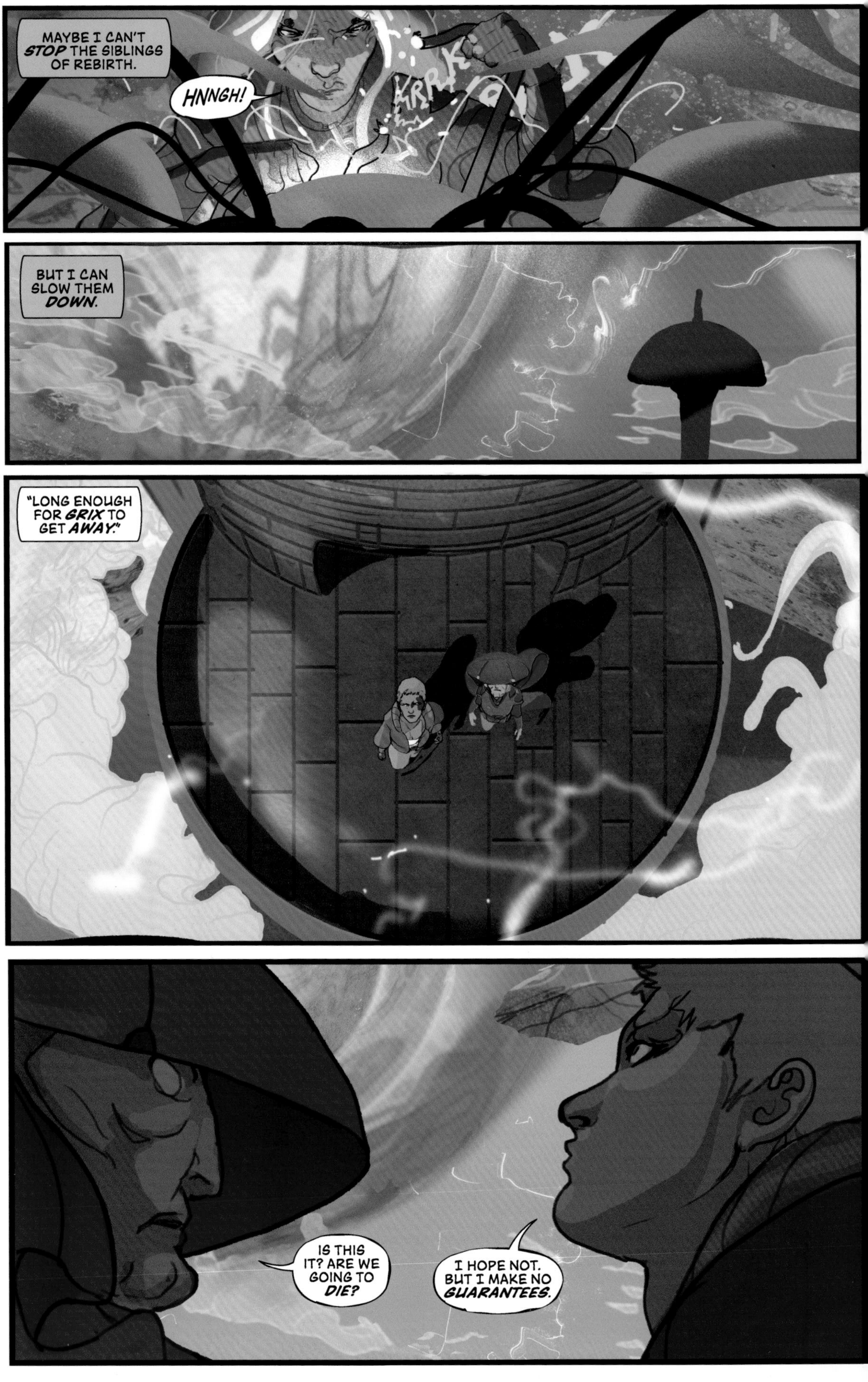
MAYBE I CAN'T STOP THE SIBLINGS OF REBIRTH.
HNNGH!
KRRK
BUT I CAN SLOW THEM DOWN.
"LONG ENOUGH FOR GRIX TO GET AWAY."
IS THIS IT? ARE WE GOING TO DIE?
I HOPE NOT. BUT I MAKE NO GUARANTEES.

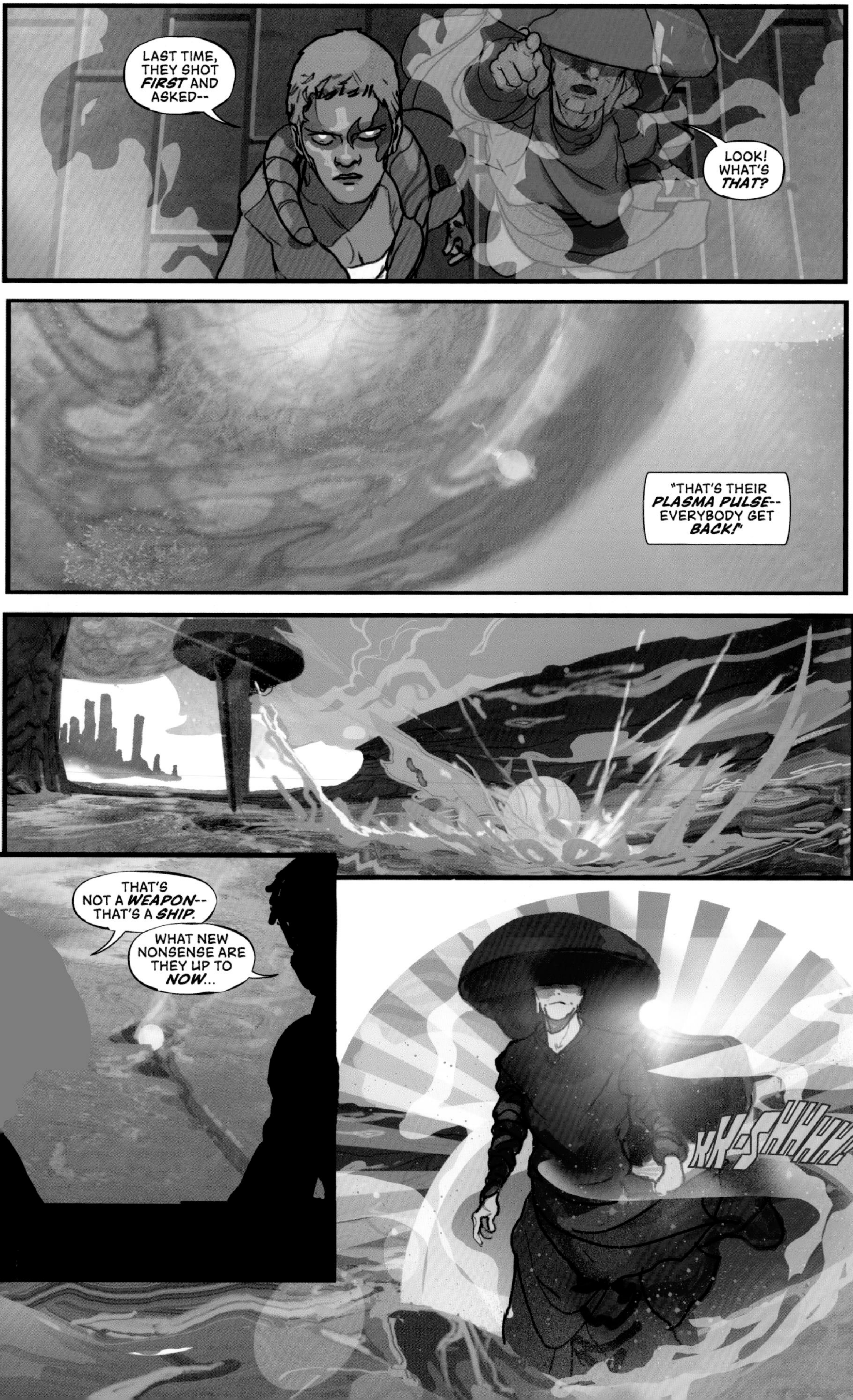
LAST TIME, THEY SHOT *FIRST* AND ASKED--
LOOK! WHAT'S *THAT?*
"THAT'S THEIR *PLASMA PULSE*-- EVERYBODY GET *BACK!*"
THAT'S NOT A *WEAPON*-- THAT'S A *SHIP*.
WHAT NEW NONSENSE ARE THEY UP TO *NOW*...
KK-SHHHH!

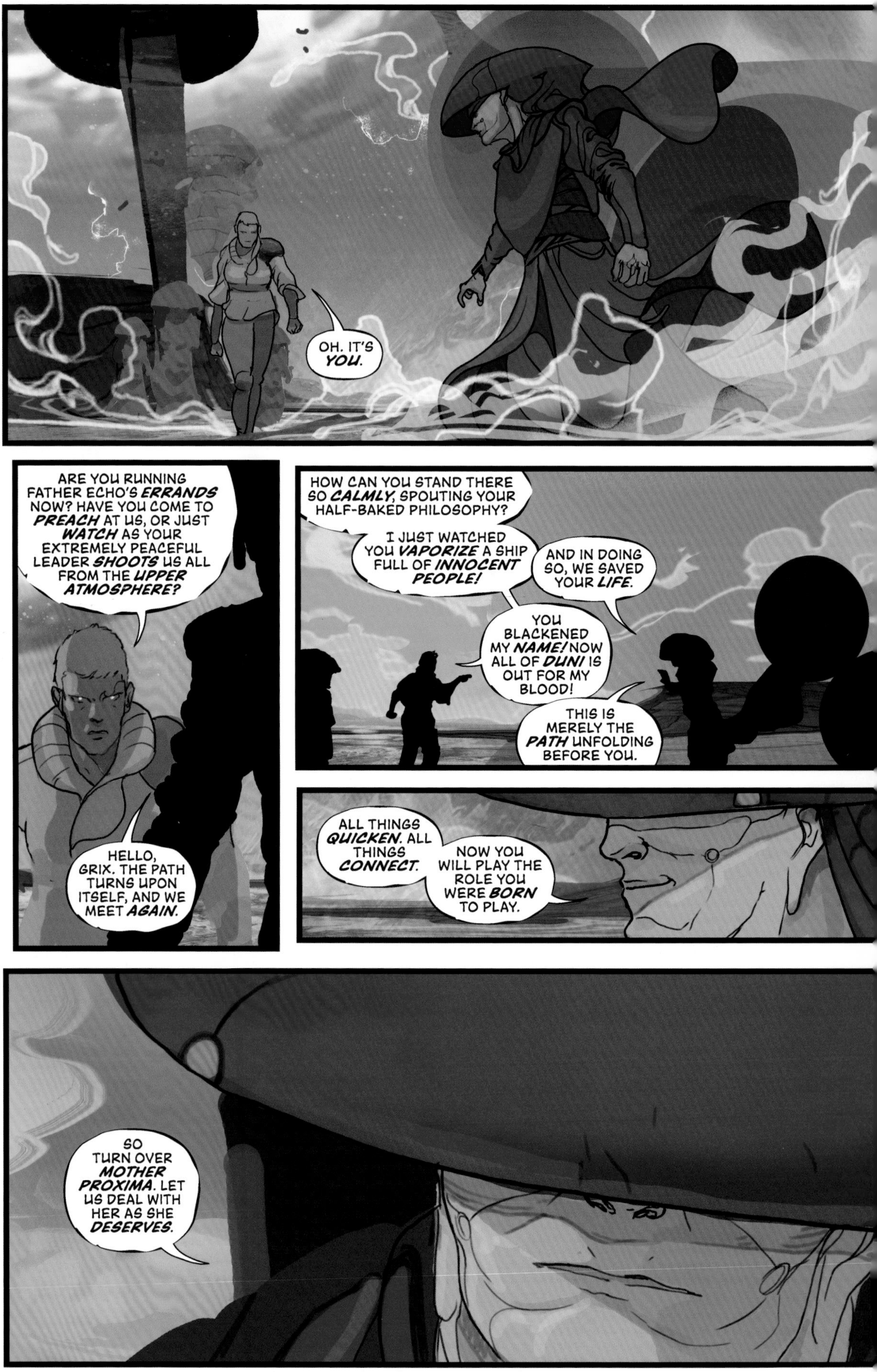
OH. IT'S YOU.
ARE YOU RUNNING FATHER ECHO'S ERRANDS NOW? HAVE YOU COME TO PREACH AT US, OR JUST WATCH AS YOUR EXTREMELY PEACEFUL LEADER SHOOTS US ALL FROM THE UPPER ATMOSPHERE?
HELLO, GRIX. THE PATH TURNS UPON ITSELF, AND WE MEET AGAIN.
HOW CAN YOU STAND THERE SO CALMLY, SPOUTING YOUR HALF-BAKED PHILOSOPHY?
I JUST WATCHED YOU VAPORIZE A SHIP FULL OF INNOCENT PEOPLE!
AND IN DOING SO, WE SAVED YOUR LIFE.
YOU BLACKENED MY NAME! NOW ALL OF DUNI IS OUT FOR MY BLOOD!
THIS IS MERELY THE PATH UNFOLDING BEFORE YOU.
ALL THINGS QUICKEN. ALL THINGS CONNECT.
NOW YOU WILL PLAY THE ROLE YOU WERE BORN TO PLAY.
SO TURN OVER MOTHER PROXIMA. LET US DEAL WITH HER AS SHE DESERVES.

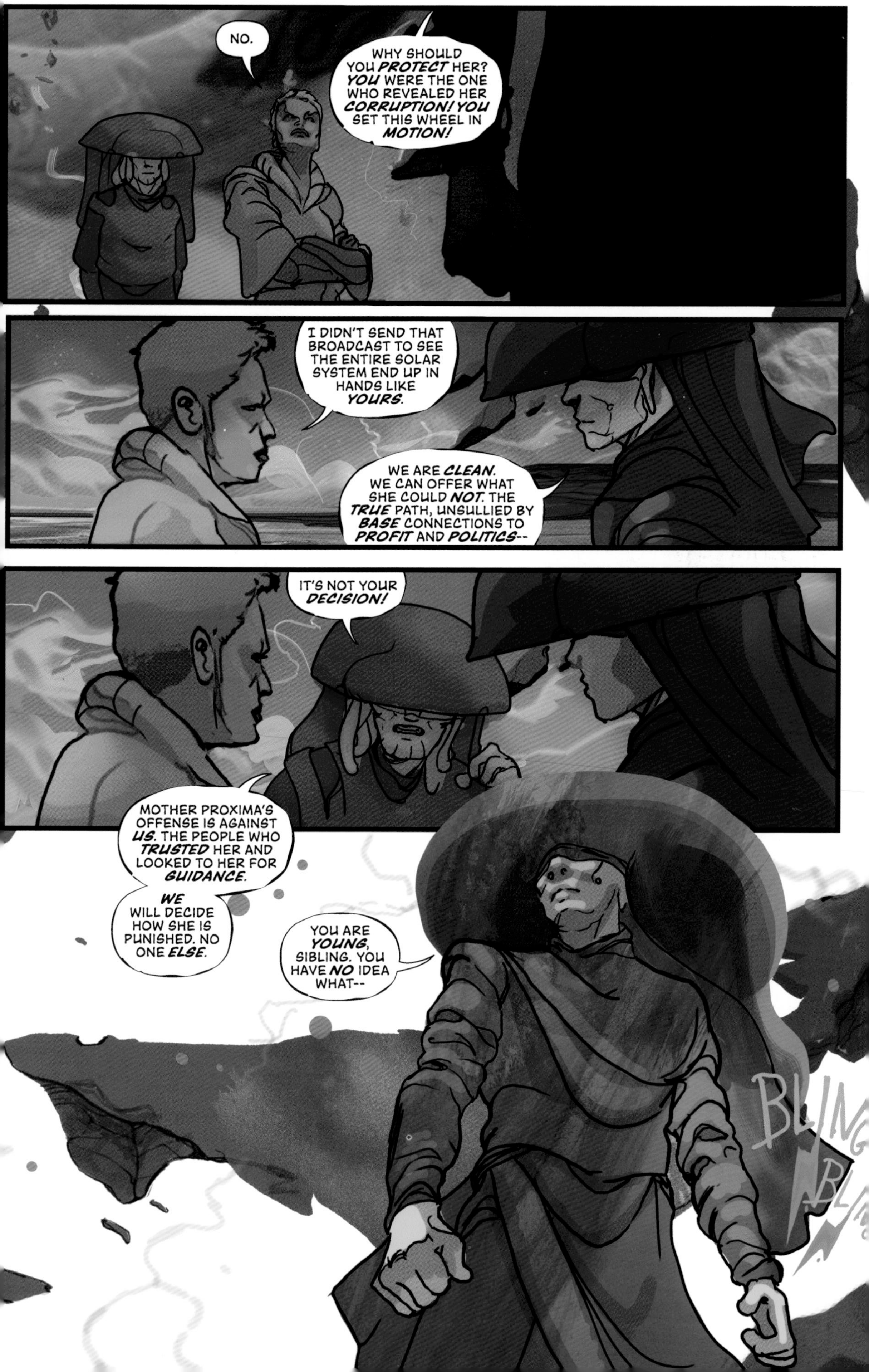
NO.
WHY SHOULD YOU PROTECT HER? YOU WERE THE ONE WHO REVEALED HER CORRUPTION! YOU SET THIS WHEEL IN MOTION!
I DIDN'T SEND THAT BROADCAST TO SEE THE ENTIRE SOLAR SYSTEM END UP IN HANDS LIKE YOURS.
WE ARE CLEAN. WE CAN OFFER WHAT SHE COULD NOT. THE TRUE PATH, UNSULLIED BY BASE CONNECTIONS TO PROFIT AND POLITICS--
IT'S NOT YOUR DECISION!
MOTHER PROXIMA'S OFFENSE IS AGAINST US. THE PEOPLE WHO TRUSTED HER AND LOOKED TO HER FOR GUIDANCE.
WE WILL DECIDE HOW SHE IS PUNISHED. NO ONE ELSE.
YOU ARE YOUNG, SIBLING. YOU HAVE NO IDEA WHAT--
BLING
BLING

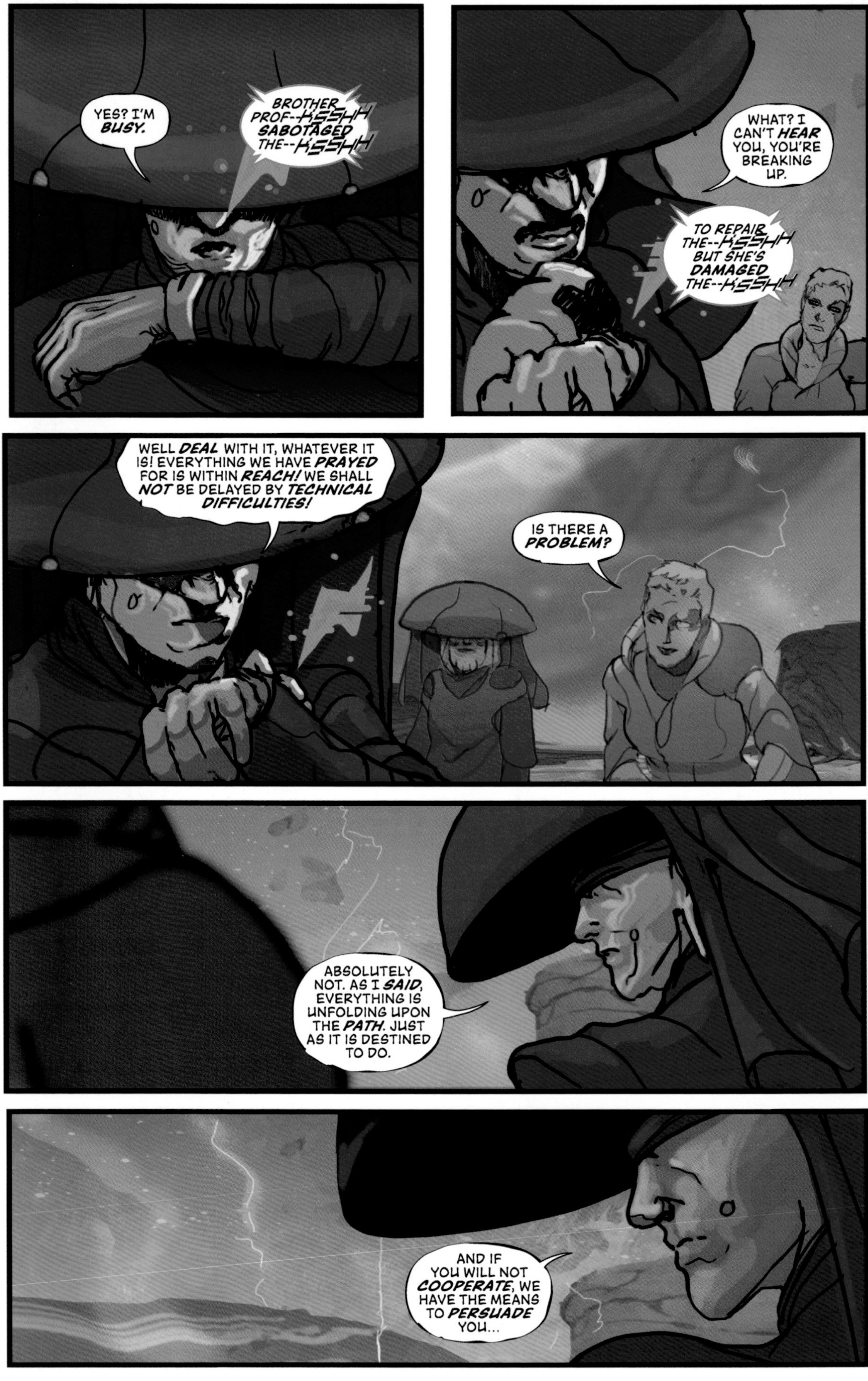
YES? I'M BUSY.
BROTHER PROF--KSSHH SABOTAGED THE--KSSHH
WHAT? I CAN'T HEAR YOU, YOU'RE BREAKING UP.
TO REPAIR THE--KSSHH BUT SHE'S DAMAGED THE--KSSHH
WELL DEAL WITH IT, WHATEVER IT IS! EVERYTHING WE HAVE PRAYED FOR IS WITHIN REACH! WE SHALL NOT BE DELAYED BY TECHNICAL DIFFICULTIES!
IS THERE A PROBLEM?
ABSOLUTELY NOT. AS I SAID, EVERYTHING IS UNFOLDING UPON THE PATH. JUST AS IT IS DESTINED TO DO.
AND IF YOU WILL NOT COOPERATE, WE HAVE THE MEANS TO PERSUADE YOU...

CONTROL!

FIRE THE *WEAPON.*

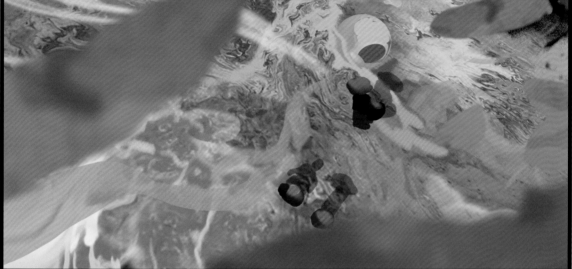

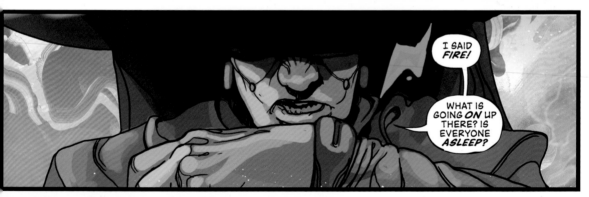

I SAID *FIRE!*

WHAT IS GOING *ON* UP THERE? IS EVERYONE *ASLEEP?*

*KSSHH* POWER SUPPLY DISRUPTION, BUT WE'RE-- *KSSHH* --VESS HAS-- *KSSHH*

VESS...THAT TRAITOROUS LITTLE *PUSTULE...*

*VESS* HAS DISRUPTED THE BIOSPHERE'S POWER SUPPLY?

I THOUGHT-- I THOUGHT SHE WAS ON *YOUR* SIDE.

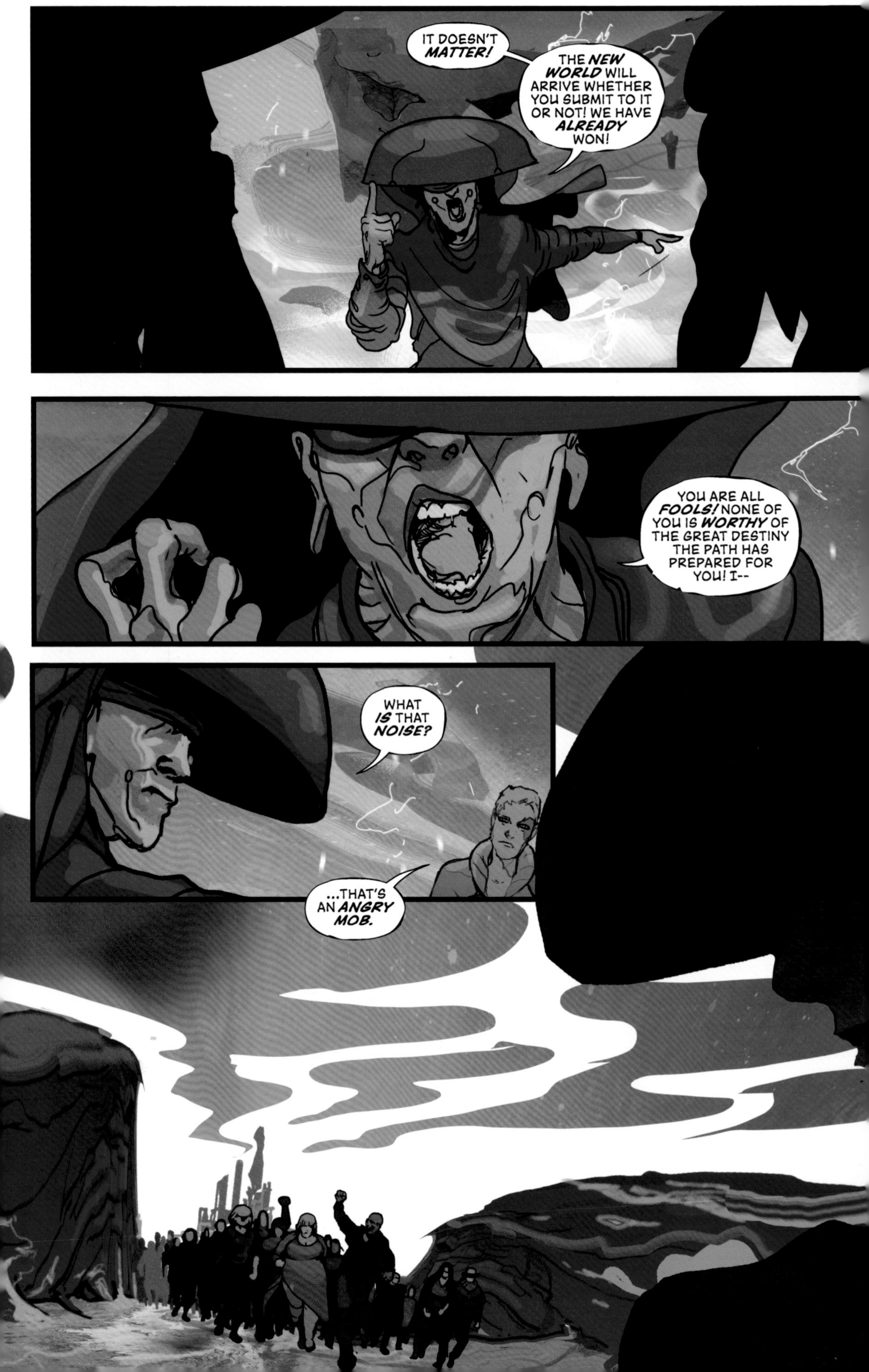
IT DOESN'T MATTER!
THE NEW WORLD WILL ARRIVE WHETHER YOU SUBMIT TO IT OR NOT! WE HAVE ALREADY WON!
YOU ARE ALL FOOLS! NONE OF YOU IS WORTHY OF THE GREAT DESTINY THE PATH HAS PREPARED FOR YOU! I--
WHAT IS THAT NOISE?
...THAT'S AN ANGRY MOB.

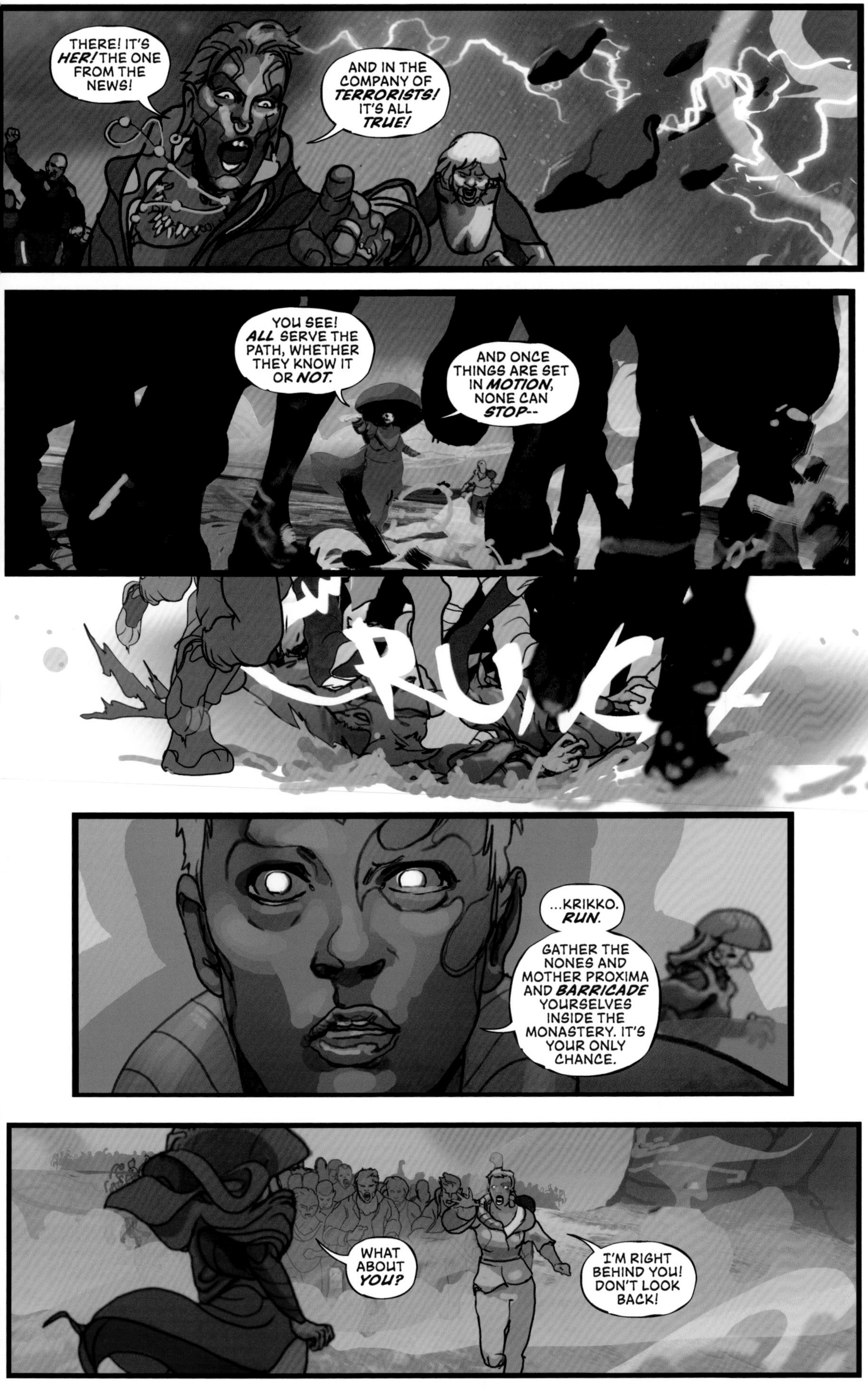
THERE! IT'S HER! THE ONE FROM THE NEWS!
AND IN THE COMPANY OF TERRORISTS! IT'S ALL TRUE!
YOU SEE! ALL SERVE THE PATH, WHETHER THEY KNOW IT OR NOT.
AND ONCE THINGS ARE SET IN MOTION, NONE CAN STOP--
...KRIKKO. RUN.
GATHER THE NONES AND MOTHER PROXIMA AND BARRICADE YOURSELVES INSIDE THE MONASTERY. IT'S YOUR ONLY CHANCE.
WHAT ABOUT YOU?
I'M RIGHT BEHIND YOU! DON'T LOOK BACK!

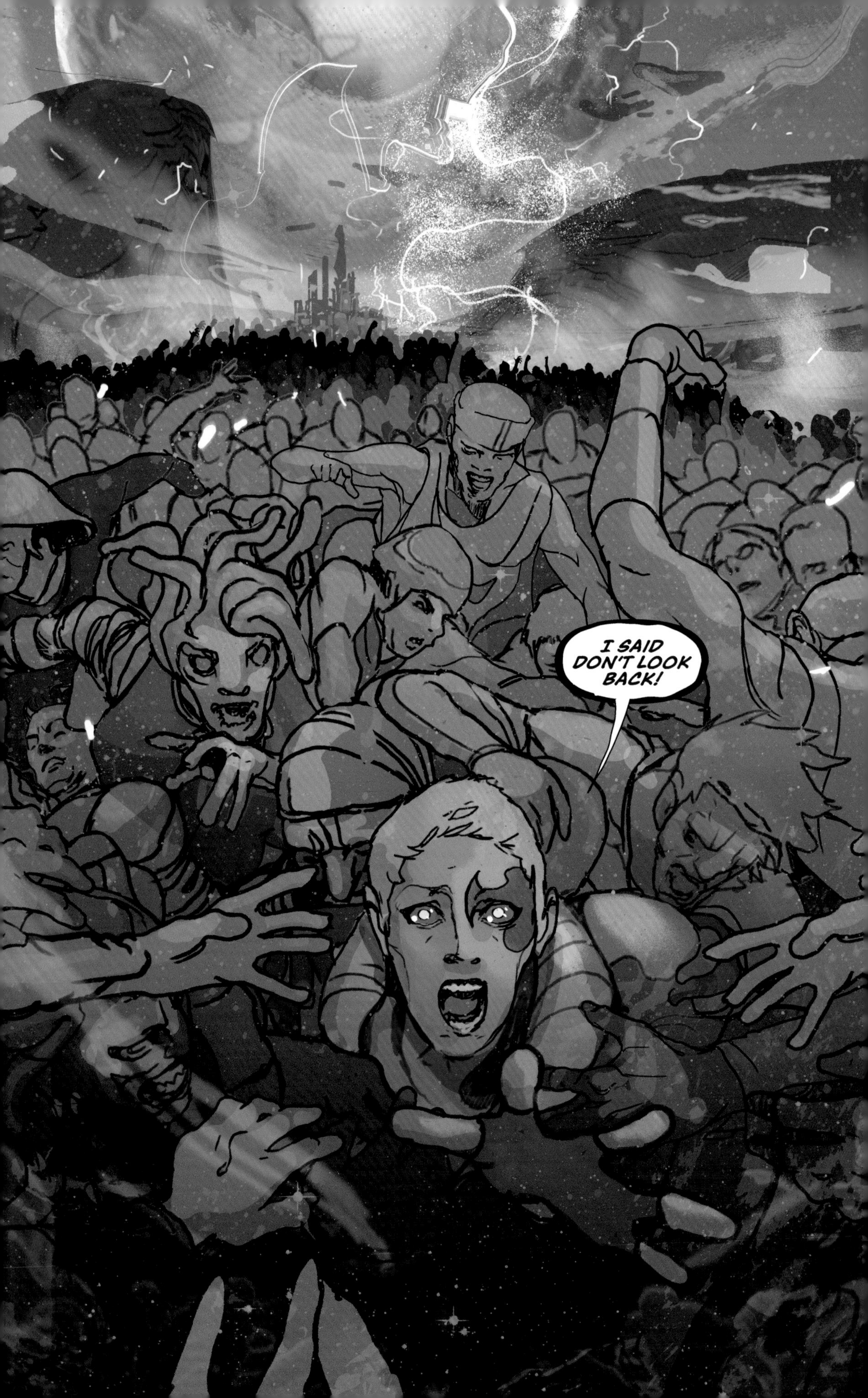
I SAID DON'T LOOK BACK!

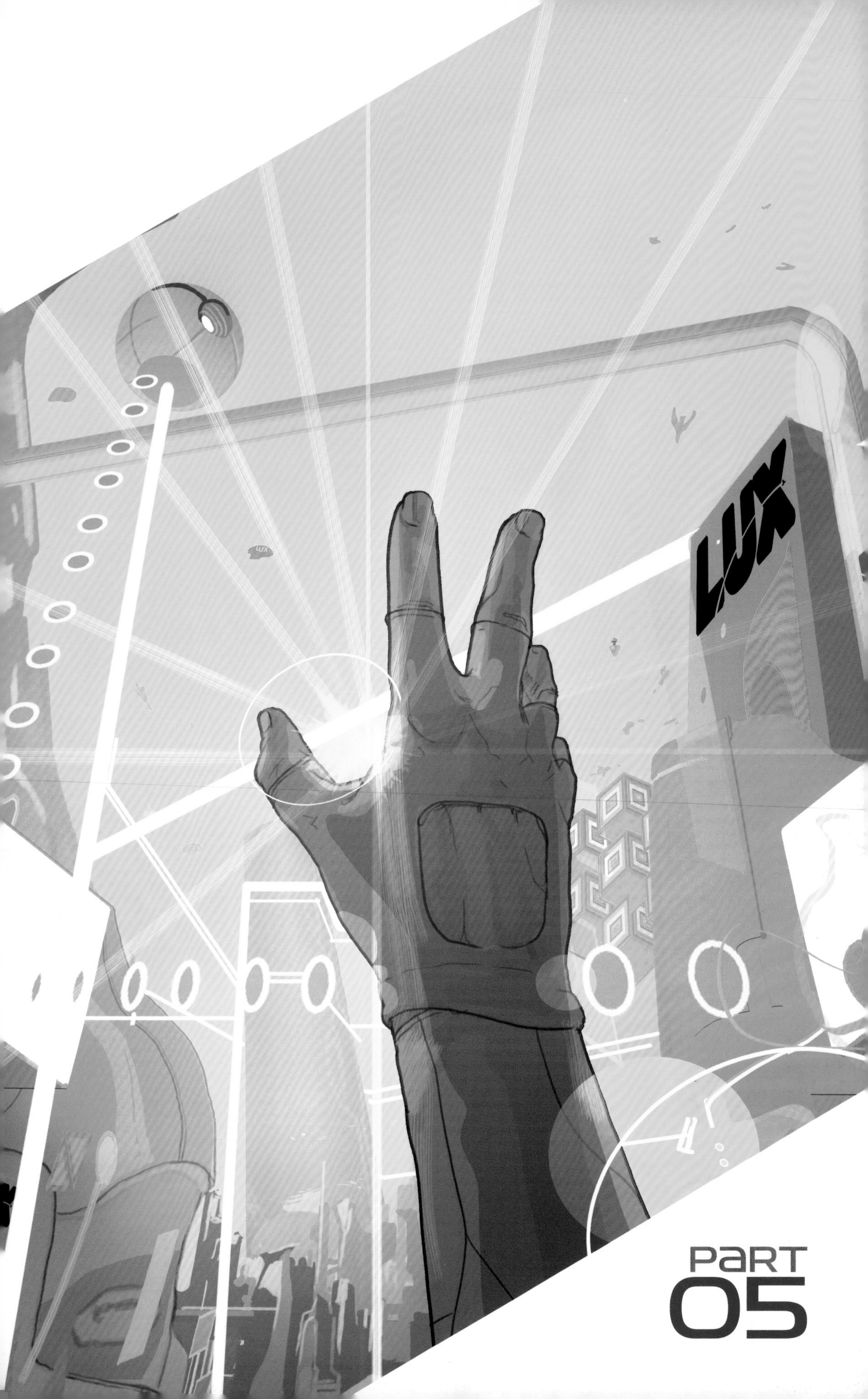
LUX

# PART 05

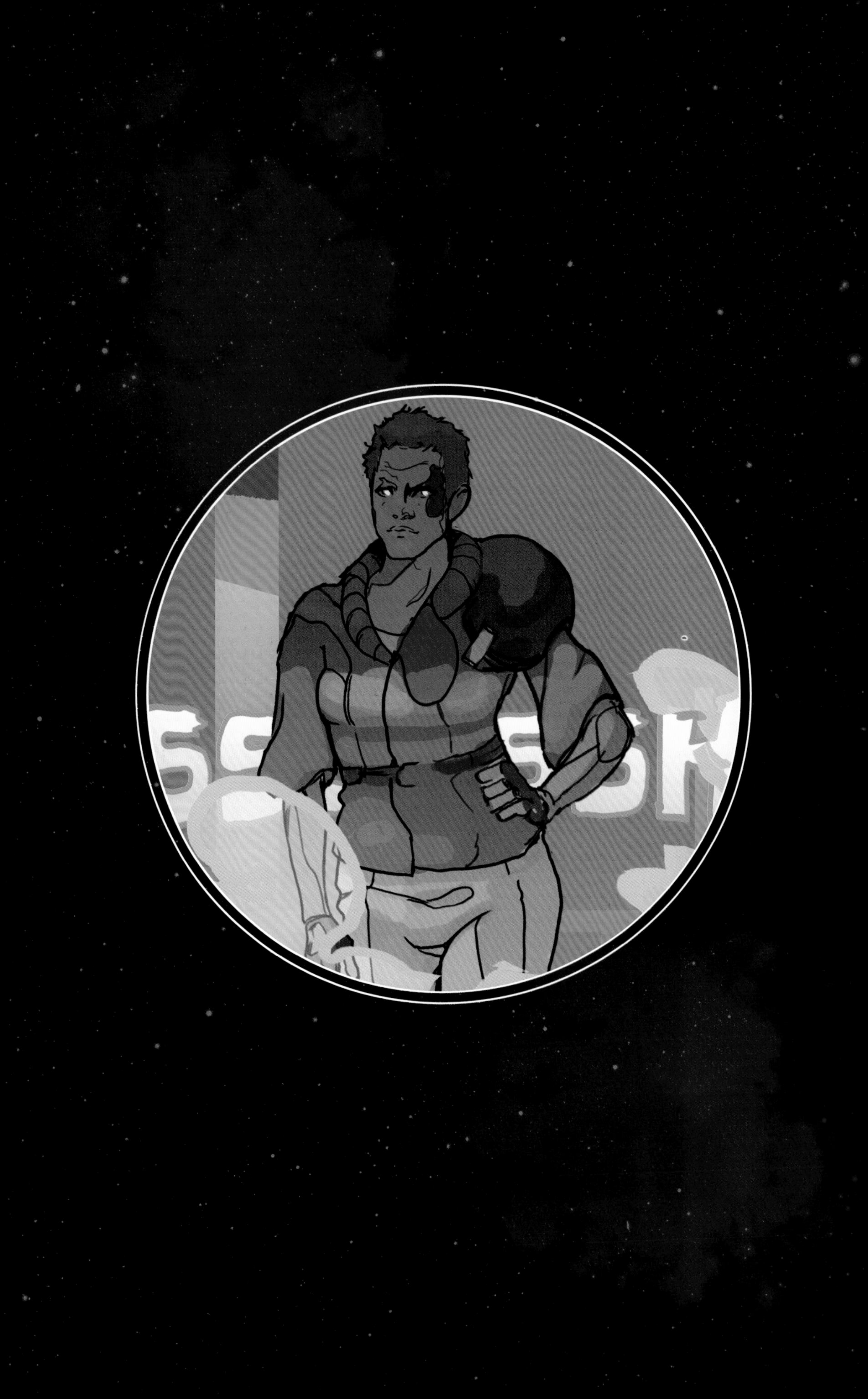

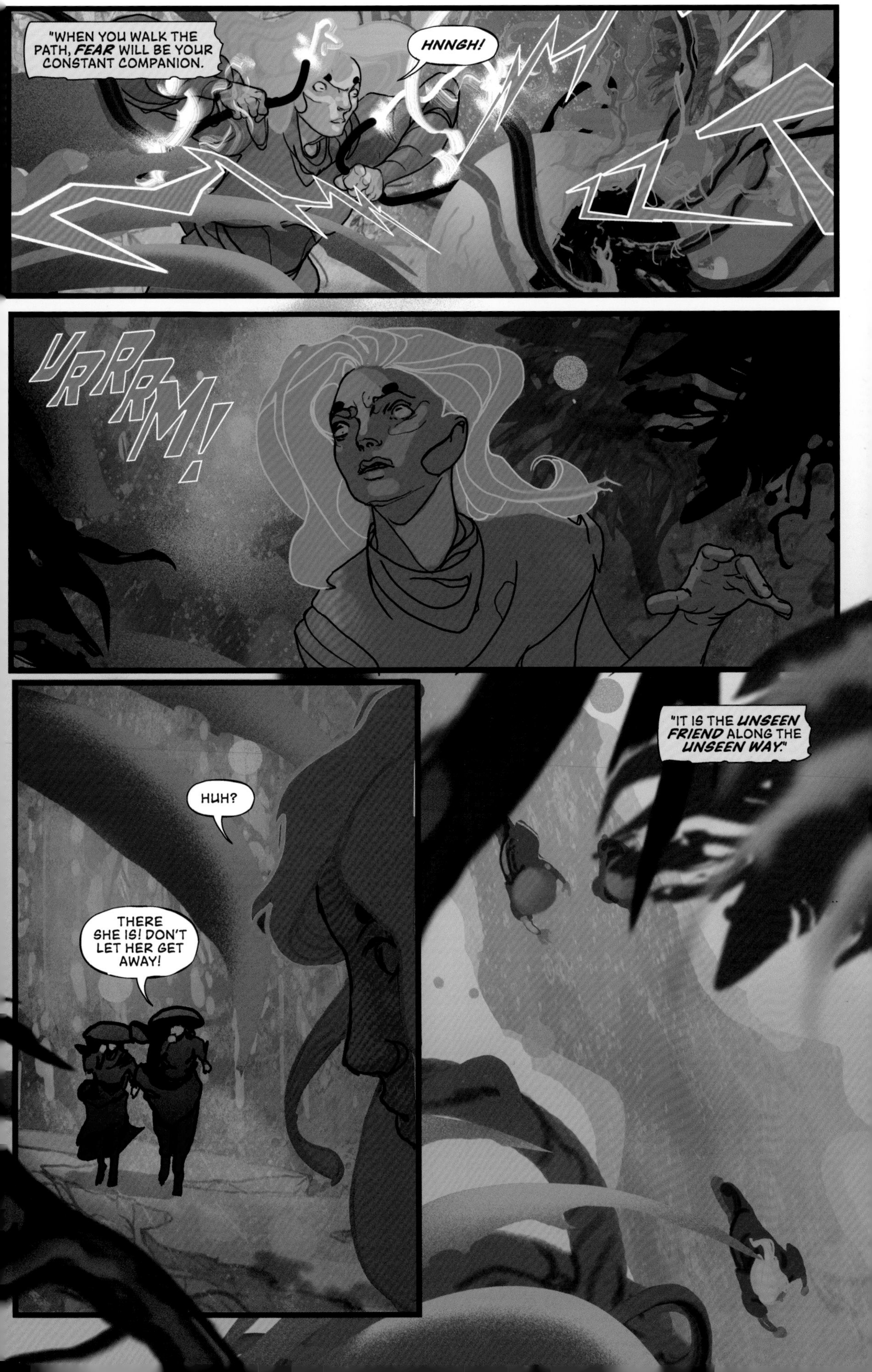
"WHEN YOU WALK THE PATH, FEAR WILL BE YOUR CONSTANT COMPANION.
HNNGH!
URRRRM!
"IT IS THE UNSEEN FRIEND ALONG THE UNSEEN WAY."
HUH?
THERE SHE IS! DON'T LET HER GET AWAY!

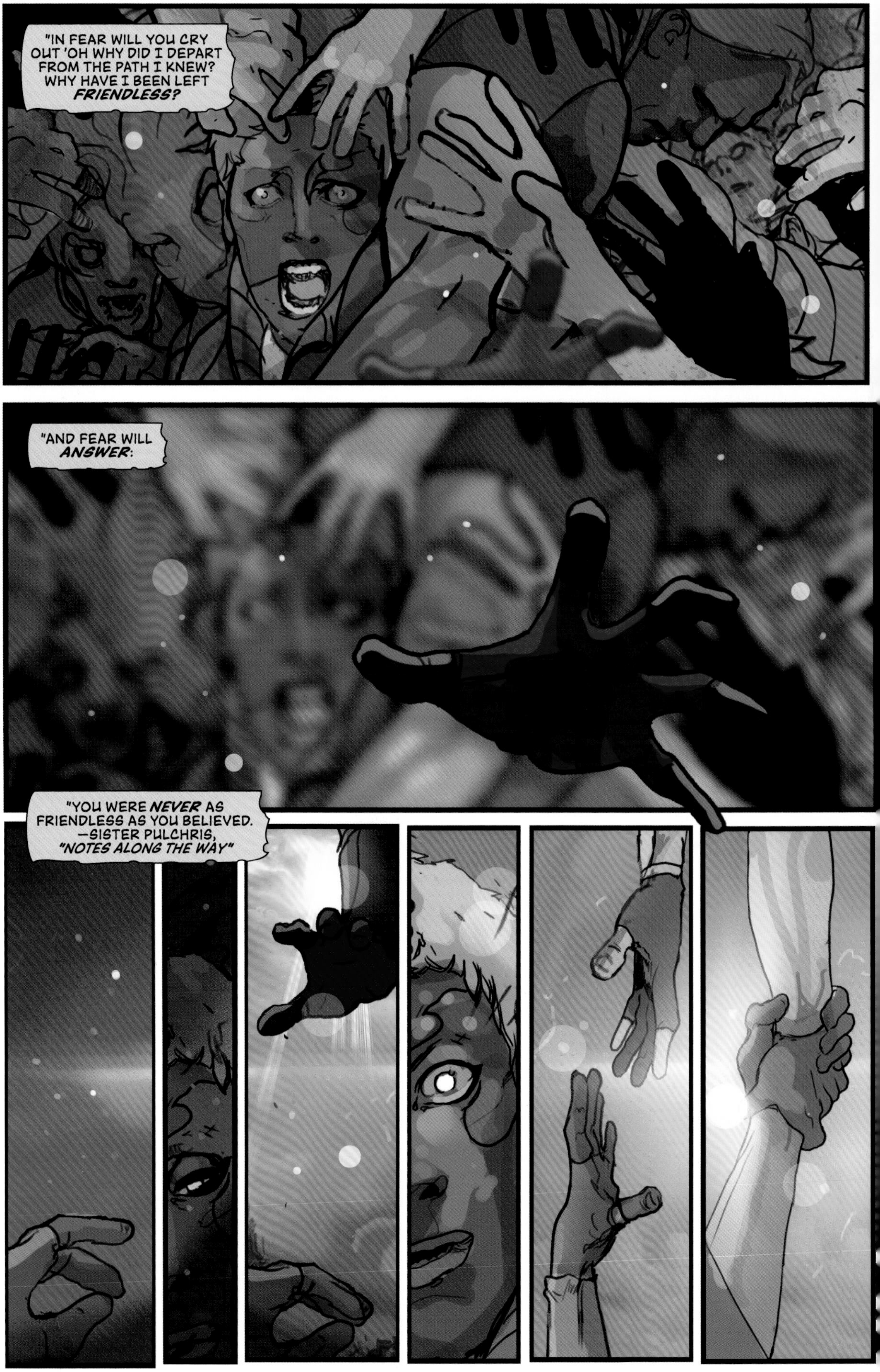
"IN FEAR WILL YOU CRY OUT 'OH WHY DID I DEPART FROM THE PATH I KNEW? WHY HAVE I BEEN LEFT FRIENDLESS?
"AND FEAR WILL ANSWER:
"YOU WERE NEVER AS FRIENDLESS AS YOU BELIEVED. —SISTER PULCHRIS, "NOTES ALONG THE WAY"

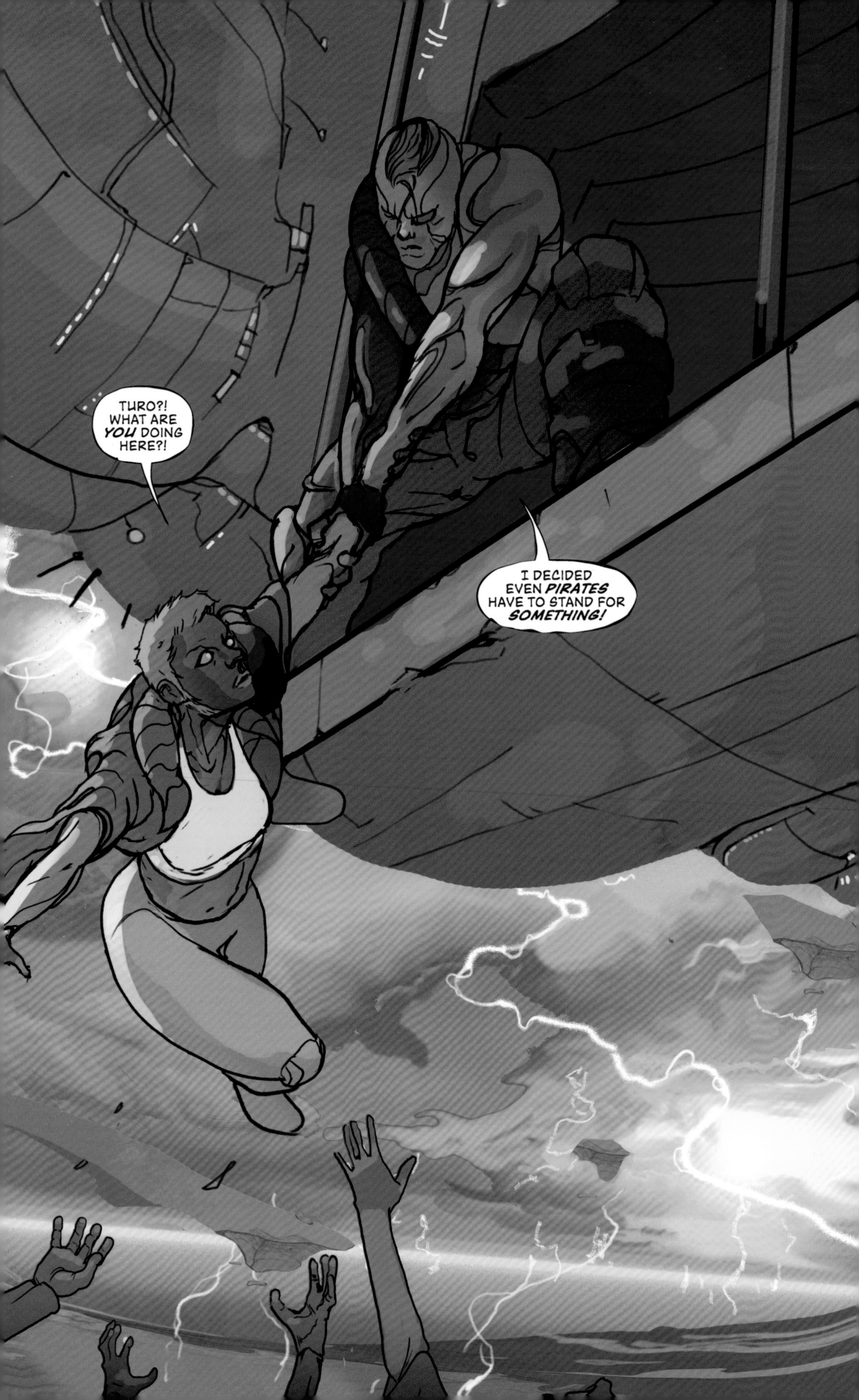
TURO?! WHAT ARE YOU DOING HERE?!
I DECIDED EVEN PIRATES HAVE TO STAND FOR SOMETHING!

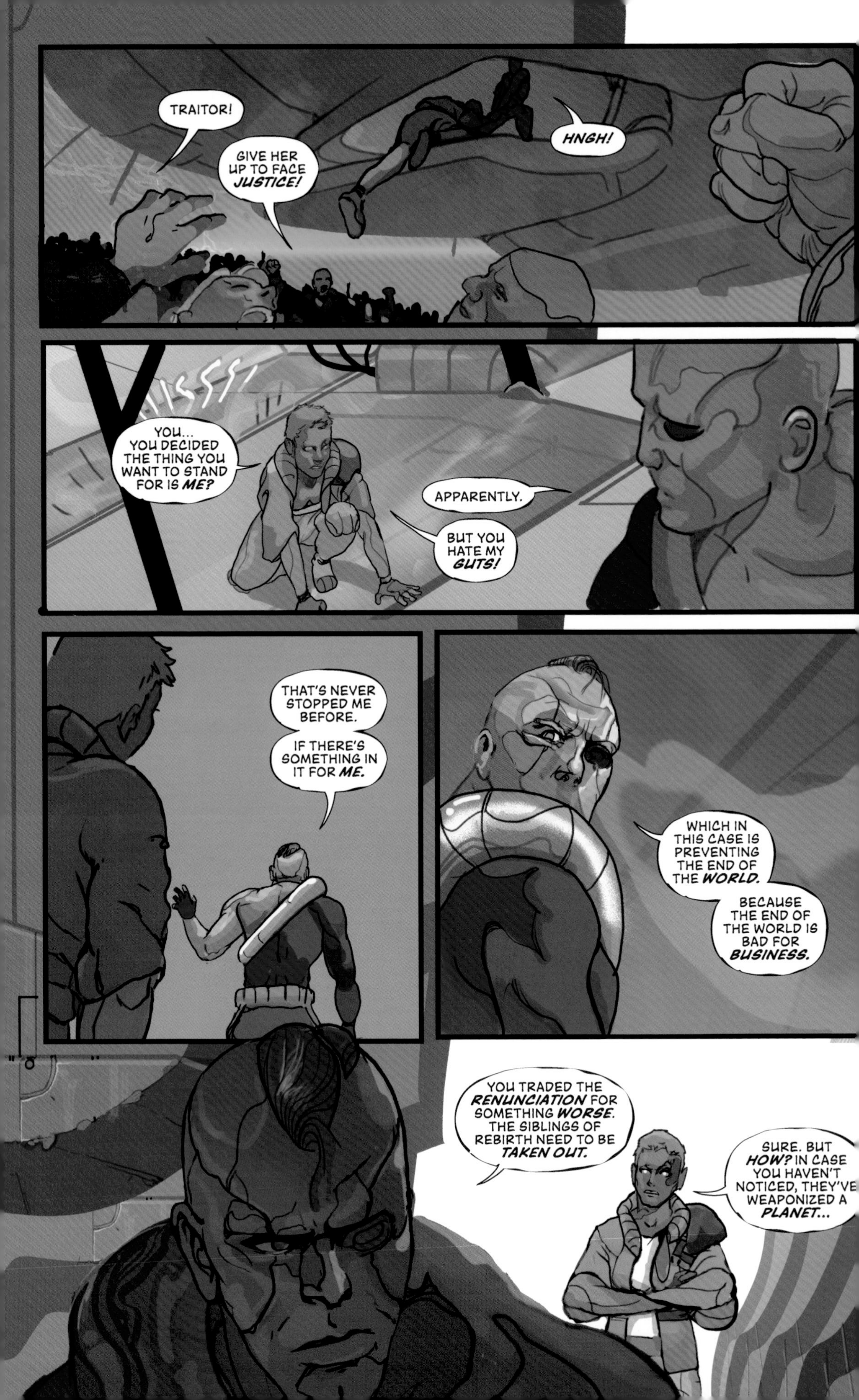
TRAITOR!
GIVE HER UP TO FACE JUSTICE!
HNGH!
HISSSS!
YOU... YOU DECIDED THE THING YOU WANT TO STAND FOR IS ME?
APPARENTLY.
BUT YOU HATE MY GUTS!
THAT'S NEVER STOPPED ME BEFORE.
IF THERE'S SOMETHING IN IT FOR ME.
WHICH IN THIS CASE IS PREVENTING THE END OF THE WORLD.
BECAUSE THE END OF THE WORLD IS BAD FOR BUSINESS.
YOU TRADED THE RENUNCIATION FOR SOMETHING WORSE. THE SIBLINGS OF REBIRTH NEED TO BE TAKEN OUT.
SURE. BUT HOW? IN CASE YOU HAVEN'T NOTICED, THEY'VE WEAPONIZED A PLANET...

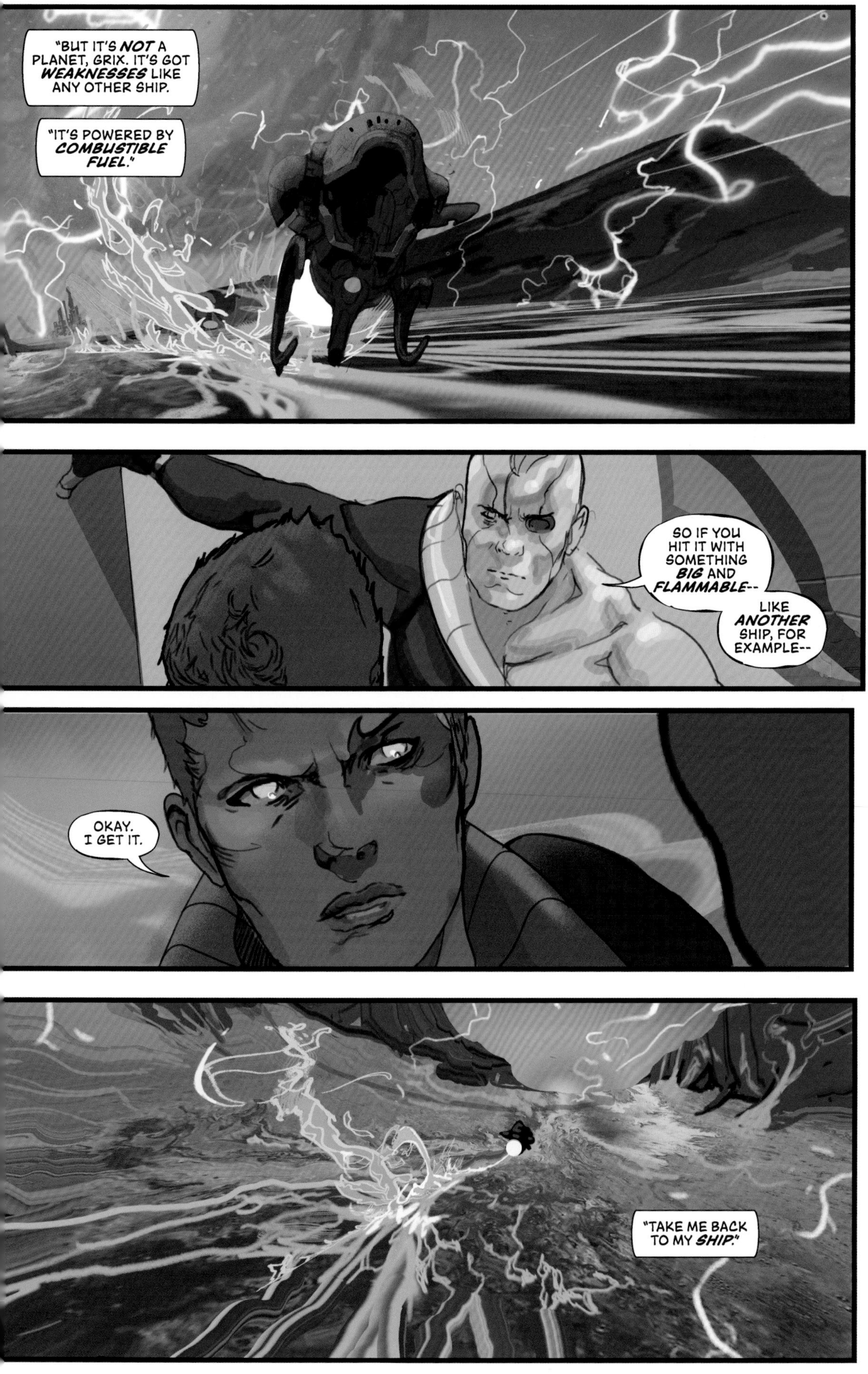
"BUT IT'S **NOT** A PLANET, GRIX. IT'S GOT **WEAKNESSES** LIKE ANY OTHER SHIP.
"IT'S POWERED BY **COMBUSTIBLE FUEL.**"
SO IF YOU HIT IT WITH SOMETHING **BIG** AND **FLAMMABLE**--
LIKE **ANOTHER** SHIP, FOR EXAMPLE--
OKAY. I GET IT.
"TAKE ME BACK TO MY **SHIP.**"

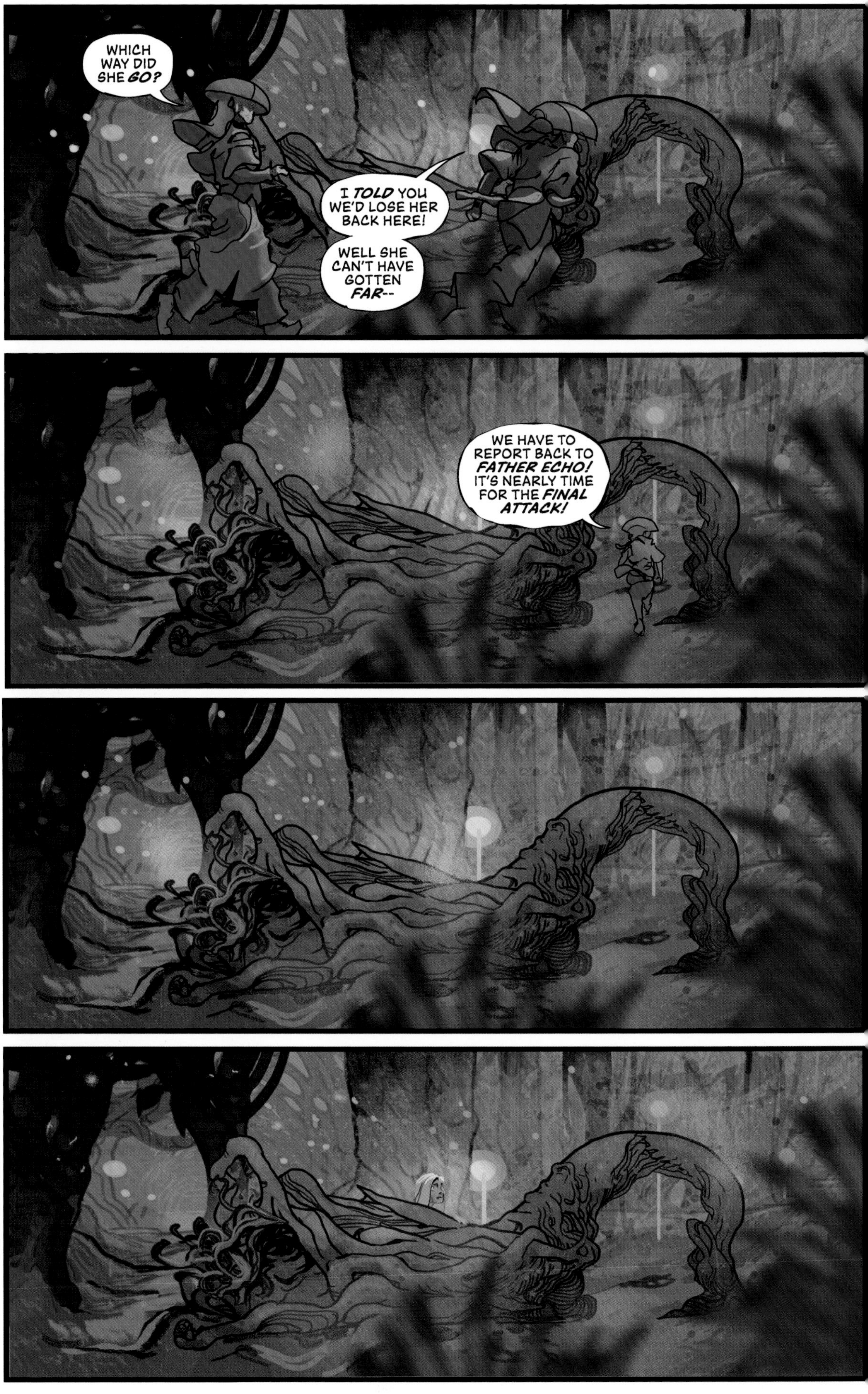
WHICH WAY DID SHE **GO?**
I **TOLD** YOU WE'D LOSE HER BACK HERE!
WELL SHE CAN'T HAVE GOTTEN **FAR--**
WE HAVE TO REPORT BACK TO **FATHER ECHO!** IT'S NEARLY TIME FOR THE **FINAL ATTACK!**

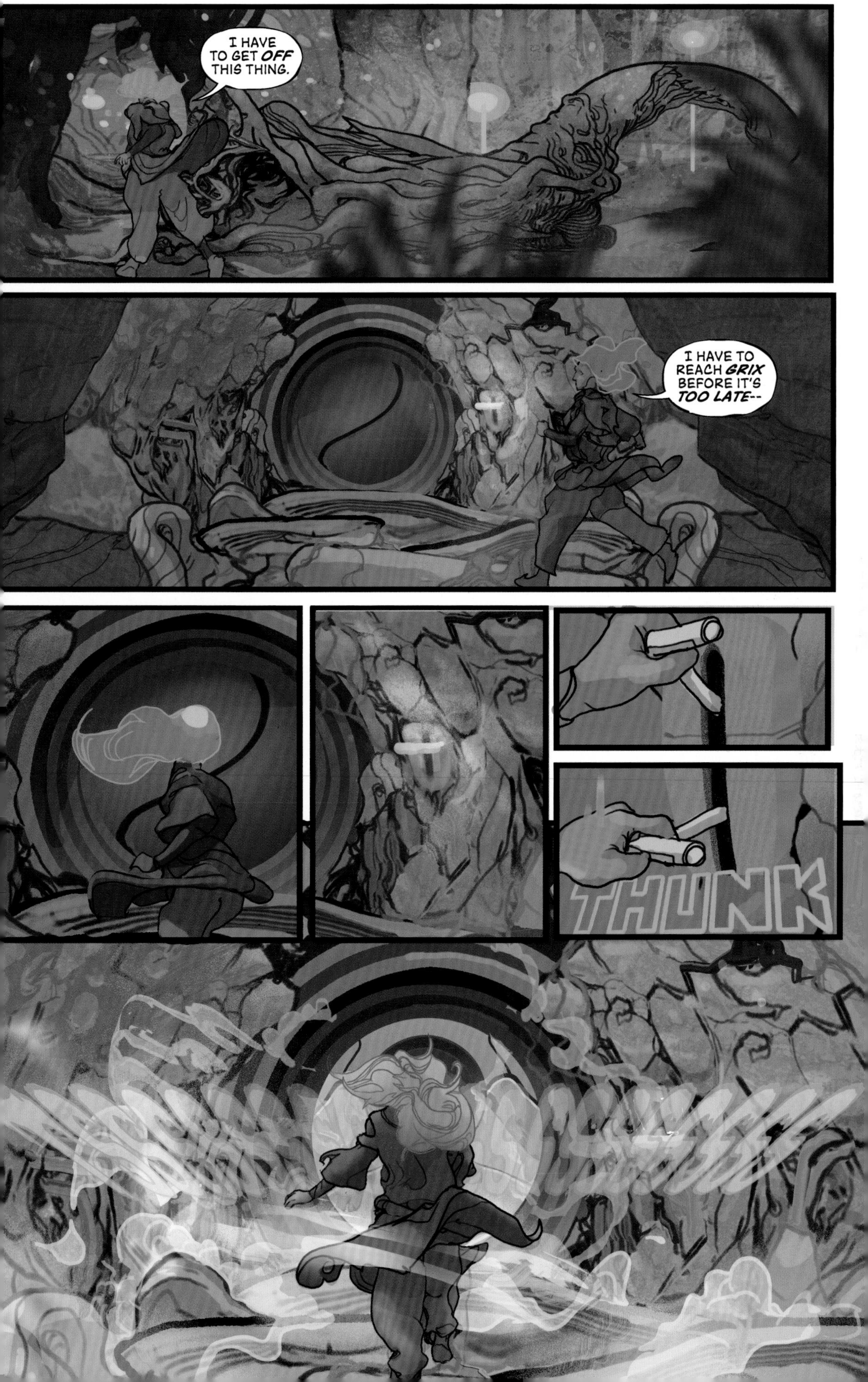
I HAVE TO GET *OFF* THIS THING.
I HAVE TO REACH *GRIX* BEFORE IT'S *TOO LATE*--
THUNK

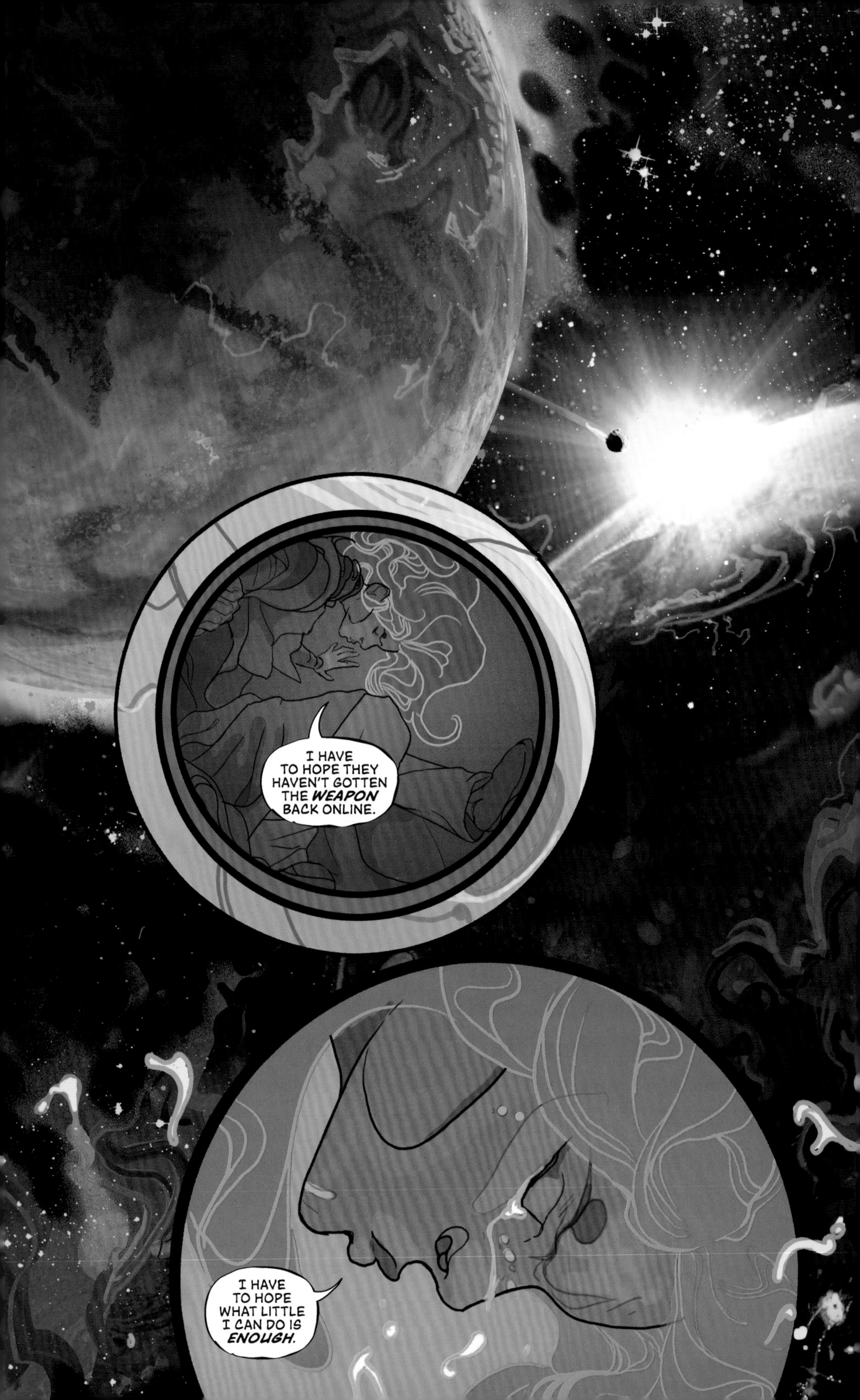
I HAVE TO HOPE THEY HAVEN'T GOTTEN THE WEAPON BACK ONLINE.
I HAVE TO HOPE WHAT LITTLE I CAN DO IS ENOUGH.

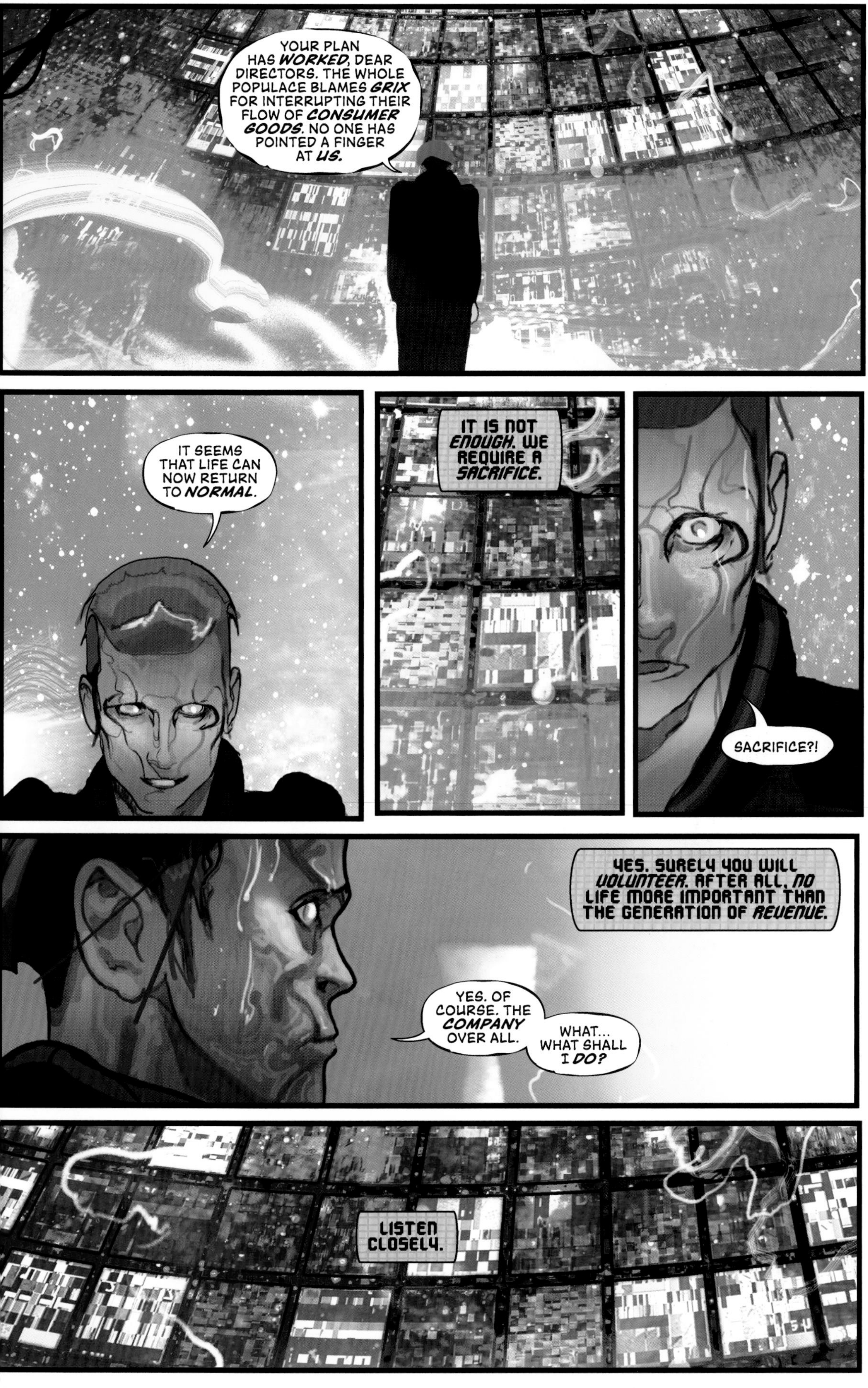
YOUR PLAN HAS WORKED, DEAR DIRECTORS. THE WHOLE POPULACE BLAMES GRIX FOR INTERRUPTING THEIR FLOW OF CONSUMER GOODS. NO ONE HAS POINTED A FINGER AT US.
IT SEEMS THAT LIFE CAN NOW RETURN TO NORMAL.
IT IS NOT ENOUGH. WE REQUIRE A SACRIFICE.
SACRIFICE?!
YES. SURELY YOU WILL VOLUNTEER. AFTER ALL, NO LIFE MORE IMPORTANT THAN THE GENERATION OF REVENUE.
YES. OF COURSE. THE COMPANY OVER ALL.
WHAT... WHAT SHALL I DO?
LISTEN CLOSELY.

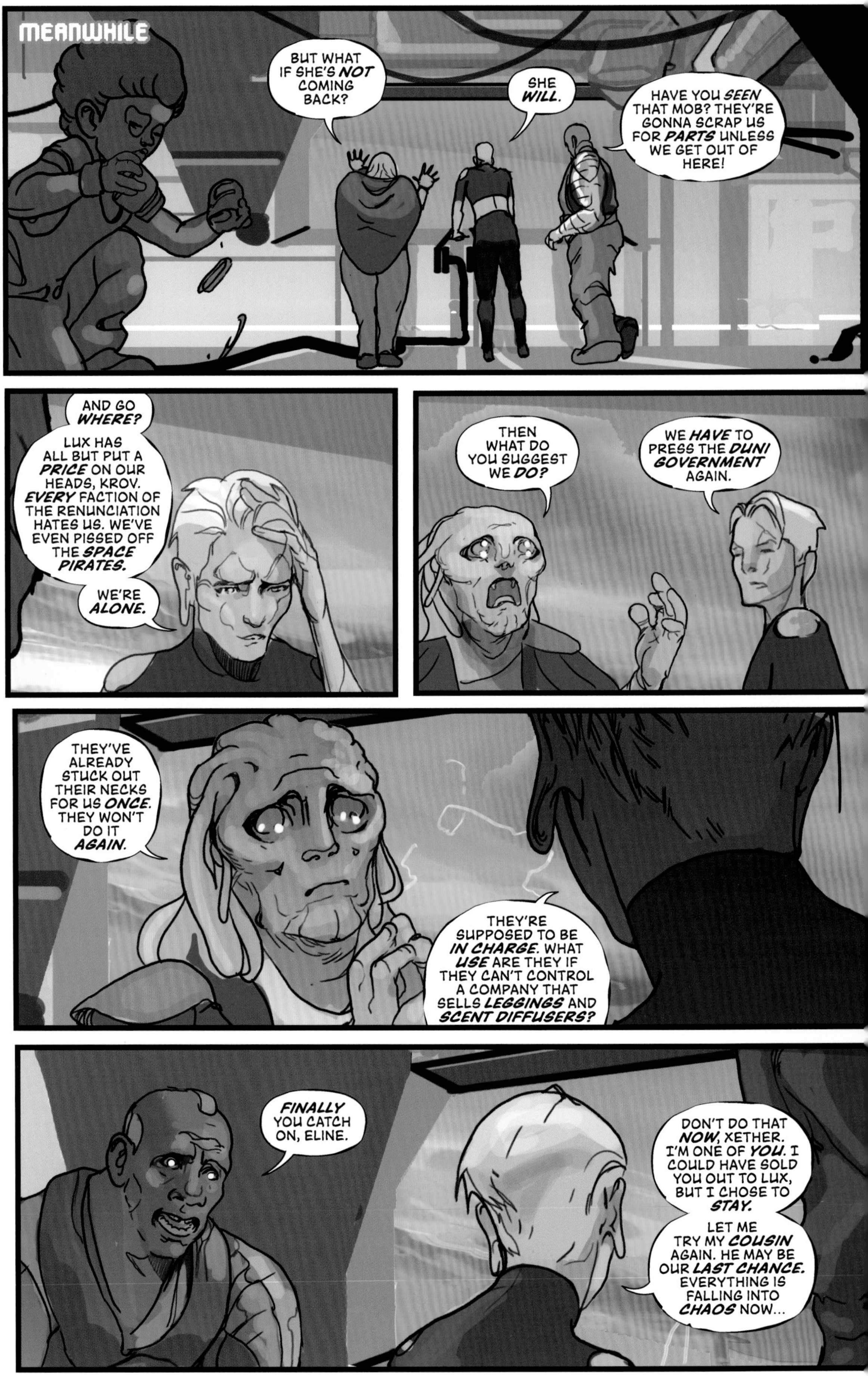
MEANWHILE
BUT WHAT IF SHE'S NOT COMING BACK?
SHE WILL.
HAVE YOU SEEN THAT MOB? THEY'RE GONNA SCRAP US FOR PARTS UNLESS WE GET OUT OF HERE!
AND GO WHERE?
LUX HAS ALL BUT PUT A PRICE ON OUR HEADS, KROV. EVERY FACTION OF THE RENUNCIATION HATES US. WE'VE EVEN PISSED OFF THE SPACE PIRATES.
WE'RE ALONE.
THEN WHAT DO YOU SUGGEST WE DO?
WE HAVE TO PRESS THE DUNI GOVERNMENT AGAIN.
THEY'VE ALREADY STUCK OUT THEIR NECKS FOR US ONCE. THEY WON'T DO IT AGAIN.
THEY'RE SUPPOSED TO BE IN CHARGE. WHAT USE ARE THEY IF THEY CAN'T CONTROL A COMPANY THAT SELLS LEGGINGS AND SCENT DIFFUSERS?
FINALLY YOU CATCH ON, ELINE.
DON'T DO THAT NOW, XETHER. I'M ONE OF YOU. I COULD HAVE SOLD YOU OUT TO LUX, BUT I CHOSE TO STAY.
LET ME TRY MY COUSIN AGAIN. HE MAY BE OUR LAST CHANCE. EVERYTHING IS FALLING INTO CHAOS NOW...

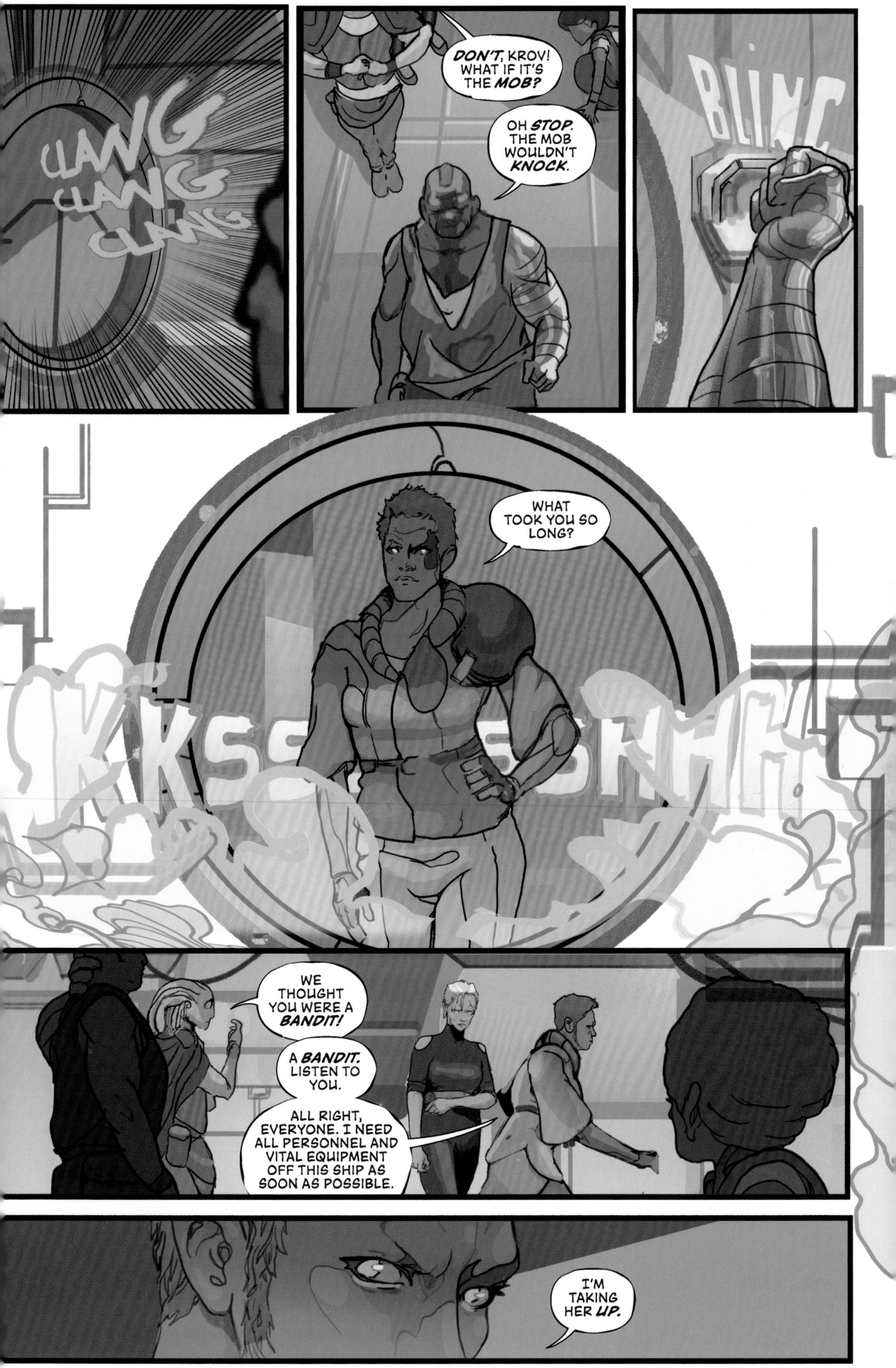
CLANG CLANG CLANG
DON'T, KROV! WHAT IF IT'S THE MOB?
OH STOP. THE MOB WOULDN'T KNOCK.
WHAT TOOK YOU SO LONG?
WE THOUGHT YOU WERE A BANDIT!
A BANDIT. LISTEN TO YOU.
ALL RIGHT, EVERYONE. I NEED ALL PERSONNEL AND VITAL EQUIPMENT OFF THIS SHIP AS SOON AS POSSIBLE.
I'M TAKING HER UP.

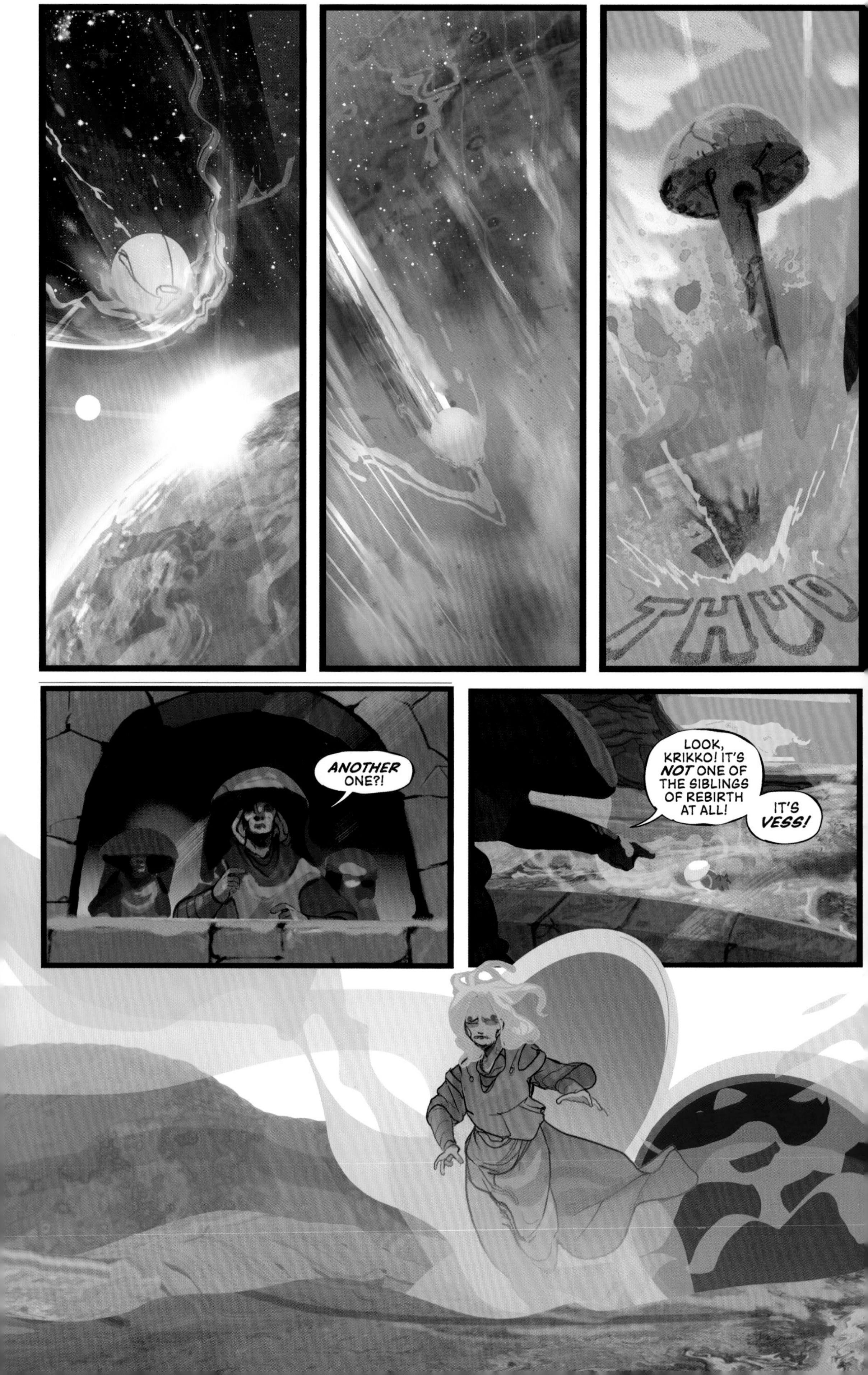
THUD
ANOTHER ONE?!
LOOK, KRIKKO! IT'S NOT ONE OF THE SIBLINGS OF REBIRTH AT ALL!
IT'S VESS!

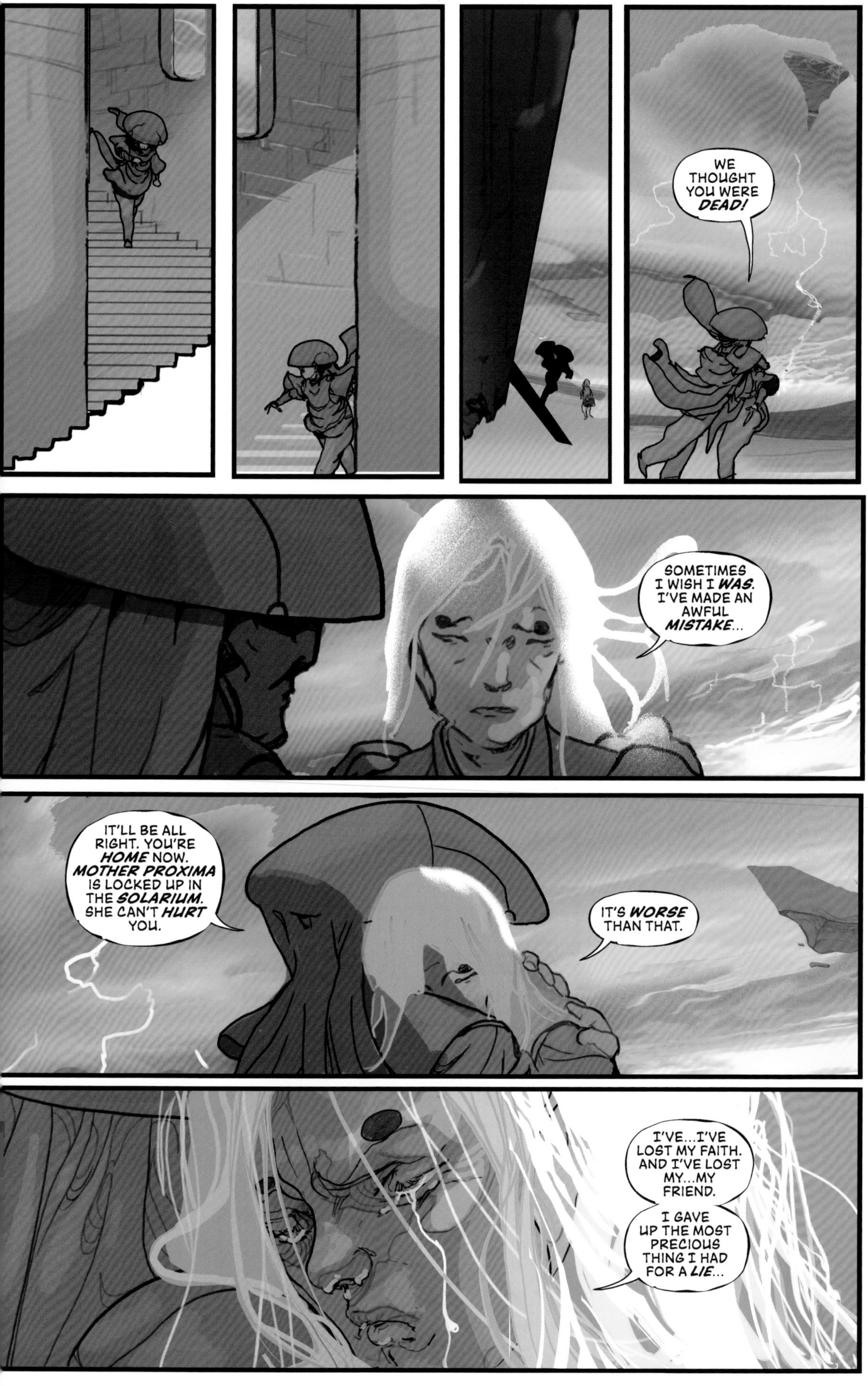
WE THOUGHT YOU WERE *DEAD!*
SOMETIMES I WISH I *WAS.* I'VE MADE AN AWFUL *MISTAKE*...
IT'LL BE ALL RIGHT. YOU'RE *HOME* NOW. *MOTHER PROXIMA* IS LOCKED UP IN THE *SOLARIUM.* SHE CAN'T *HURT* YOU.
IT'S *WORSE* THAN THAT.
I'VE...I'VE LOST MY FAITH. AND I'VE LOST MY...MY FRIEND.
I GAVE UP THE MOST PRECIOUS THING I HAD FOR A *LIE*...

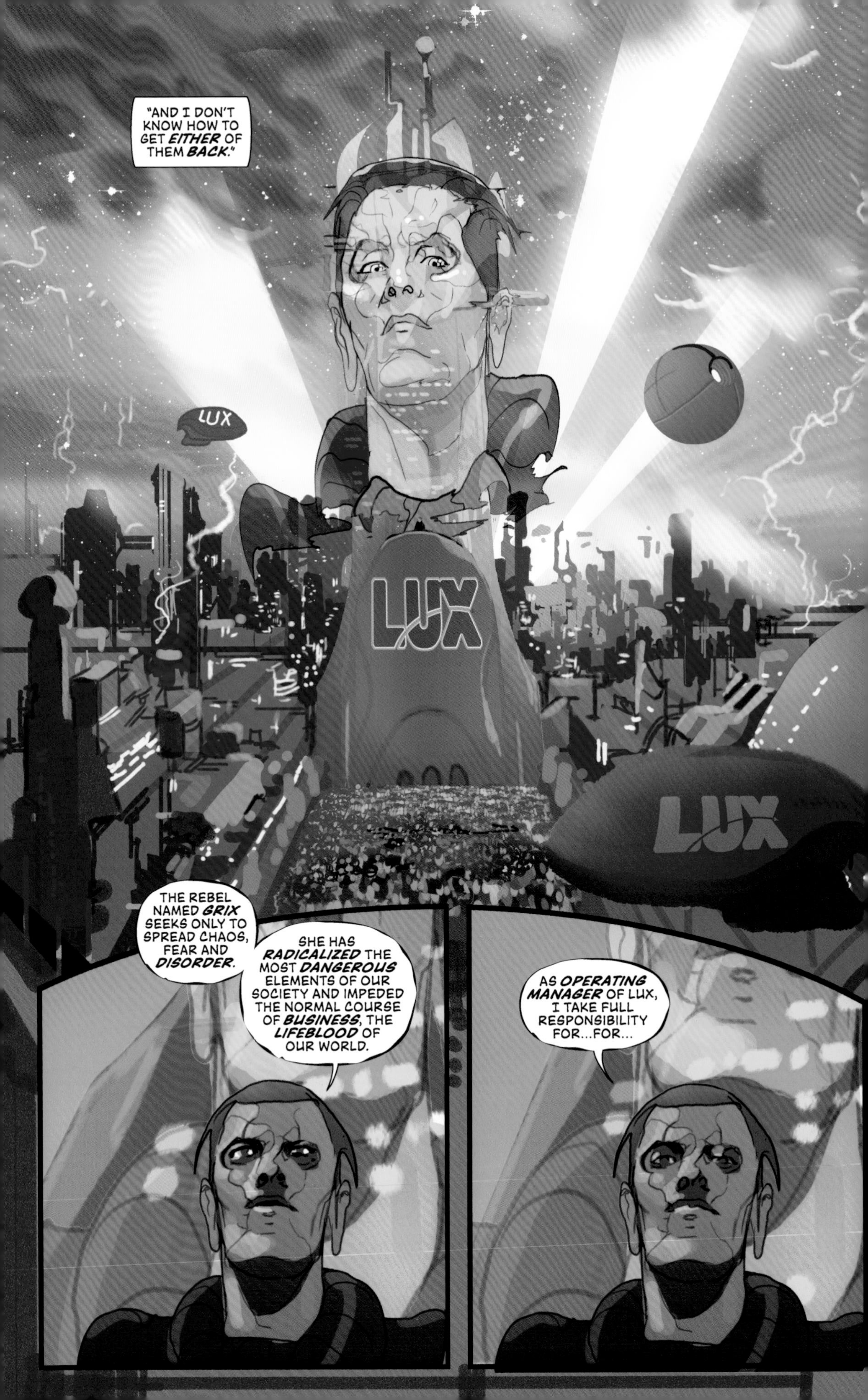
"AND I DON'T KNOW HOW TO GET EITHER OF THEM BACK."
LUX
LUX
LUX
THE REBEL NAMED GRIX SEEKS ONLY TO SPREAD CHAOS, FEAR AND DISORDER.
SHE HAS RADICALIZED THE MOST DANGEROUS ELEMENTS OF OUR SOCIETY AND IMPEDED THE NORMAL COURSE OF BUSINESS, THE LIFEBLOOD OF OUR WORLD.
AS OPERATING MANAGER OF LUX, I TAKE FULL RESPONSIBILITY FOR...FOR...

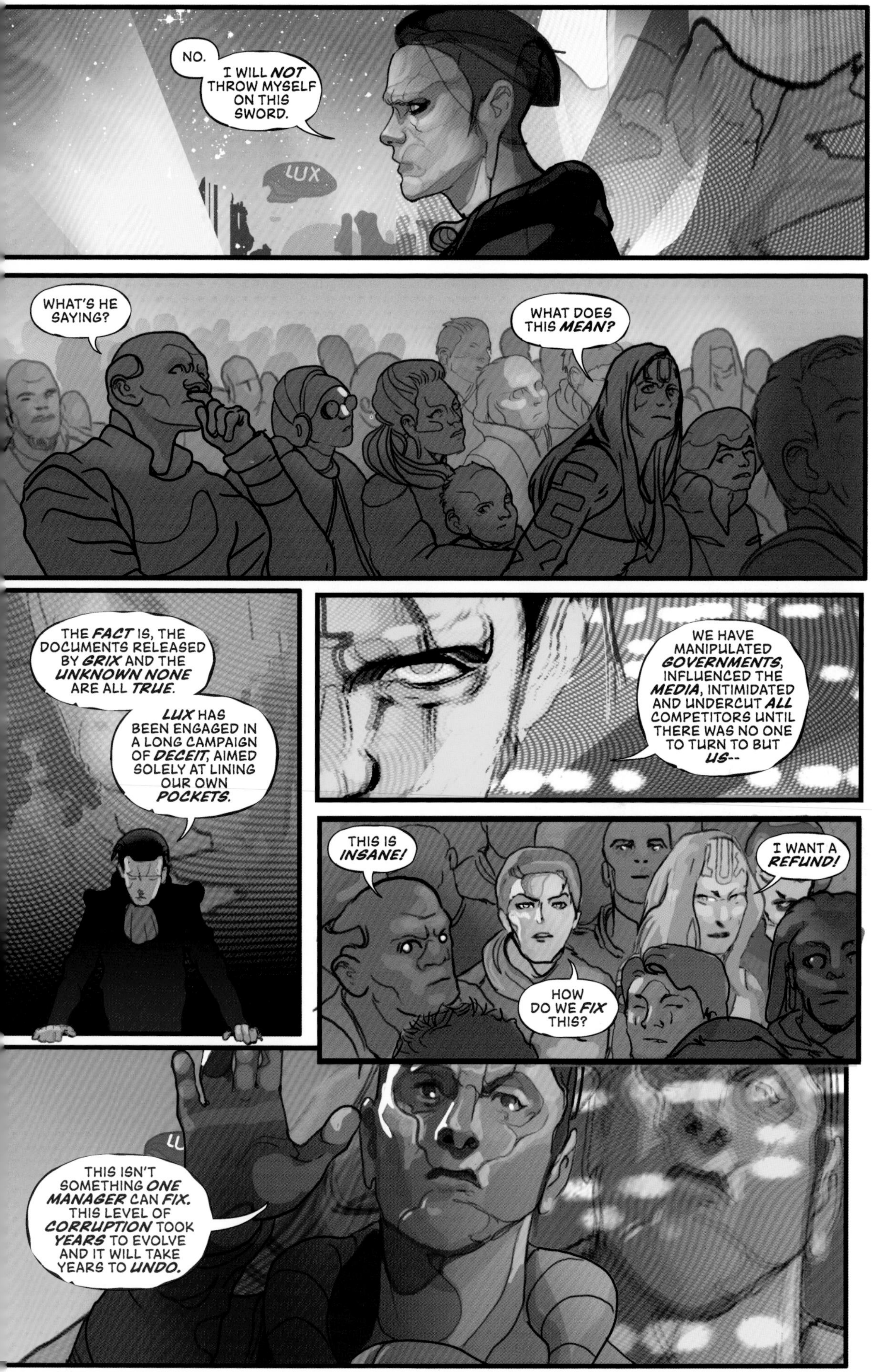
LUX
NO.
I WILL NOT THROW MYSELF ON THIS SWORD.
WHAT'S HE SAYING?
WHAT DOES THIS MEAN?
THE FACT IS, THE DOCUMENTS RELEASED BY GRIX AND THE UNKNOWN NONE ARE ALL TRUE.
LUX HAS BEEN ENGAGED IN A LONG CAMPAIGN OF DECEIT, AIMED SOLELY AT LINING OUR OWN POCKETS.
WE HAVE MANIPULATED GOVERNMENTS, INFLUENCED THE MEDIA, INTIMIDATED AND UNDERCUT ALL COMPETITORS UNTIL THERE WAS NO ONE TO TURN TO BUT US--
THIS IS INSANE!
I WANT A REFUND!
HOW DO WE FIX THIS?
THIS ISN'T SOMETHING ONE MANAGER CAN FIX. THIS LEVEL OF CORRUPTION TOOK YEARS TO EVOLVE AND IT WILL TAKE YEARS TO UNDO.

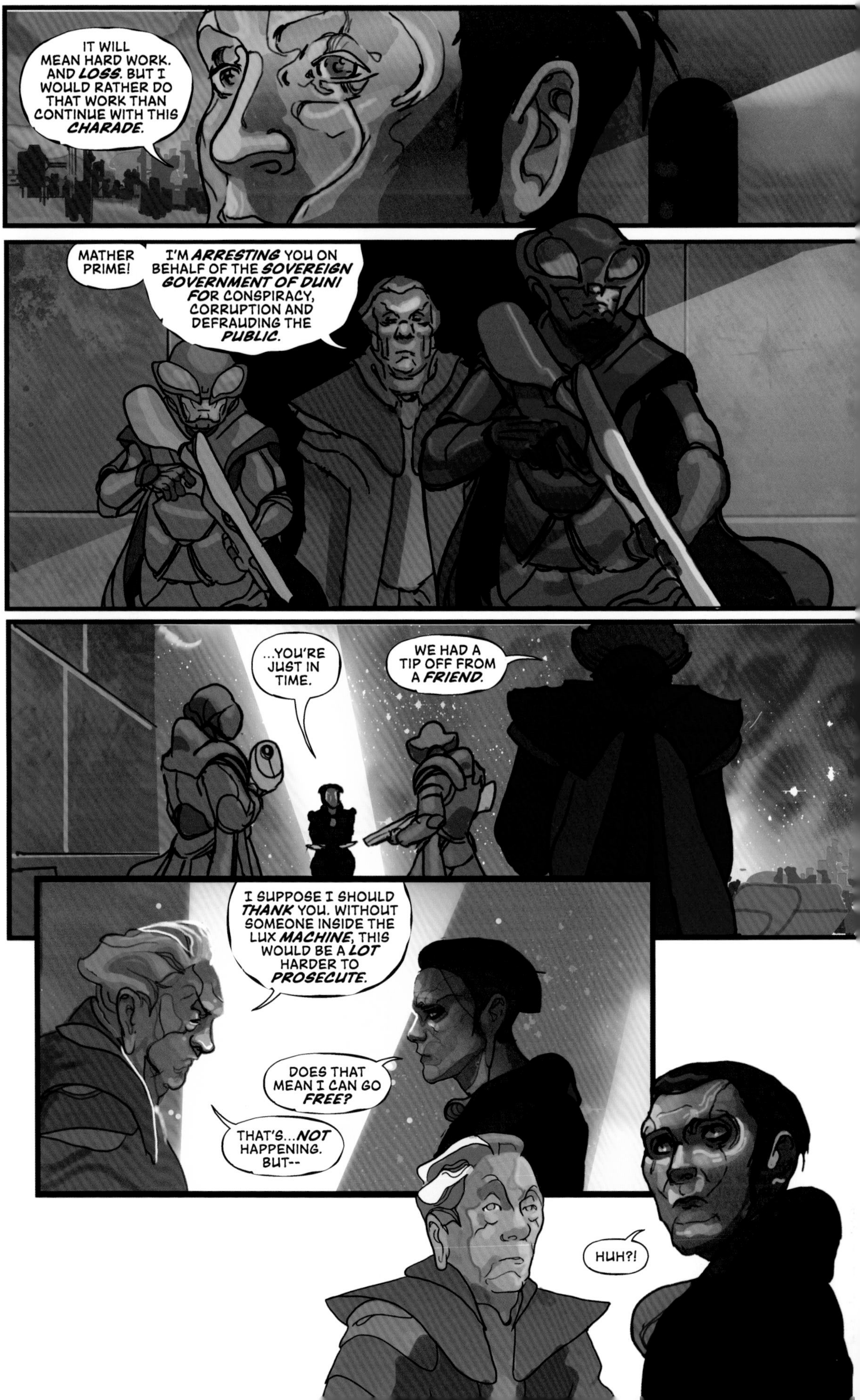
IT WILL MEAN HARD WORK. AND LOSS. BUT I WOULD RATHER DO THAT WORK THAN CONTINUE WITH THIS CHARADE.
MATHER PRIME!
I'M ARRESTING YOU ON BEHALF OF THE SOVEREIGN GOVERNMENT OF DUNI FOR CONSPIRACY, CORRUPTION AND DEFRAUDING THE PUBLIC.
...YOU'RE JUST IN TIME.
WE HAD A TIP OFF FROM A FRIEND.
I SUPPOSE I SHOULD THANK YOU. WITHOUT SOMEONE INSIDE THE LUX MACHINE, THIS WOULD BE A LOT HARDER TO PROSECUTE.
DOES THAT MEAN I CAN GO FREE?
THAT'S...NOT HAPPENING. BUT--
HUH?!

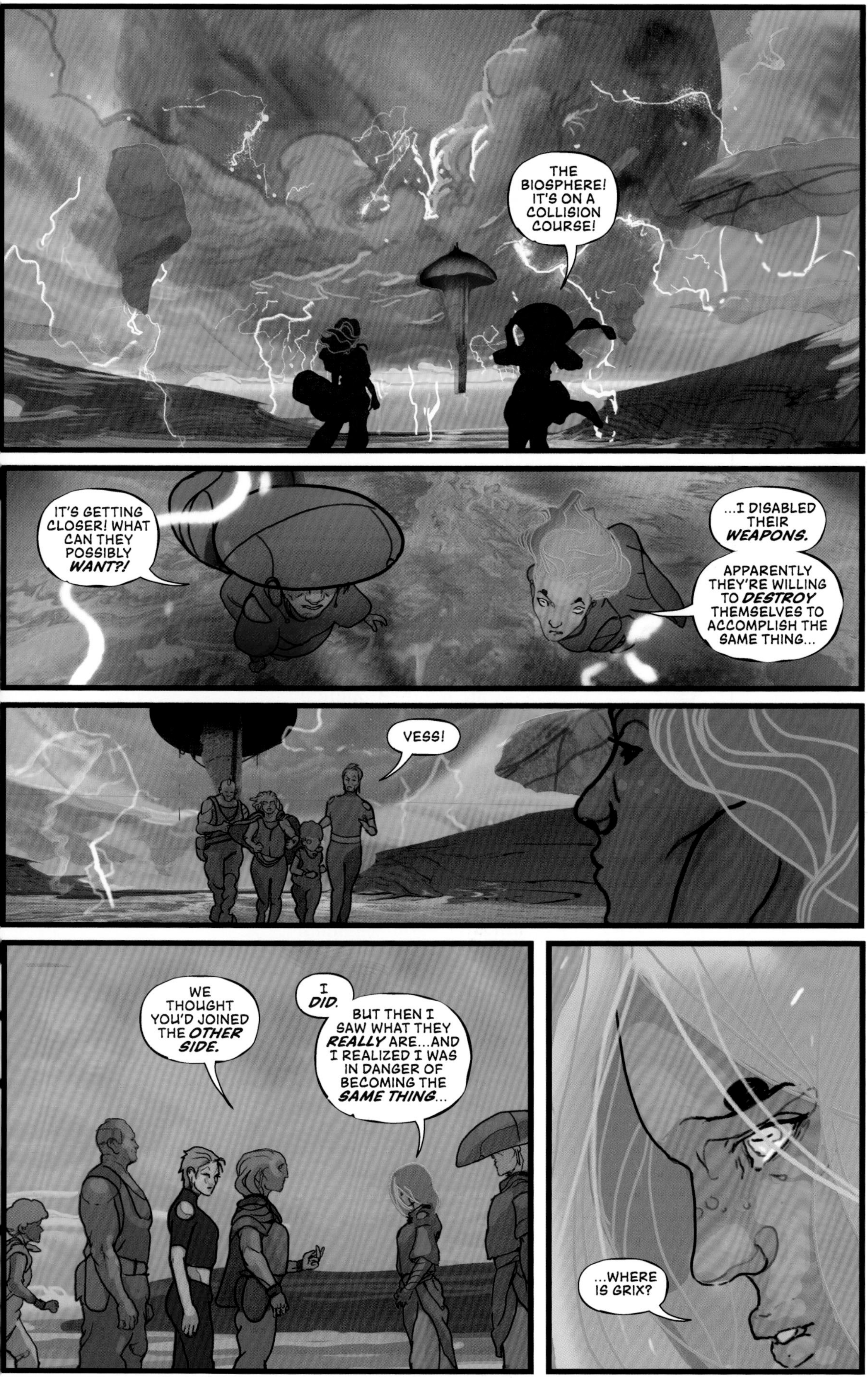
THE BIOSPHERE! IT'S ON A COLLISION COURSE!
IT'S GETTING CLOSER! WHAT CAN THEY POSSIBLY *WANT?!*
...I DISABLED THEIR *WEAPONS.*
APPARENTLY THEY'RE WILLING TO *DESTROY* THEMSELVES TO ACCOMPLISH THE SAME THING...
VESS!
WE THOUGHT YOU'D JOINED THE *OTHER SIDE.*
I *DID.*
BUT THEN I SAW WHAT THEY *REALLY* ARE...AND I REALIZED I WAS IN DANGER OF BECOMING THE *SAME THING*...
...WHERE IS GRIX?

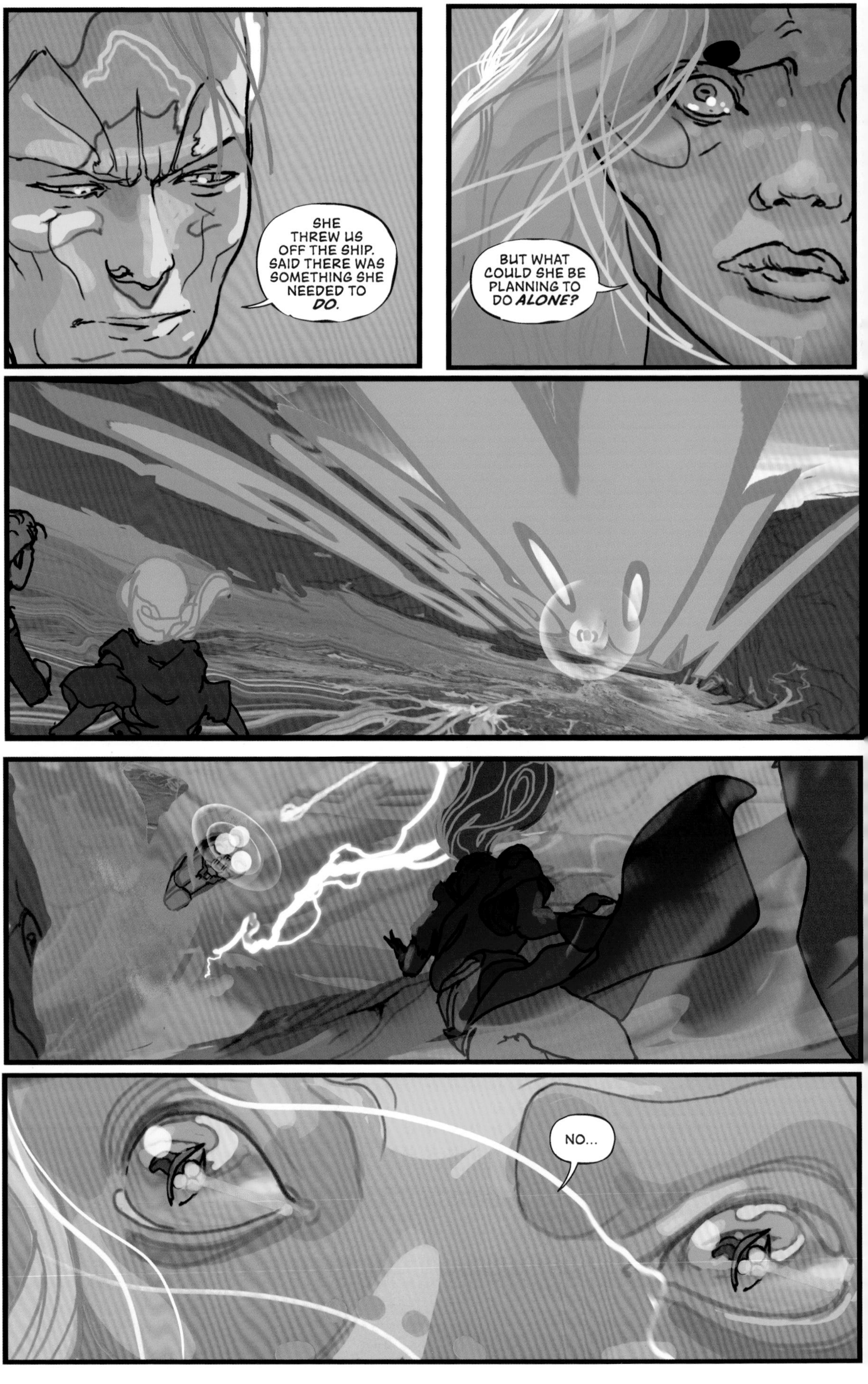
SHE THREW US OFF THE SHIP. SAID THERE WAS SOMETHING SHE NEEDED TO *DO*.
BUT WHAT COULD SHE BE PLANNING TO DO *ALONE?*
NO...

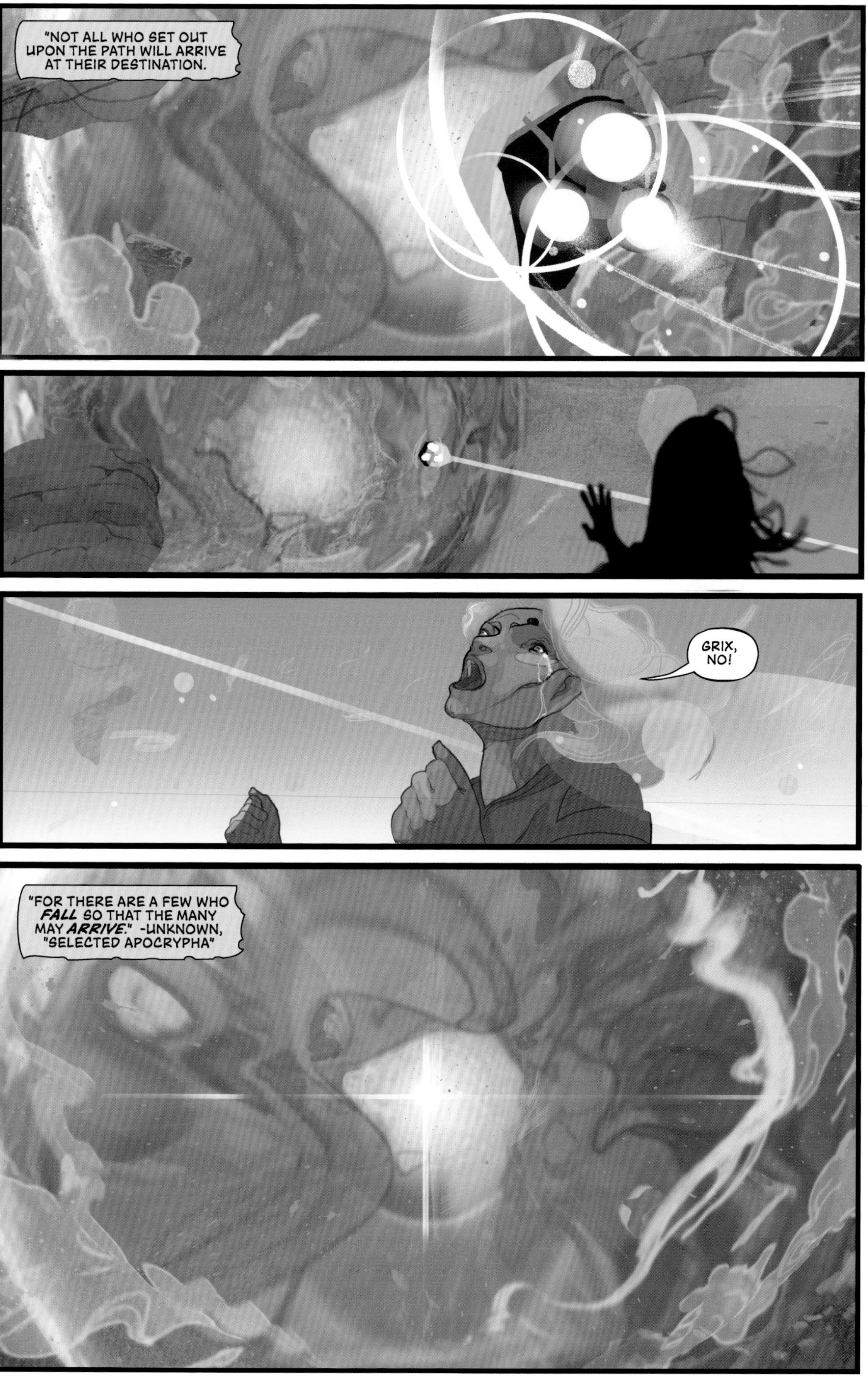
"NOT ALL WHO SET OUT UPON THE PATH WILL ARRIVE AT THEIR DESTINATION.
GRIX, NO!
"FOR THERE ARE A FEW WHO FALL SO THAT THE MANY MAY ARRIVE." -UNKNOWN, "SELECTED APOCRYPHA"

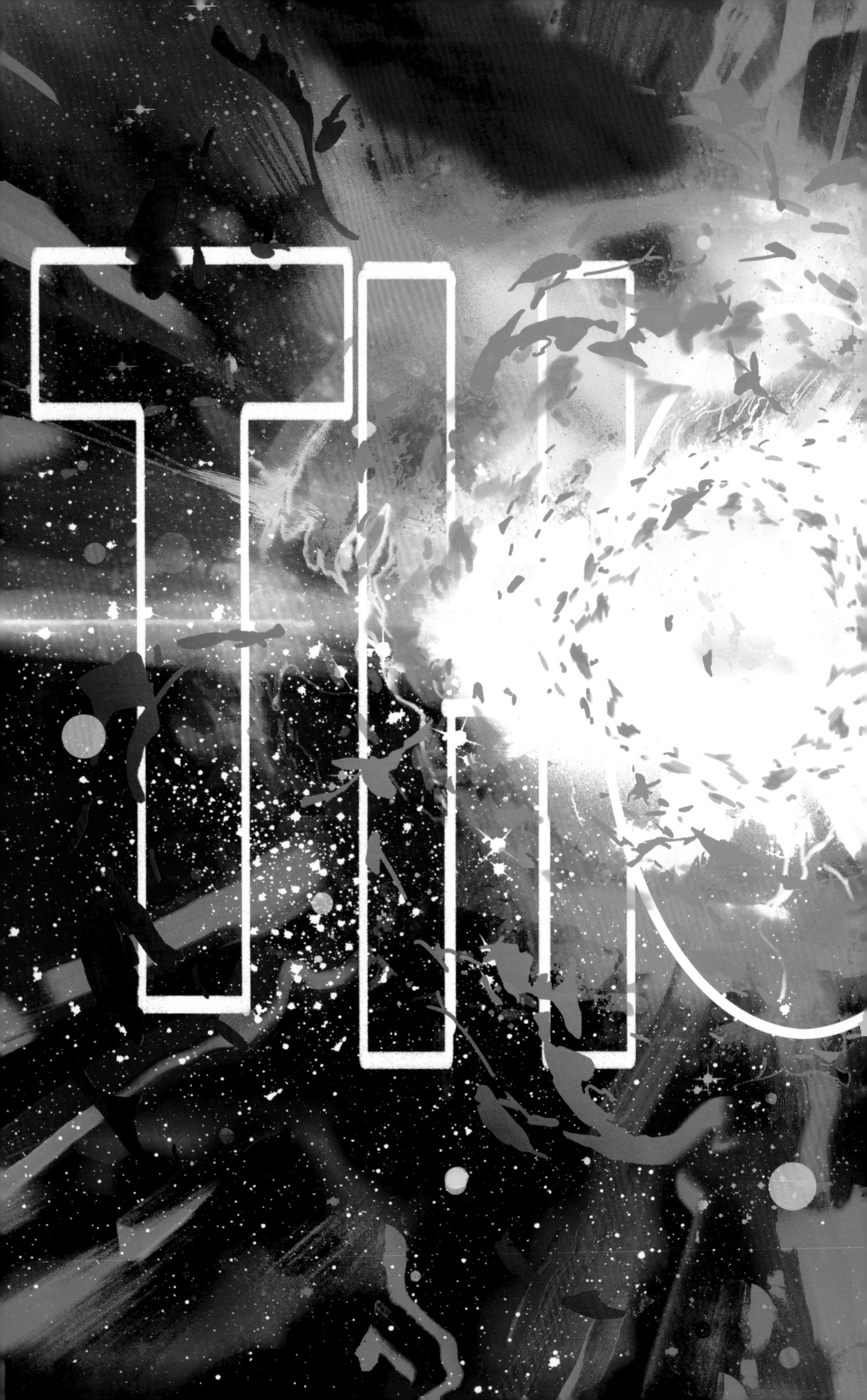

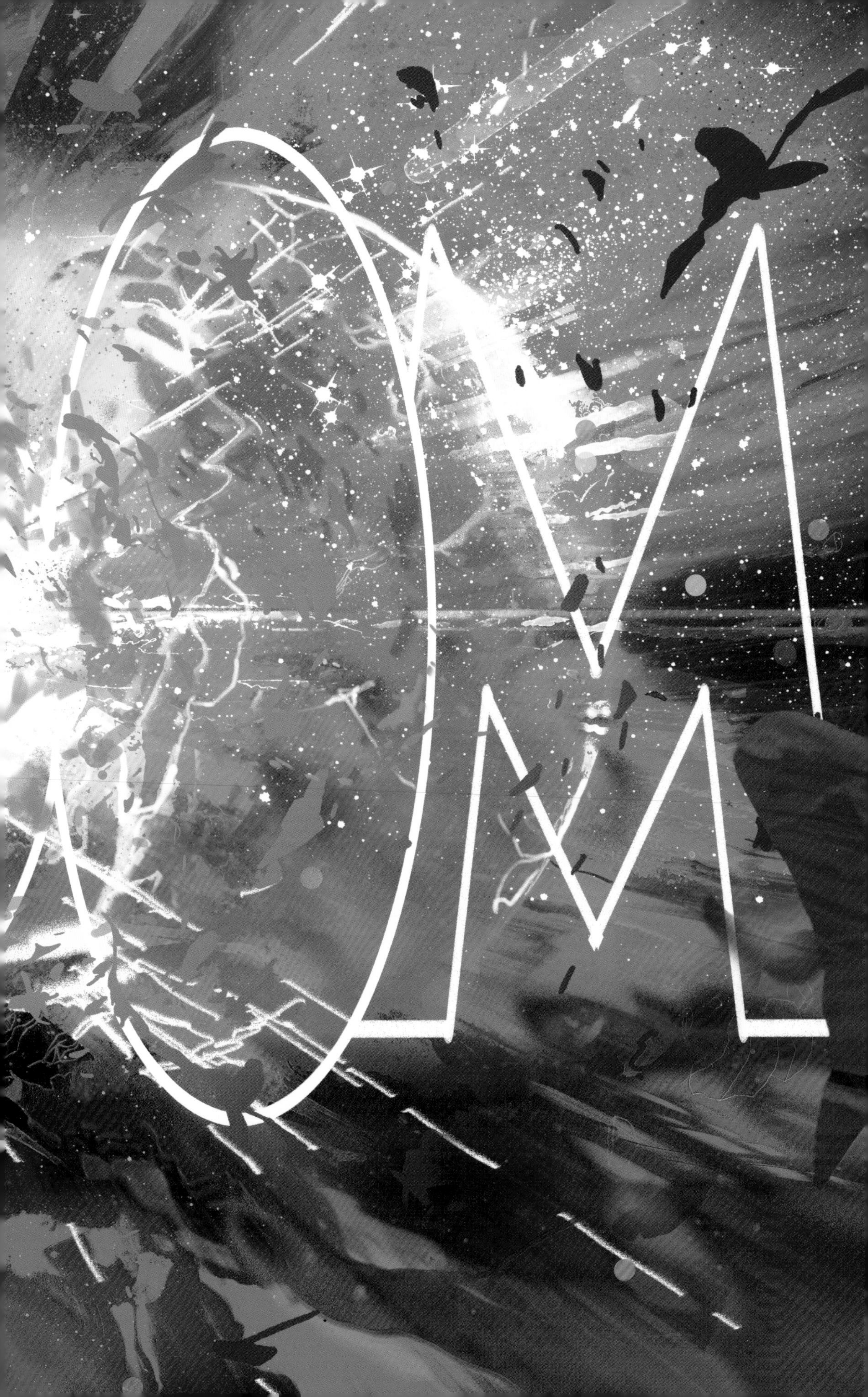
OM

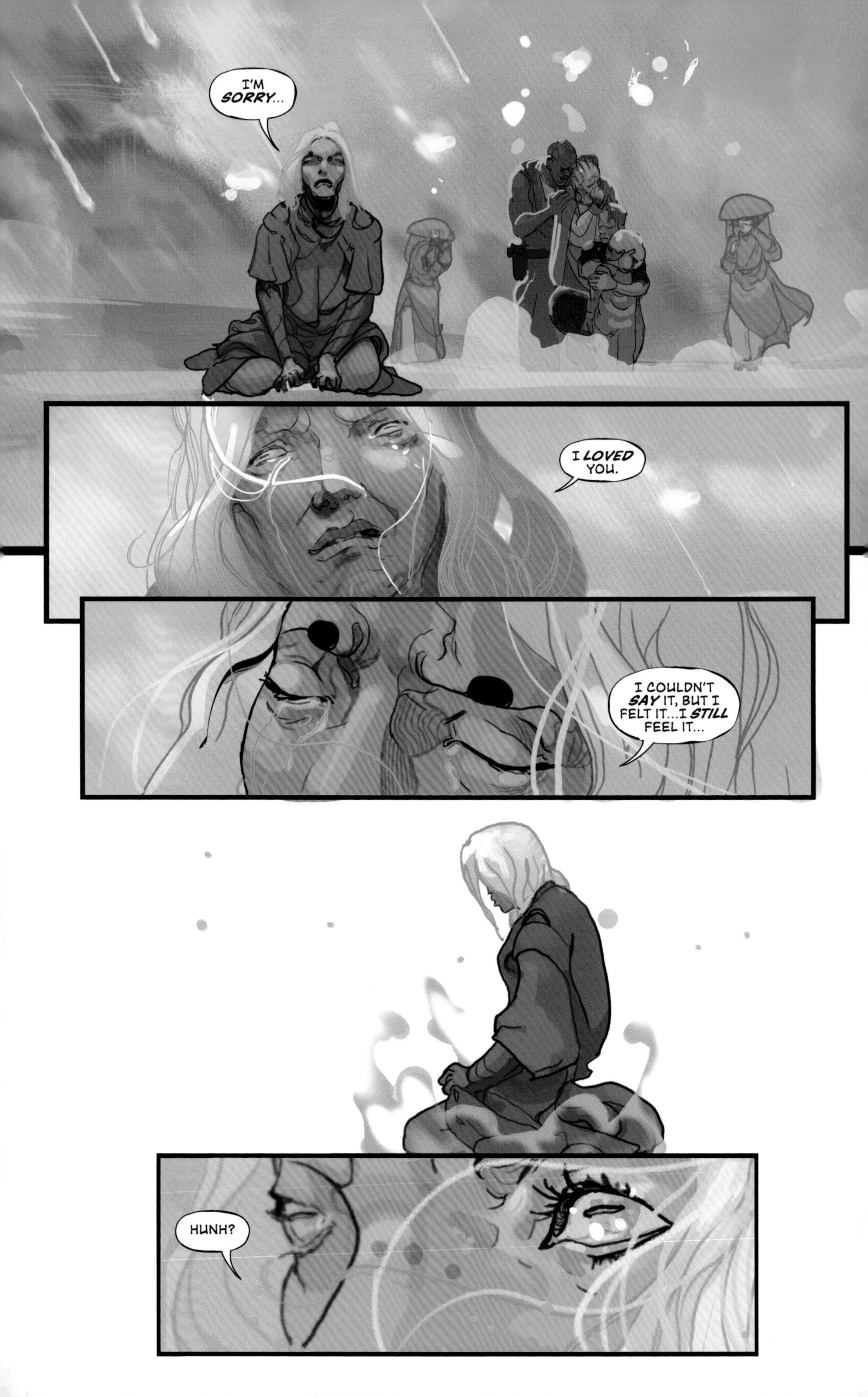
I'M SORRY...
I LOVED YOU.
I COULDN'T SAY IT, BUT I FELT IT...I STILL FEEL IT...
HUNH?

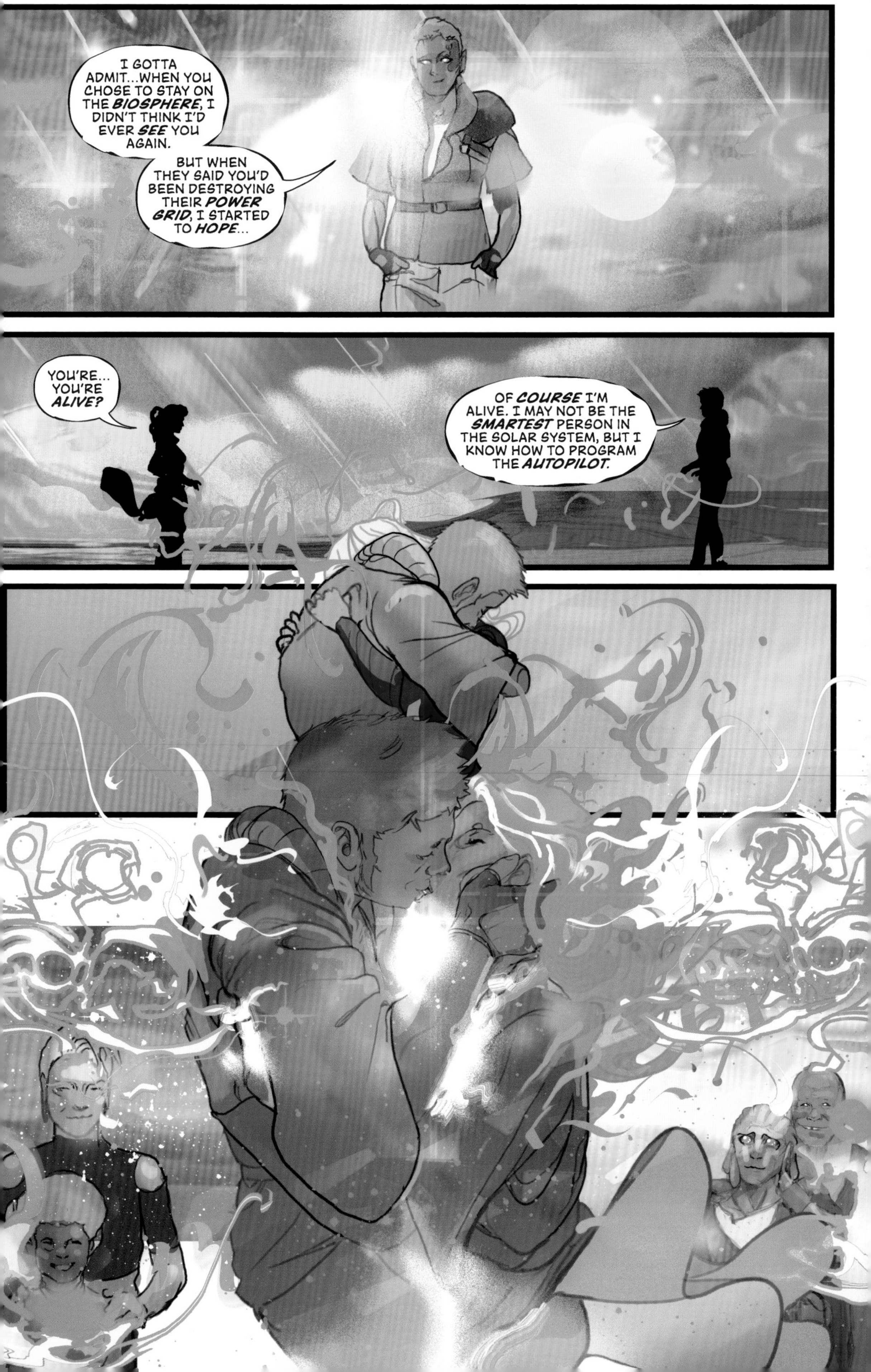
I GOTTA ADMIT...WHEN YOU CHOSE TO STAY ON THE *BIOSPHERE*, I DIDN'T THINK I'D EVER *SEE* YOU AGAIN.
BUT WHEN THEY SAID YOU'D BEEN DESTROYING THEIR *POWER GRID*, I STARTED TO *HOPE*...
YOU'RE... YOU'RE *ALIVE?*
OF *COURSE* I'M ALIVE. I MAY NOT BE THE *SMARTEST* PERSON IN THE SOLAR SYSTEM, BUT I KNOW HOW TO PROGRAM THE *AUTOPILOT*.

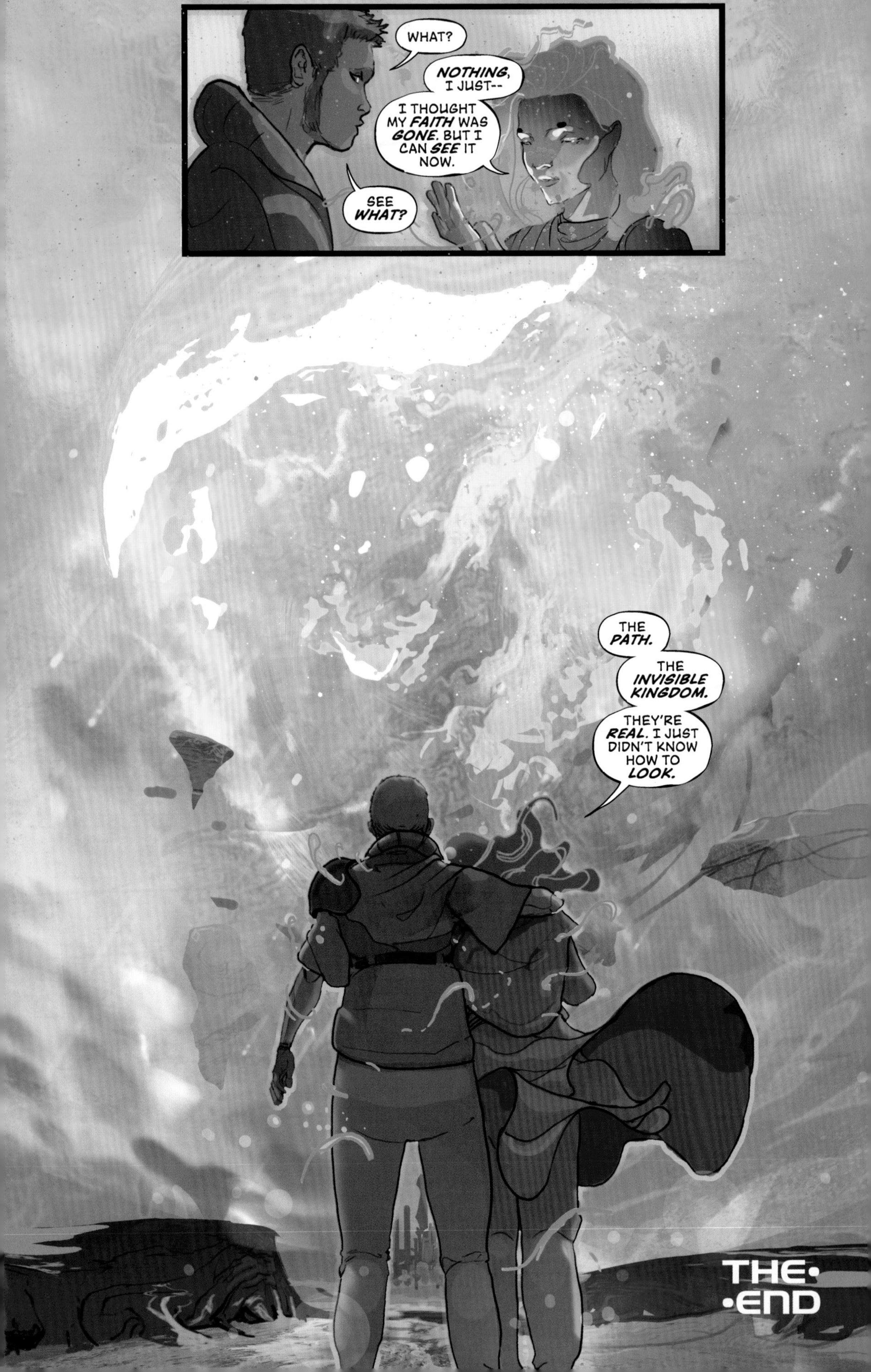
WHAT?
NOTHING, I JUST--
I THOUGHT MY FAITH WAS GONE. BUT I CAN SEE IT NOW.
SEE WHAT?
THE PATH.
THE INVISIBLE KINGDOM.
THEY'RE REAL. I JUST DIDN'T KNOW HOW TO LOOK.
THE END

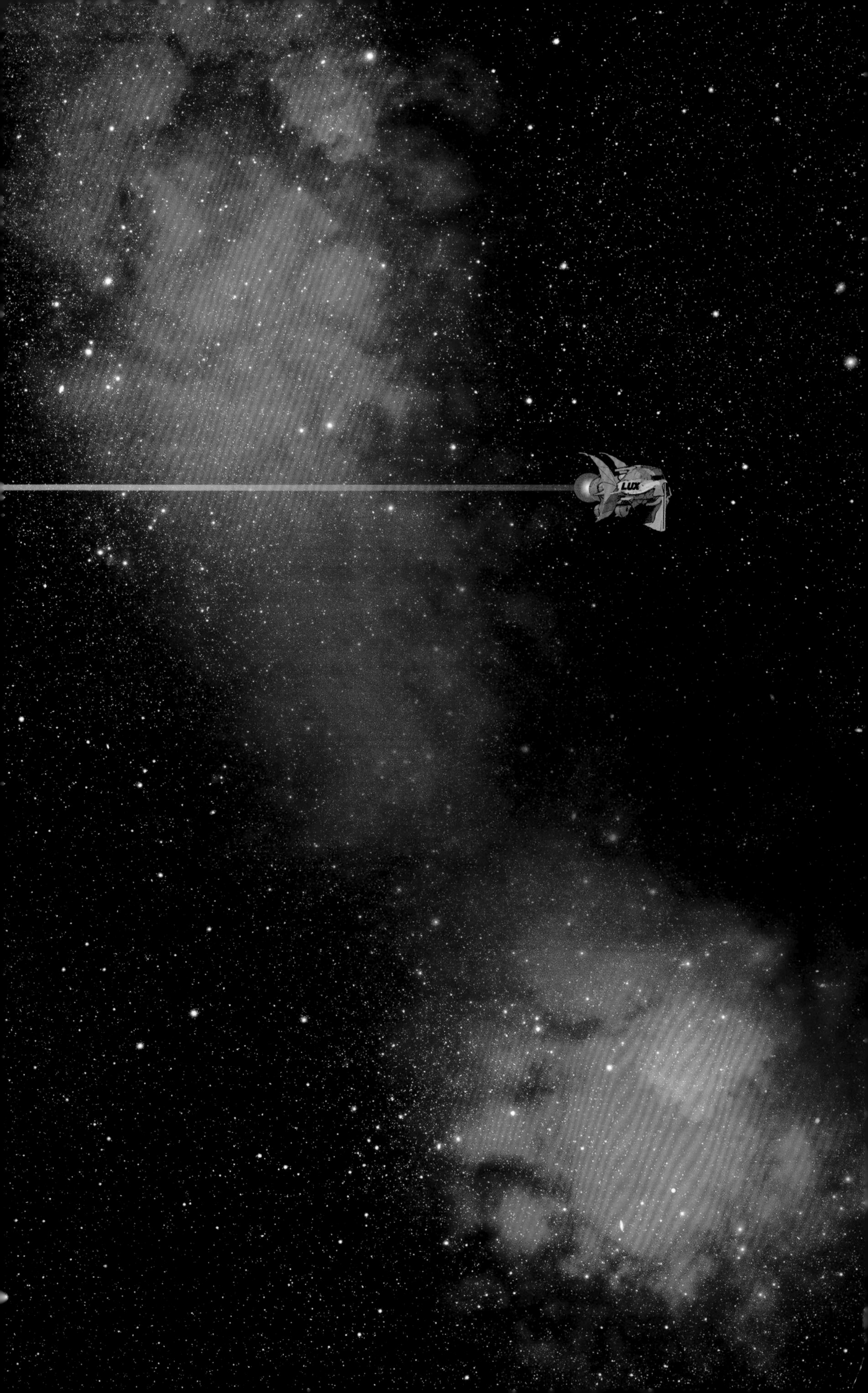
LUX

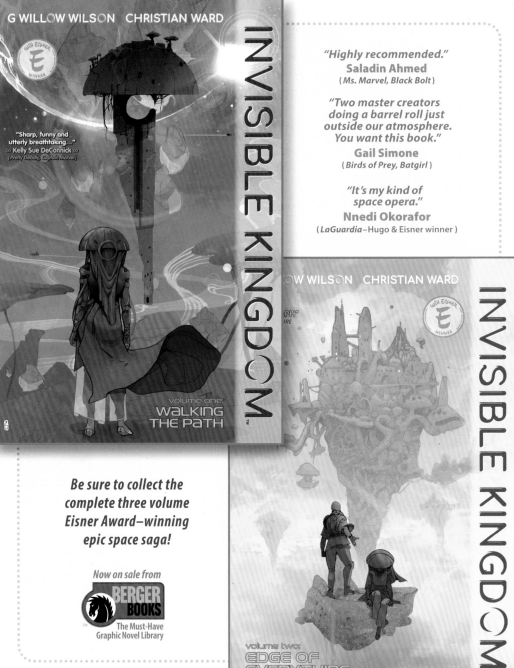

"Highly recommended."
**Saladin Ahmed**
( *Ms. Marvel, Black Bolt* )

"Two master creators
doing a barrel roll just
outside our atmosphere.
You want this book."
**Gail Simone**
( *Birds of Prey, Batgirl* )

"It's my kind of
space opera."
**Nnedi Okorafor**
( *LaGuardia*–Hugo & Eisner winner )

*Be sure to collect the
complete three volume
Eisner Award–winning
epic space saga!*

Now on sale from

The Must-Have
Graphic Novel Library

Invisible Kingdom Volume Three: In Other Worlds, May 2021.

Text and illustrations of Invisible Kingdom™ © 2021 G. Willow Wilson and Christian Ward. The Berger Books Logo, Dark Horse Comics® and the Dark Horse logo are trademarks of Dark Horse Comics LLC, registered in various categories and countries. Berger Books® is a registered trademark of Karen Berger. All rights reserved. No portion of this publication may be reproduced or transmitted, in any form or by any means, without the express written permission of Dark Horse Comics LLC. Names, characters, places, and incidents featured in this publication either are the product of the author's imagination or are used fictitiously. Any resemblance to actual persons (living or dead), events, institutions, or locales, without satiric intent, is coincidental.

Published by
Dark Horse Books
A division of
Dark Horse Comics LLC
10956 SE Main Street
Milwaukie, OR 97222
DarkHorse.com
ComicShopLocator.com
1 2 3 4 5 6 7 8 9 10
First Edition: May 2021
Ebook ISBN 978-1-50672-152-1
ISBN 978-1-50672-151-4
Printed in China

Names: Wilson, G. Willow, 1982- author. | Ward, Christian (Christian J.), artist. | Cipriano, Sal, letterer.
Title: In other worlds / script, G. Willow Wilson ; art, Christian Ward ; letters, Sal Cipriano. Description:
First edition. | Milwaukie, OR : Dark Horse Books/Berger Books, 2021. | Series: Invisible Kingdom; volume III
Identifiers: LCCN 2020045279 | ISBN 9781506721514 (trade paperback) | ISBN 9781506721521 (ebook)
Subjects: LCSH: Comic books, strips, etc. Classification: LCC PN6728.I574 W49 2021 | DDC
741.5/973--dc23 LC record available at https://lccn.loc.gov/2020045279